UPHEAVAL AND CONTINUITY

UPHEAVAL
and
CONTINUITY

A Century of German History

Edited by
E. J. FEUCHTWANGER

Preface by
KLAUS SCHULZ

UNIVERSITY OF PITTSBURGH
PRESS

© 1973 OSWALD WOLFF (PUBLISHERS) LIMITED, LONDON
Published 1974 in the U.S.A. by the University of Pittsburgh Press

Library of Congress Catalog Card Number: 73–17691

ISBN 0–8229–1113–2 (cloth)
ISBN 0–8229–6083–0 (paper)

MADE AND PRINTED IN GREAT BRITAIN BY
THE GARDEN CITY PRESS LIMITED
LETCHWORTH, HERTFORDSHIRE
SG6 1JS

Contents

	page
Preface by Klaus Schulz	9
E. J. Feuchtwanger *Introduction*	11
Golo Mann *The Second German Empire: the Reich that Never Was*	29
Wolfgang Abendroth *The Absolutism of the Hohenzollern State and the Rise of the Social Democratic Party*	47
Walter Jens *The Classical Tradition in Germany—Grandeur and Decay*	67
R. Hinton Thomas *German and English Intellectuals—Contrasts and Comparisons*	83
Kurt Sontheimer *The Weimar Republic—Failure and Prospects of German Democracy*	101
F. L. Carsten *The Historical Roots of National Socialism*	116
Martin Broszat *National Socialism, its Social Basis and Psychological Impact*	134
Theo Sommer *Germany's Strategic Position in the European Power Balance*	152
Peter C. Ludz *Experts and Critical Intellectuals in East Germany*	166
Alfred Grosser *Epilogue: Germany in our Time*	183
Suggestions for Further Reading	189
Contributors	192

Editorial Note

Most of the essays collected together in this volume were delivered as lectures in the winter of 1971–72 at the London School of Economics and University College, London, under the general title *Germany 1871–1971*. Two of the speakers in the series, Alfred Grosser and Peter C. Ludz, have, in place of their lectures, written contributions especially for this volume. The Introduction by the Editor was also specially written for this version in book form.

The contributions of Wolfgang Abendroth, Walter Jens, Kurt Sontheimer, Martin Broszat, Peter C. Ludz and Alfred Grosser were translated from the German, mostly by the Editor. The essays of Golo Mann, R. Hinton Thomas, F. L. Carsten and Theo Sommer appear in their original English version.

A German edition of this volume appeared under the title *Deutschland—Wandel und Bestand*, Kurt Desch Verlag, Munich, in May 1973.

E. J. FEUCHTWANGER

Preface

When I became Director of the German Institute in London three years ago, I soon became aware of the gaps in my own knowledge of English history. It was no consolation to me that many of my British friends fared no better in their knowledge of German history, and I therefore sought ways of improving matters. As a result, the first Anglo-German Seminar for teachers of history took place in Heidelberg in the summer of 1971. German and British historians, university and school teachers from both countries met to inform themselves about the post-war history of Germany and to discuss together. The preparations for this seminar reached back into 1970. My British partners wanted to put the starting date for the seminar in 1945. I had to make it clear to them that this was unthinkable for Germans—particularly in the historic year 1971.

1945 cannot be explained without reference to 1933, and Hitler's seizure of power in March 1933, with the support of 44 per cent of the German electorate, is again closely tied up with 1918 which in turn is linked with Bismarck's unification of Germany. My British friends had some difficulty in understanding my arguments, but the organisers of the second seminar—scheduled to be held in Britain in August 1973—will be able to start without qualms in 1945 and have no need to turn back to Disraeli and the Victorian period. Great Britain as a state comprising the whole United Kingdom is a product of the eighteenth century and not of the late nineteenth century. Herein lies a fundamental difference in the historical awareness of Britons and Germans, which both parties need to see clearly. This was also the basis of the lecture series, Germany 1871–1971, which the German Institute arranged in collaboration with University College and the London School of Economics between October 1971 and May 1972. My thanks are due in the first place to the lecturers themselves, to the publishers, Mrs. I. R. Wolff (London) and Kurt Desch (Munich), and especially to the editor, Dr. Feuchtwanger.

I am sure this book will be useful to both Britons and Germans. The last hundred years of German history are still the subject of controversy in our own country. This is to be welcomed, for only through coming to grips with what has developed from the past can we hope to change the present. This should be the concern of Britons and Germans particularly at the present time when Britain is making a new start by linking herself to the Continent, while the Germans in the Federal Republic are abandoning the dream of the old national state.

KLAUS SCHULZ

London, 1973

Introduction

by E. J. FEUCHTWANGER

The Germans have over the last century experienced more frequent
and profound upheavals in their mode of national existence than
almost any other major nation. It is true that the absence of a
revolution on the French or Russian or even the English seventeenth-century model has often been regarded as a root cause of
many of Germany's ills. Even without such a revolution, however,
the transformations in the life of the German people since the
middle of the last century have indeed been far reaching. On the
one hand there have been the drastic and violent changes in the
shape of the territorial and political framework : from the loose
German Bund including many of the German-speaking subjects of
the Hapsburg Empire to Bismarck's *kleindeutsch* Prussia-Germany,
through the truncated Republic of 1918 and Hitler's temporarily
bloated *Grossdeutsche Reich* on to the Federal Republic and the
German Democratic Republic of today. On the other hand, in
spite of the absence of a classically complete revolution, the social
and economic upheavals have been scarcely less profound : the
rapid industrialisation of the later nineteenth century, the mobilisation of the First World War followed by the economic crises of
the twenties and thirties, the totalitarian control of society and
economy in the Third Reich followed by the vast population movements at the end of the Second World War.

Nevertheless, from the perspective of the 1970s the continuities
are as impressive as the discontinuities. The great dividing lines
1870, 1918, 1945 no longer appear as absolute as they did in the
past. The formation of the Second Reich is no longer seen in terms
of cataclysmic events which took place in 1870 or 1866, activated
by a single statesman of superhuman proportions. A long process
of socio-economic development prepared the way for unification by
Prussia and even Bismarck is perceived to be acting to some extent
in response to inescapable political and economic pressures. The
Second Reich, both in its internal and external policies, is seen in
terms of an intensification of these pressures and the discrepancy
between the forces of modernity and a backward-looking political

structure. The First World War resolved tensions in Germany which had become well nigh intolerable before 1914 and the Revolution of 1918 was a consummation which had been all too long delayed. The failures of the Weimar Republic can again be to a large extent explained by this element of political retardation inherited from the imperial past. The very violence and extremism of the Nazis has made it necessary to search meticulously for the roots of the evil in previous history and to establish the continuities between the Third Reich and its immediate antecedents. The profound changes in social attitudes and political mores which all observers find in post-war Germany are now in turn felt to have been prepared, albeit unconsciously, by the draconian treatment of the body politic dispensed by the masters of the Third Reich. Thus a continuous web of development can be established over the whole of the last century or more of German history, more significant in many ways than the dramatic turning points which have in the past more obviously attracted attention.

The continuities of the German story are perhaps the more evident because of the upheaval of perspectives that has taken place among historians and their public. In the past generations of Germans were taught to regard the national state as the ultimate value, the creation of a German nation state in the nineteenth century as the climax of their history. The events of the twentieth century have shown up the impermanence of these achievements and have put in doubt the value systems enshrined in them. In paving the way for German unification, in binding the Germans to the new Reich and in gaining their acceptance of its political methods German historians played a rôle of exceptional importance. They placed the emphasis on the state, conceived in an Hegelian idealistic sense, on the great men and the great decisions, on authority and *Realpolitik*, on power and the primacy of foreign policy. They neglected industrialisation, the clash of classes and economic interests, the tensions produced by outmoded political structures, the 'bonapartist' methods by which domestic conflicts were transcended by adventurous policies abroad. A cluster of other socio-political attitudes accompanied this historical perspective, social Darwinism, survival of the fittest at home and abroad, imperialism and the need for Germany to have a place in the sun before it was too late; any attack on the existing social and political structure was regarded as tantamount to treason and even mild reformism was fairly oppositional, liberalism and democracy were Western, non-German and decadent. It was not only historiography that fostered such attitudes, but the work of German historians played an important part in the process of legitimising and sub-limating the Second Reich and all its features.

One has only to draw this picture with a few broad strokes of the brush to realise how profound a change of perspective has taken place among historians and social scientists and is now gaining general acceptance. The emphasis has entirely changed. The first and most fundamental question that is now asked is whether the creation of a German national state, excluding as it did a sub-stantial part of the German-speaking population of Central Europe, was worth while and desirable at all. Golo Mann, in his gently self-deprecating way, confessed in his lecture to a nostalgia for the German Confederation, but admitted that his preference may well be part of a predilection for sinking ships and lost causes. Elsewhere he has called the events of 1866 the first partition of Germany. 1866 does now look like the watershed. The cards tumbled in favour of a *kleindeutsch* solution to the German national problem, fashioned by Prussia. From this there followed a chain of other events : German liberalism succumbed to the success of Prussian arms, the semi-feudal structure of Prussia remained intact and was indeed transferred to a wider German sphere, in a revolution accomplished from above a constitution was imposed and annexations, of Hanover and other long established legitimate entities, were perpetrated. It is these aspects of the cataclysmic events of 1866 and 1867 that now command most attention, no longer the diplomatic genius of Bismarck or the military glory of Moltke and the Prussian armies. Thus a great deal of the work done in our generation by German historians has been concerned with the deeper economic and social currents that produced the need for a larger unified trading area and brought it about that Prussia outdistanced Austria—for instance Herbert Böhme's great work, to mention only one example among many. It is these underlying developments which enable us to perceive the continuity of German history. Nevertheless, the events of 1866 and the years immediately before and after, were not the inevitable by-product of economic forces and do constitute a revolution from above. When Golo Mann at the beginning of his lecture spoke of Bismarck's Reich as something essentially new he meant just that —something was created which did not organically grow. We are now much more conscious of the weaknesses and failures of the Second Reich and perhaps the pendulum has swung too far the other way. For all its shortcomings it did supply the framework for a dynamic growth of population and resources in central Europe and in so far as its creation was, as Böhme and others have shown, the result of long-term economic pressures, these did find through it a creative release. It seems doubtful if a reformed German Confederation or the ideal of *Mitteleuropa*, such as was conceived by Schwarzenberg and Bruck in the early 1850s, could have been adequate for this purpose. Nevertheless the structural faults of the Hohenzollern Reich are glaringly obvious to us now. First of all there were the constitutional and political anomalies and Golo Mann listed many of them in his lecture: the absence of full ministerial responsibility, the curious relationship between Prussia and the Reich, with the Chancellor himself as the only major link, the anachronistic three-tier electoral system in Prussia. There were the growing burdens imposed upon the new Reich by its international situation, especially the 'hereditary enmity' with France, entirely spurious and nonsensical as Golo Mann rightly called it, but nevertheless unhappily reinforced by the annexation of Alsace-Lorraine. As time went on these burdens were compounded by the new imperialism; Golo Mann again explained vividly in his lecture how paltry and merely 'fashionable' were the intellectual roots of this movement, how insignificant its concrete benefits. But, alas, its consequences in terms of heightened international tension were real and serious enough.

Among the many unhealthy situations in Imperial Germany the political alienation of the Social Democratic Party, the most authentic expression of the aspirations of the German working class, proved to be one of the most fateful. This is the theme of Abendroth's lecture and he deals with it from an avowedly Marxist standpoint. It is in many ways an appropriate subject for a Marxist historian. With the Gotha Congress of 1875 Marxism became the official doctrine of the unified German Social Democratic Party and, whatever the back slidings in practice, it remained so substantially until 1959. It was no less important that the attitudes of the German middle classes and the policies of the state also conformed to the Marxist pattern in the Second Reich and were, with only minor exceptions, unremittingly hostile to the workers and to social democracy. This was particularly the case in the twelve years from 1878 to 1890 when the party was illegal. Abendroth sees this as a period when, in a dialectical process, the proletarian consciousness of the German working class deepened and the Social Democratic Party became firmly committed to its Marxist destiny. By contrast Abendroth regards the following twenty-four years till 1914 as a period when the party increasingly lost its way and failed to give the German working class the guidance which was its due. It was a time of growing electoral success, ending in the Reichstag elections of 1912, when the party became the largest in that assembly. The party grew into a mass movement which the Imperial régime, however fundamental its continuing hostility, could not suppress. The prospect of attaining power by democratic parliamentary methods led to the formation of the classical revisionist doctrine, of which Edward Bernstein was the most prominent exponent. The rise of a mass labour movement, with political and trade union wings, produced a vast bureaucracy of functionaries, made the more self-sufficient by the isolation into which it was forced by the hostile Hohenzollern state. This army of functionaries had a vested interest in stability and lost its revolutionary élan. Even before 1914 Robert Michels, in a pioneer study of party sociology, had diagnosed this bureaucratisation and its consequences. The moment of truth came, as is well known, in August 1914, when the German Social Democratic Party, in a complete volte-face and in defiance of its long cherished beliefs, came out in support of the war and voted for the war credits in the Reichstag. Abendroth points out that a group of leaders, which included Rosa Luxemburg and Karl Liebknecht, opposed this surrender to the prevailing tide, as they had opposed the move towards reformism and growing accommodation with the existing order earlier on. Their resistance heralded a permanent split in German Social Democracy and in the Second International. The volte-face of 1914 was, however, only in part, perhaps in small part, due to theoretical and practical shortcomings of the party; in a much more fundamental way it followed from the massive tidal wave of patriotic fervour which gripped the working classes as much as the rest of society. Abendroth as a Marxist admits this and concedes that even the left wing leaders had not foreseen anything like it. Is it really possible to fit this great upsurge of nationalist emotion, which swept the working class in Germany and everywhere else, into the Marxist pattern by the cry of 'false consciousness'? The more realistic explanation is likely to be that the European working classes were more fully integrated into their respective societies than Marx had foreseen and that there was a good deal of myth about proletarian consciousness. In Germany the workers had at least to some extent shared in the great growth of material prosperity experienced under the Second Reich and had accepted many of its values and ideals. German Social Democracy may have been alienated from the Second Reich as a political structure, but this is not synonymous with saying that the German workers in their millions had not found a place of sorts in Imperial Germany as a society.

Nevertheless, the cleavage in Wilhelmine Germany that is so neatly encapsulated in the Kaiser's famous reference to the Social Democrats as *vaterlandslose Gesellen* was of profound significance both in domestic and foreign policy, especially after the departure of Bismarck, and accounts for what one might call the 'bonapartist style' in the conduct of affairs. The more evident it became that there was a lack of consensus stretching right across society the more difficult it was to admit it. Popular caesarism at home and assertive imperialism abroad papered over the cracks. The proliferating associations and pressure groups of the turn of the century, particularly those with a strong ideological commitment like the Pan-German League and the Navy League, played their part in this. On the left, among Social Democrats and left wing liberals, there was the hope that a move towards a full parliamentary system could succeed. There were occasions when the acceptance of ministerial responsibility or the reform of the Prussian three-tier electoral law seemed imminent. On the other hand, the nationalist agitation from the right, with its imperialist expansionist social-darwinist and racialist overtones, was in the main successful in supporting the established order and in stemming the tide of social change and the demand for political advancement. The confrontation between these conflicting tendencies was further heightened by the war. The pressure for democratisation had by 1917 become almost irresistible but was being countered by expansionist, annexationist demands of the political right backed by the continuing practice of an acclamatory style of government.

Golo Mann expressed the view in his lecture that the war aims, fabricated by irresponsible bodies such as the *Zentralverband der Deutschen Industrie* and more or less officially accepted, were a lunatic by-product of the war rather than a major cause in itself. In this he differs somewhat from the views of Fritz Fischer and his supporters, who see a more complete continuity of cause and effect between the pre-1914 bellicosity of German foreign policy and the failure to seek a compromise peace during the war. In all this the position of the Social Democratic Party was crucial. The political fault line in Wilhelmine Germany, rather ineffectually hidden from sight during the days of patriotic fervour, the *Burgfrieden*, in the first few years of the war, is also the chief element of continuity across the Revolution of 1918 and one of the main reasons for the weaknesses and eventual failure of the Weimar Republic.

Sontheimer stresses, like many commentators, how the ruling classes of Imperial Germany in their hour of defeat, when, as Thomas Mann put it, they had become *windelweich* (as weak as a

* *

jelly), rushed to embrace the democratic system they had so long resisted in order to save something of their privileged position. But it was only for a brief moment in 1919 that the democratic parties of the Weimar Coalition had the support of a majority of Germans. By 1920 the self-confidence of all the many sections of the German people who had identified themselves with the Imperial Régime was rapidly recovering : psychologically they had divested themselves of the burden of defeat and shifted it onto the new republic and its supporters—the stab-in-the-back legend was part of this process. Among the many continuities from Imperial to Weimar Germany the attitude of the conservative Right in all its many shadings, forms one, the various attitudes and habits of the Social Democrats another. Men like Ebert, Scheidemann and Noske conducted themselves with reasonable resource and dignity when they were catapulted into power in circumstances of appalling difficulty in November 1918. But even at that stage they were pathetically dependent on the advice of civil servants and generals of the old régime, as Carsten points out. It was hardly surprising that their first priority was to prevent Germany from being engulfed by a revolution on the Russian Soviet model. Knowing as we do the degeneration of the Russian revolution we must praise them for their foresight rather than blame them for having prevented a more thoroughgoing transformation of German society at that stage. But as the threat to the new republic began to come increasingly from the Right, the Social Democratic leaders proved lacking in the most elementary sense of self-preservation. Their long experience of being second-class citizens in Imperial Germany and their confinement to a kind of political ghetto had given them an inferiority complex in the face of their former masters. They bent over backwards to stick to the rules of a liberal-democratic system when their opponents had no intention of playing the game. An anti-republican judiciary would not save the President of the Republic himself, Ebert, from being hounded to his death by slanderous accusations.

Another continuous thread in the tumultuous German story of the nineteenth and twentieth centuries is formed by the seamless web of intellectual life. Several of our contributors address themselves to the development of German ideas and the German mind : this is the theme of Walter Jens and Hinton Thomas and a specific if sinister strand in this development is a major subject for Sontheimer and Carsten. In the age of classicism German thought was in the mainstream of European ideas. Jens takes the special case of classical antiquity and its place in German culture and he

2—UAC • •

shows how the Greek ideal was in men like Schiller, Hölderlin,
Humboldt and even Hegel a force for liberation and change. The
German intellectual élite at the turn of the eighteenth and nineteenth centuries watched the French Revolution with fascination
and detachment. For the most part they applauded it, at any rate
in its early stages; the Greek city state seemed to them the ideal
towards which the Revolution was reaching out. The classical
heritage in Germany, however, soon ceased to have any critical
impact on existing social attitudes and relationships. Instead it
was used by the possessing classes as yet another element through
which they differentiated themselves from and buttressed themselves against the masses. A classical education, and the content of
education in nineteenth-century Germany consisted, through the
work of Humboldt, very largely of the study of the classics, became
an ornament for the bourgeoisie. It could lead to a self-conscious
aestheticism and élitism, as with the Stefan George circle. From
there it was but a short step to a general contempt for the manifestations of modern mass civilisation, democracy, parliaments,
parties and so on. Thus the classical tradition in Germany, once
a force for social criticism, became a pillar of the established order
and potentially a factor reinforcing the move to the extreme right.

On a broader front, our contributors, in common with many
other writers on the history of ideas in Germany, trace the separation of German thought from the main stream of Western
European development and describe what flowed from it. There is
the growing antagonism to the West of the German national movement which can be observed, as Carsten points out, early on in
writers like Ernst Moritz Arndt and Turnvater Jahn and which
soon exhibited racialist overtones. What was still vestigial in the
early part of the nineteenth century became the central theme in
writers like Lagarde and Houston Stewart Chamberlain at the end
of the century. Along with the theories in which racial inter-
pretations of history, social darwinism and anti-semitism jostled
each other, there were movements such as Stöcker's Christian
Socialists, the Pan-German League and the Agrarian League
(*Bund der Landwirte*) which represented these theories in the
practical politics of Imperial Germany. Another strand in the
separation of the German world of ideas from the West goes back
to the development of German idealism. Through Hegel there was
transmitted a view of the state, of the individual and of freedom,
three essential components of man's social existence, which put the
stress on the collectivity and perceived freedom for the individual
as arising in its highest form only through identification with the

community. This made it much easier to regard authoritarian policies, which emphasised national unity, as particularly suited to Germans, while parliaments and parties could be seen as factors of disintegration and degeneration. Intellectuals especially were perceived as destroyers of that instinctive unity of the folk invoked by so many German writers and publicists. Heine was, as Professor Hinton Thomas points out, the prototype of the critical rootless intellectual and also a Jew, and such people occupied a prominent place in the demonology of the conservative nationalist Right in German politics. The rôle of the intellectual in German politics was in fact highly ambivalent. On the one hand he was put on a pedestal, because German *Kultur* was, in contrast to the shallow pragmatism of the Anglo-Saxons, seen as deeply rooted in fundamental philosophical positions. The intellectual was concerned with the pure inward life of the spirit, a pursuit unsullied by preoccupation with the real world, let alone the sordid political sphere. Thomas Mann's *Betrachtungen eines Unpolitischen* (Meditations of a Non-Political Man) are mentioned in this connection by Jens and Hinton Thomas. At the other extreme there was the intellectual, bred of cities, destructive, subversive, restless, a poisonous weed. In England, as Hinton Thomas points out, intellectuals were neither so revered nor so reviled, nor were power and spirit ever so dialectically polarised. Yet another attitude which coloured German intellectual life, certainly once industrialisation had seriously got under way, was the nostalgia for the simple rural life, close to the soil, the equating of a strong farming population with racial health; on the other hand suspicion of urban civilisation, materialism and the drab rationality of business and commerce.

Many of these ideas and attitudes are not peculiar to Germany. Gobineau and Houston Stewart Chamberlain were not Germans and were among the most extreme exponents of the racialist view of history. But in Germany these ideas assumed special importance and a particular form because of the tension caused by the continued existence of archaic political structures and an exceptionally rapid industrialisation process. The groups and classes most exposed to the discomforts of swift social transformation became the most fertile breeding ground for anti-liberal ideologies. The agrarian interest was, especially after 1890, under pressure economically and increasingly facing a declining future in an industrialised, urbanised nation. The political and social strength of the East Elbian Junkers was, however, still such that on tariffs and other matters they could make their needs prevail. The agrarians, threatened by the ever-increasing power of industry and finance, were not surprisingly a mainstay of the nationalist, racialist, anti-semitic tendencies of the period. In quite a different economic context there was the stratum of white-collar employees, lower middle class in social and psychological orientation and rapidly increasingly in numbers. This group felt an acute need to differentiate themselves from the proletariat proper and they were helped in this by the paternalist and bureaucratic traditions of German industry. They wanted to see themselves as *Privatbeamten*, civil servants in the private sector but sharing the prestige of those in the public sector. Such men, insecure and anxious about their status, were again especially receptive to the ideologies of the extreme right; as Carsten mentions, one of their principal organisations, the *Deutschnationaler Handlungsgehilfenverband*, was affiliated to the Pan-German League. Thus it was that ideas which were not unique to Germany attained particular political importance there.

The defeat of 1918 and the circumstances of Weimar Germany aggravated these tendencies to the point of neuroses. A number of new factors, mainly stemming from the war and the experience of mass mobilisation and mass killing, were now also at work and one of our contributors, Martin Broszat, deals with them extensively. They were again not peculiar to Germany, but to be found there in particularly acute form. Throughout Europe the war damaged severely the optimistically progressive, liberal, humanitarian image of man. It mobilised and socialised vast masses of men who had previously been completely left out of the political process, particularly the peasants in many countries including Germany. It exposed them to highly emotional nationalism and to the experience of dynamic and dramatic political events. Another development very relevant to the rise of fascism in Europe was the transfer of military modes of action into the political sphere and the use of paramilitary formations, some of which derived their line of descent directly from the war-time armies by way of volunteer corps and so-called *Freikorps*. The type of the perpetual soldier who could not, after four years in the trenches, adjust to civilian life was easily recruited into the uniformed formations of fascist movements. Another characteristic of fascist and extreme right-wing movements was cultivation of youth and the ability to attract young people. These and other common denominators of European fascism were combined in Germany into a particularly explosive mixture through the addition of further elements of social resentment. There was the deep trauma of the lost war, starkly contrasting with the dynamic ascent of Germany between 1870 and 1914. Some of the economic groups which had already experienced stress from social change before 1914 now suffered from it in redoubled form, for instance farmers and white collar workers. The middle classes in general were exposed to unprecedented economic insecurity, through the inflation of the 1920s, through the growth of large economic combines, department stores—this affected the small shopkeeper especially—insurance companies and banks, in the final years of crisis of the Weimar Republic, through unemployment and slump. Broszat, like Sontheimer, shows the influence of these pressures on voting patterns : at the beginning of the Republic the apparent success of the democratic parties, including a 20 per cent vote for the *Deutsche Demokratische Partei*, a party dedicated to making good the past failures of German liberalism, seemed to augur well for the future. At last the German middle class seemed prepared to accept the parliamentary system and close the psychological gulf separating it from the working class. But after a fleeting moment older and more deeply ingrained attitudes and habits reasserted themselves : much of the voting strength of the German middle class was switched to the *Deutschnationale Volkspartei*, the main vehicle for the conservative landowners, civil servants, protestant clergy and others who had set the tone in Imperial Germany. In the mid-twenties, this party temporarily participated in republican cabinets, but basically it was anti-republican and in the final crisis it became, under the control of Hugenberg, Hitler's respectable ally. The drift from the Liberal parties to the right was not compensated for by the fact that the more right-wing of the two liberal parties, the *Deutsche Volkspartei*, became, through the figure of Streseman, one of the main supports of the republic. During the final agony of the republic the electoral strength of both liberal parties was reduced virtually to vanishing point. Almost the entire voting strength of the German middle class, at least the Protestant part of it, had gone over to Hitler. All this is traced in detail by Broszat and he notes, as does Jens in a different context, how the traditional culture patterns of the German middle class bolstered their respect for authority above them and their contempt for the proletariat beneath them. Thus the very class which should have been the buttress of liberalism and stability became a prey to extremism.

Following Sontheimer's lecture, there was a prolonged discussion on the causes of Weimar's collapse, in which Walter Laqueur, James Joll and A. J. Nicholls also took part. There was general agreement that the explanation had to be pluralistic and that any mono-causal account such as the 'orthodox' Marxist line that fascism is the inevitable product of capitalism *in extremis*, is quite inadequate. Joll stressed that the slump of 1929 to 1932 was the second economic catastrophe in a decade and therefore psychologically so much harder to bear. Nicholls felt, speaking of Brüning's Memoirs, that even at that late stage there were political choices to be made and that Brüning himself pursued what was essentially a *Katastrophen-politik* and was thinking in terms of a restored monarchy rather than a survival of the Republic. The importance of anti-semitism in the advance of the Nazis was much discussed and there was a general disposition to agree with Walter Laqueur who stressed the importance of anti-semitism in giving Nazi ideology its cutting edge and its fanatical activists, but who considered its electoral importance with the broad masses relatively slight.

Just as some political tendencies of Imperial Germany were taken to extremes under Weimar so some of the intellectual trends of the pre-1914 period reappeared in the twenties distorted by the traumas of war and defeat. To the older ideologies of the right there were now added strands such as the cultural pessimism of Oswald Spengler, the Conservative Revolution adumbrated by a number of writers from Moeller van den Bruck to Ernst Niekisch, and calls for a charismatic leader and a corporate state. What all these attitudes had in common and what distinguished them from the heady optimism of pre-1914 political thinking was a feeling of dis-comfort and malaise concerning western civilisation paired with a conviction that it was on its way out. This conviction was not without a certain amount of *Schadenfreude*, for if Germany had fallen on evil days then surely the downfall of the West as a whole could not be far off. Nihilism and lust for destruction coloured the anti-democratic thinking of Weimar; but it was also accompanied by revolutionary romanticism, dreams and prophecies, perhaps satisfying from an aesthetic but hardly realistic from a political point of view. Stefan George and Ernst Jünger were no doubt major literary figures; their political influence was baneful and their personal position became tragic when the Nazis came to power. Let it be remembered, however, that the Weimar period was also one of the liveliest and most creative in the history of modern European culture, the influence of which on the arts is still felt today. The critical and experimental tradition in the arts which flourished so much in the twenties was as much part of a continuity linking Weimar Germany with the past as were the ideologies of the right which helped to put the Nazis into power. Unfortunately, as James Joll and Walter Laqueur pointed out in discussion, the brilliant social criticism of the *Simplizissimus* and Maximilian Harden made hardly any political impact before 1914. Similarly,

the intellectual establishment in the Universities and elsewhere was
solidly anti-republican under Weimar, and the critical intelligentsia,
whose names are still remembered now, remained an impotent
minority.

While our contributors devote much space to the roots and causes
of Nazism they have little to say about the Third Reich itself. This
omission is not due to any reluctance to face up to the subject, but
an indication that it does represent the greatest discontinuity in
the last century of German history. For all the gigantic claims it
made and the unprecedented havoc it wrought, the Third Reich
left only the most miniscule and incidental positive achievement,
but it did accomplish a monumental demolition job. It was essential
to the technique and process of the Nazi take-over of power that a
total political transformation should not be accompanied by a social
transformation equally far-reaching. In fact the failure to accomplish any kind of socio-economic revolution was the basic cause of
the first major crisis of the régime, the 30 June 1934. In the longer
run and especially during the years of radicalisation in the later
stages of the war, however, the Hitler régime undoubtedly removed
unwittingly some of the obstacles to modernity and some of the
elements of retardation in the fabric of society which are so frequently alluded to in these pages. Nazi ideology was poised in
curious ambivalence between revolutionary anti-capitalist, anti-
establishment attitudes and insistence on a large range of traditional bourgeois values. The Nazi state, for all its competing
bureaucracies and confusions, could be very modern in the technological methods it employed and it was positively a pioneer in
the technique of social manipulation. It demonstrated to all its
citizens that an ideology, however absurd, could shape social reality,
in fact it could be said that Nazism gave a better demonstration of
the power of ideology than many left-wing and Marxist régimes
of the modern world, with their much more conscious and elabor-
ate ideological prescriptions. On the level of social consciousness the
Nazi régime thus did remove some archaic blockages, though not
in the way Hitler intended it.

The great legacy of the Third Reich, however, was the purely
negative one of destroying Germany's position in Europe, her
territorial integrity and whole sectors of her population and
demolishing the traditional homesteads of many of her people in
her cities and more permanently along her eastern borders. One of
our contributors, Theo Sommer, discusses the implications of Germany's profoundly changed international position in an age which
has harnessed nuclear energy for military purposes. His analysis

makes it clear, once more, that from a strategic point of view the division of Germany and the integration of the two parts into their respective power blocs is for the foreseeable future irreversible. Naturally this was not recognised in East or West in the years immediately after 1945. Even the Soviet Union for a time considered its interests best served by championing German reunification, but by the fifties came out, increasingly openly, in favour of making the division permanent and internationally acknowledged. The Germans on both sides of the dividing line favoured the West overwhelmingly—even in the East this was clearly indicated by the rising of 1953. This was the underlying reason why the Soviet Union had to give up any hope of unifying Germany under its auspices; by the same token the West was able to stick to its prescription of German unification by free elections, but gradually, as the facts of the nuclear stalemate began to assert themselves, it ceased to be a position of strength.

Both German states were therefore in a sense founded on a false prospectus. In the case of the Federal Republic, as Alfred Grosser pointed out in his lecture and elsewhere, this meant that everything including the Basic Law had a deliberately transitory and temporary aspect. Moreover, the Federal Republic came into existence on the initiative of the Western victor powers; its institutions were created not by an assembly elected by the German population, but by bodies appointed by the Allies. Yet in spite of this apparent lack of legitimacy the Federal Republic has never in its existence had to face the challenges which the Weimar Republic did. Nevertheless, the anxieties which Grosser and so many others have expressed about the security and permanence of democratic institutions in the Federal Republic stem not only from the past record but also from the awareness that this state was built on assumptions which could have proved a danger for democracy. The problem of coming to terms with the past, to which Grosser devoted much attention, was made so much more difficult by the genesis of the Federal Republic. If this state was called into existence to create a bulwark against Soviet expansion, was it then not the main fault of the Nazis that they had been anti-Bolsheviks prematurely? This kind of argument was frequently heard in the fifties and served then to legitimise the politics of the extreme right. It has died away, not only because of the passage of time and the arrival of new generations, but also because from the mid-sixties the Federal Republic has increasingly moved away from its origins in the Cold War. The attack from the extreme right which proved fatal to Weimar has always faltered at the first fence under Bonn. The more optimistic interpretation that a fundamental change of social structures and attitudes had cut away the ground from under the traditional conservative authoritarian behaviour patterns has turned out, by and large, to be correct. It is one of the more fortunate discontinuities of German history, the result in the main of the upheavals of the Third Reich and the Second World War.

In their analysis of the current situation our contributors concentrated their attention on Ostpolitik and its consequences internationally and domestically for both German states. There was general agreement that the various treaties and agreements signed between the Federal Republic, the Soviet Union, Poland and the DDR in practice amount to an international recognition of the division of Germany and will lead in due course to the admission of two Germanies to the UN. There was also agreement that this situation has enhanced the international standing of the Federal Republic and is likely to present considerable problems for the leadership of DDR. The FRG has benefited from dropping a pretence, as Grosser has called it (*So tun als ob*), which had previously condemned it almost to impotence. For the leaders of the DDR the fear of contamination which might arise from increasing contacts between East and West is real enough. The dilemma began to face the Ulbricht régime when the Soviet Union decided that a move towards detente was in its global interests. Walter Ulbricht himself proved too inflexible to follow the new line and had to go. The Soviet leaders probably forced his retirement—Professors Ludz and Grosser share this view. The policy of the DDR under Honecker remains contradictory : on the one hand the régime has shown itself genuinely anxious to reach agreements with the Federal Republic in order to demonstrate its loyalty to the Soviet Union, to upgrade its international status and perhaps also for economic reasons; on the other hand East German propaganda has continued to shower abuse on Bonn and the DDR leaders clearly intend to keep any concessions resulting in increased freedom of movement and contact to the absolute minimum. Too much in the way of concrete results should therefore not be expected from Ostpolitik. Ludz makes it clear that little liberalisation can be hoped for in the internal affairs of the DDR. In surveying the role of the intelligentsia, so-called, in the DDR, he shows how indirectly and circuitously the still small voice of conscience has to operate within the East German system. Nevertheless, he concludes that the intellectuals, in their various guises, do constitute a potential for change even within these very restricted parameters.

In the Federal Republic extent and speed of Ostpolitik led to

a near break-down of the consensus on foreign affairs which had
previously existed between the parties. Although the CDU in the
end abstained in the crucial votes on the Eastern treaties in May
1972, its decision to refrain from outright opposition was clearly
governed by electoral considerations. The CSU, its Bavarian wing,
would have preferred rejection of the treaties. Fundamental dis-
agreements about the meaning of Ostpolitik and foreign policy
orientation were a feature of the election campaign of the autumn
of 1972, but the CDU chose not to highlight them because of the
evident satisfaction of the electorate with Willy Brandt's foreign
policy. It remains to be seen whether the decisive result of the
election will remove Ostpolitik from the arena of controversy or
whether events will again make it a cause of deep divisions.

The consensus between the parties which has made it relatively
easy to work a democratic system in the Federal Republic up to
now is also potentially threatened by domestic events. Radicalism
on the left, epitomised by the New Left, but also appearing in
many other, possibly more important and enduring guises, has
become a factor throughout the Western World, even though it
has not so far recaptured the dynamic of its finest hour in 1968. The
German universities are still strongly affected by left-wing radicalism; this may not be an unhealthy development, given the past
record, though it carries dangers of a new type of intolerance. The
SPD, securely in office with a larger majority, may feel stronger
pressure from its left wing, now that the chances of carrying a
programme of reforms are greater and the dangers of rocking the
boat are less. More important than extremism on the left, which
is essentially a minority taste in modern Germany, is the backlash
from the right. The law and order cry still evokes a particularly
strong response in Germany; one has only to remember the dis-
proportionate fears provoked by the Baader-Meinhof Gang and
there are other indications that a right-wing backlash is a possibility.
Much depends on the course pursued by the CDU and even in
May 1972, when the federal elections might still have been nearly
eighteen months in the future, Grosser foresaw this as the crucial
problem of domestic politics in the FRG. If now, after the elections,
the CDU turns strongly to the right, this could open up an ideological gulf unprecedented in the Federal Republic and somewhat
reminiscent, given the very different circumstances, of the political
fault line that divided Imperial Germany and proved fatal to the
Weimar Republic. It depends probably more on the CDU than
the SPD, for the Coalition renewed by the elections of November
1972 could not, by its very nature, move far into a left-ward direc-

tion. One has only to articulate these possible dangers to feel that they are not very likely to materialise. Some on the left and the right may feel that a breakdown of consensus is precisely what the Federal Republic needs, but its social structure makes this unlikely. One hesitates to predict a Scandinavian future for West German politics, but this model may well be more applicable now than it ever was in the past.

Upheaval and continuity has seemed a suitable title for this collection of essays in which distinguished academics reflect on a turbulent century of German history. When they were first read in London in the winter of 1971-72 members of the general public and students flocked in their hundreds to hear them, a tribute to the distinction of the authors and to the great concern felt abroad for the affairs of Germany. This concern is due not only to the impact of Germany's dramatic and terrible history in the twentieth century on the whole world, but also to the feeling that many of the great problems of human society in the developed world have been experienced in particularly acute form in Germany in our time.

The Second German Empire: the Reich that Never Was

by GOLO MANN

The German Empire of 1871 was something essentially new. During the following half-century, far from settling down, merging into the landscape and gaining in self-confidence, it in a sense never lost its novelty. Herein lies a profound difference between Germany on the one hand and France and Britain and many lesser European States on the other. Not even Russia was new at that period, nor, incidentally is the Soviet Union new today, in spite of its absurd name. The United States, as it evolved from the Civil War, became something new, first as a nation, and then as a world power, but certain American traditions going back to the beginning of the eighteenth century survived all the changes and are noticeable even today.

Most similar to the German case is obviously the Italian and for centuries Italy and Germany have been sisters in fate. Differences in national character and, more important, differences in the dimensions of power may explain why Italy, equally unaided by tradition, did not play the same disturbing and fatal role as the new Germany. I, for one, consider the unification of Germany, as it took place under Bismarck and after him, as inevitable, even though I am by no means in sympathy with it. My own sympathy is rather with the German Confederation, the German *Bund* of Metternich's time, it is much more with Lord Acton or with Franz Grillparzer, the great Austrian poet, who had so much political insight and foresight, than with, say, the historian Heinrich von Treitschke. But then Acton himself admitted that he was a friend of sinking ships, a poetic or nostalgic rather than a realistic inclination. The German Confederation was well and wisely conceived in 1815, perhaps the last product of ancient European statecraft, but it proved to be merely static and conservative, unable to come to grips with newly emerging problems, desires or necessities. By 1848 it was already at the end of its tether. This was the age of the national state, and it would have been futile to demand that the Germans and the Germans alone should have excluded themselves from what was, with increasing stridency, the spirit of the times. The unification of Germany, by the now defunct and almost forgotten Kingdom of Prussia, was at once inevitable and absurd, artificial and harmful. Would anyone in, say, 1630, have foretold that a successor of the Elector of Brandenburg, by far the weakest and poorest of the six Electors, residing in a godforsaken little town called Berlin, would one day become the ruler of Germany?

It was no longer a matter for ridicule at the time of the Congress of Vienna, and both Talleyrand and Gentz saw it coming. The British politicians who actively helped Prussia to acquire the Rhineland and Cologne were not trying to bring it about; they merely thought of having a comparatively solid power protecting the Rhine, the west of Germany and the new Netherlands against a restless France.

The acquisition of the Rhineland and of half of Saxony made Prussia by far the biggest and most universal German State. She was now again mainly German, in spite of her Polish provinces, and this gave her a character which Austria did not have and could never acquire. In Germany time was henceforth working for Prussia and at least some Prussian politicians knew it. Bismarck's achievements, brutally skilful as they were, did not come out of the blue, as for instance A. J. P. Taylor would have us believe. This is on the assumption that the Germans, or the most active and energetic of them, wanted national institutions far more efficient than the German *Bund* could give. Austria had no solution—this became clear in 1849: to combine the supra-national Hapsburg Monarchy with a German national state meant squaring the circle. The Republican solution, the destruction of Prussia, proved equally impossible in 1848; the powers that be were still far too strongly entrenched, the forces of democracy, the middle classes and the proletariat, still far too weak. There remained only the Prussian solution, provided the ruling classes or caste of Prussia themselves wanted it. In fact, they did not want it; for reasons of their own neither the King, nor the Junkers, nor the Church, nor the military wanted it. To drive these groups into a direction which they detested, into the war against Austria, into the North German Federation, and then the new Reich was Bismarck's most nerve-racking task, far harder than to win over the essentially helpless lesser German States from Mecklenburg to Bavaria by conquest, demagoguery or by secret bribes. I cannot here raise the question how that intellectual or political force called nationalism, in this case German nationalism, actually arose—this would be an unfair undertaking in itself. I only want to stress here that German

Nationalism was not in any way a coalition of the ruling classes, the Monarchs, the nobility, the bureaucracy, the army and so forth. The outbreak of violent, viciously anti-French nationalism in 1840 was not welcome to Metternich nor to the King of Prussia; it was a spontaneous combustion articulated by mediocre and obscure poets and publicists.

There is the thesis, and for a later period it has much to be said for it, that the German ruling classes, including now the new capitalists and entrepreneurs in heavy industry, chose to whip up nationalism against France, or later against Britain or Russia, in order to cheat the nation of the solution of its internal problems and in order to choke rising democracy. This is largely true for the age of the Kaiser, but it is certainly not true for the age of the last Prussian kings. Nor did Bismarck invent or favour German national-ism—far from it. He consciously decided to make use of this new force, so unpalatable to him, because it was there and would not be appeased until it was at once satisfied, tamed and corrupted. Had the citizens of Prussian been allowed to vote on the question of war or peace with Austria in 1866 they would have voted for peace with an overwhelming majority. Marx and Engels, these two omniscient men, expected revolution in Berlin and a mutiny of the troops in June 1866. Again had the Bavarians in 1869 been allowed to vote on the question of independence or joining Prussia within a new Empire, they would clearly have voted for independ-ence, again with a great majority. This can be proved, but it does not prove much. It is the quality and the character of those who oppose a certain development that counts. The Prussian Parliament made peace with Bismarck after Sadowa, capitulating in the face of success. The Bavarian patriots who in the spring of 1871 made most excellent speeches against Bavaria joining the Reich, against Prussian militarism, against materialism and greedy capitalism in Berlin, and so forth, they were mere conservatives who had nothing dynamic to offer. They simply wanted good old Bavaria to remain what she was, agrarian, catholic, conservative, peaceful, pious, gemütlich, but that was exactly what she could not in any circum-stances remain. In 1870 the unfortunate King Ludwig, Wagner's friend, wrote to his brother : it was sad and horrible beyond descrip-tion, but he had been forced to declare war on France and join Prussia and become a Prussian satellite, because leading opinion in the Bavarian cities had been such that the dynasty would have been swept away had he resisted this national trend. The business community, chambers of commerce, the great newspapers, the universities and the liberal bourgeoisie were all for the Reich and remained so in Bavaria, I may say until the present day. The Hohenzollernreich was made by a minority, that is quite true, but so was the American Revolution or the American Union. The immense energies which the new Germany developed after 1871 must already have been there, potentially, before that year of decision. These energies demanded new institutions, new channels, new opportunities and Bismarck understood this.

As to the means he used they are, at first glance, quite in harmony with the rules and the spirit of the age. This was an age of daring political experiments, of paradoxical, insincere alliances, between monarchy and plebiscite, between the House of Savoy and Garibaldi, between Louis Napoleon and the Roman Church, between Karl Marx and Abraham Lincoln. Bismarck, before he turned liberal or pseudo-liberal, had toyed with a kind of royalist socialism, his flirtation with Lassalle. When some months before his war with Austria, he suddenly proposed an all-German National Assembly in Frankfurt, to be elected by universal suffrage, a Berlin satirical weekly announced that it must cease publication for it could never produce better jokes than Herr von Bismarck. There was an element of joke, of bluffing, of cynical improvisation in Bismarck's proposals, but then he did admit the principle of universal suffrage for the Reichstag though not for the Prussian Landtag. During those years Bismarck's contemporaries saw clearly that he was in many ways a pupil of Napoleon III, but this was lost sight of by posterity. When in 1862 he left Paris to become Prime Minister in Berlin he took with him a certain amount of advice which a leading Bonapartist, the Duc de Persigny, had given him. Returning to Paris in 1868 he asked de Persigny with a laugh : 'Well, how have I followed your lessons?' 'Indeed,' Persigny answered, 'I must admit that the student has surpassed his master.' It was an age of great political gambling, of calculated risks of many renversements des alliances, of limited wars deliberately embarked upon and quickly ended.

Bismarck provoking Austria to war and then France was not so different from France and Sardinia deliberately needling Austria into war in 1859. Neither the Crimean nor the Italian war however had the permanently poisoning consequences of the Franco-German War. There is the difference and it appears again and again in the history of Hohenzollern Germany. German colonialism in Bismarck's later years, German imperialism under the Kaiser was no more immoral than French or Belgian colonialism. German nationalism under the Kaiser was not essentially different from American or British nationalism. German success in industry and trade was not exceptionally worthy of blame. When Bismarck and Bismarck's successors whipped up fear and war hysteria, because they wanted the military budget increased, artificially created invasion scares were not lacking in England during that period for similar reasons. But whatever the Germans did, even when it was a pale and unsuccessful imitation of what other powers did, turned out to be different, had different effects and caused different reactions. This is the strange phenomenon, of which the underlying causes must be manifold. Germany's central position in Europe may be one, the radically new and unhistorical character of the second Reich may be another of far greater importance. There were no traditions which could help to direct and guide its ever-growing expansive and flamboyant energies. Hence in the minds of the leaders there was a lack of instinct, of measure, of *Augenmass*, as Bismarck used to say, a deep feeling of insecurity in spite of all boastful strength. After all, it had been a principle of the ancient wisdom of European statecraft, accepted by German politicians themselves, that the *corpus germanicum* was something too vast and manifold to form a single state like France, that its organisation must be loose and complex, in the interests of Europe as well as of the Germans. Now all of a sudden a German National State did exist, and it had come into being not in a comparatively static and innocent age like the eighteenth century, but in the most dynamic of ages. An Austrian Statesman who had been the luckless Prime Minister in 1866, Belcredi, wrote in 1871, 'I doubt whether this new nationalist state, the Reich, can ever be a national state in the sense that it would draw all German speaking peoples into its orbit. There is for this new state only one chance, namely to dominate the whole of Europe, an ambition in which no European nation has ever succeeded so far. If the new Reich does not succeed in this, it is in permanent danger and one day it will be divided.' This was written in 1871. Henry Adams, the American historian and philosopher of history, wrote twenty-six years later : 'For this last generation since 1865, Germany has been the great disturbing element in the world and until her expansive forces are exhausted I do not see how either political or economic equilibrium is possible. Russia can expand without bursting anything, Germany cannot. Russia is in many respects weak and rotten, Germany is immensely strong and concentrated.' Adams wrote again four years later from St. Petersburg : 'Germany from this point of view is a powder magazine, all her neighbours are in terror, for fear she will explode, and sooner or later explode she must.' There we have two prophesies which came to be fulfilled. The Austrian saw the mere mechanism of the eternal

European power game, that the new Germany did not fit into it, she could not become a normal state like the others, she had to expand forever, far beyond any national frontier, or she would be destroyed. The American saw it more from the perspective of the domestic economy. Was it sheer guesswork in both cases? The answer to this question depends on one's taste. I for one would answer no, it was not merely happy guess work. Did both men foresee the inevitable? There again I would answer no. I refuse to accept that kind of fatalism in history. There would have been ways to avoid the first disaster let alone the second, that of 1939 to 1945. The Austrian and the American both saw dangerous possibilities, the realisation of which became not less but more probable as time went on.

It is the merit of Bismarck to have kept international affairs under strict control as long as he ruled. The adventurer of the 1860s became the experienced Statesman, the over-cautious and over-subtle protector of peace in the seventies and eighties. I cannot enter into this aspect of his work here but it is, I think, generally accepted that the revolutionary did in fact turn into a second Metternich. That goes for external affairs, but not for domestic politics. It is impossible here to discuss Bismarck's strong and strange personal character, so attractive in some ways and so repulsive in others. Essentially, he always remained a man of conflict, passion and power, and not of consensus. Always fearing for the security of his own work, his new empire, he renounced an aggressive foreign policy and tried to appease foreign countries with skill and tact. But he needed conflict and he sought, found and created it within his new Germany. He had come to power in 1862, for reasons of internal constitutional conflict; domestic conflicts threatening danger for the monarchy and for the possessing classes had to exist as late as 1890 so that he could stay in power. A. J. P. Taylor in his little book *The Course of German History*, published during Hitler's War and in my humble opinion one of the most intelligent essays on the topic, has described the Bismarck constitution as a fake, as the mere trappings of a liberal or parliamentary government. Some ten years later in his Bismarck biography he described the same constitution as containing all the essentials of a modern democratic state. As we know that outstanding scholar has always had the courage to revise his judgement, such as, for instance, when one day he discovered that Adolf Hitler was a man of peace and never intended to do any of the things he did. Personally I would choose neither Taylor's first nor his second position but an intermediate one. The prerogatives of the new parliament, the Reichstag, were by no means to be despised. This parliament and within it the leading party of the 1870s, the National Liberals, created in that decade the institutions essential to an industrial and commercial society. It is, of course, true that the Prime Minister or Chancellor depended on the Emperor, the King of Prussia, alone and not on a majority in the Reichstag. Of the seven Imperial Chancellors between 1871 and 1918 (excluding the very last, Prince Max of Baden) only two, Caprivi and Hohenlohe, fell from power as mere victims of extra-parliamentary conflict and intrigues. The five others, Bismarck, Bülow, Bethmann, Michaelis and Hertling, had to retire or were dismissed by the Emperor only after they had been defeated in the Reichstag. The parties in the Reichstag could, if they wanted to, make work impossible for the Chancellor but never until 1917 did they have the slightest influence on the choice of his successor.

In the main the imperial constitution proved to be static, because of its infinite and immensely awkward complications, and it was incapable of development. Almost, for it did develop slowly, far too slowly, before 1914, but with considerable speed between 1914 and 1918. The first German Republic, the Democracy of 1919, was not entirely an improvisation; developments pointed clearly in its direction in the years before and the Reichstag had the main say in that development. It happened under the pressure of war, but this indicates that technically it would have been possible during the years of peace. That it did not happen was only in part due to the unfortunate set-up of the constitution itself. In greater part it was due to the firmly entrenched power of the Prussian conservatives, to the socialist scare among the bourgeoisie and to the mediocrity of those who stood or pretended to stand for democratic progress. I must touch here upon the absurdities of the constitution of the Second Reich. The American and Swiss Federations provided for a national Government, the new Germany did not. The Reich Chancellor was nothing but the President of the Bundesrat, the Federal Council, which was supposed to be a kind of Government and was in fact a conference of State Governments, controlled by Prussia and ranging down to the principality of Schaumburg-Lippe and the Republic of Lübeck. Bismarck could not even appear before the national Parliament, the Reichstag, as Reich Chancellor, but only as Prussian Foreign Minister. Prussia had created the Reich and made up about three-fifths of the Reich in area and population. The constitution separated the two entities and Bismarck took care that they should remain separated. The Prussian Parliament was elected by the absurd three-class franchise which gave a secure majority to the Conservatives, and had the strange effect of leaving the Social Democrats without a single seat in the Prussian Lower House at a time when they were already polling the highest vote of all parties in the whole of Germany.

No party or individual, only the Federal Council, the *Bundesrat*, could initiate bills to be voted on by the national Parliament. The *Bundesrat* was controlled by Prussia, Prussia in turn was controlled by the Conservative Agrarians, later by a combination of Agrarians and industrial capitalists in both Houses, not to speak of the King Emperor himself, his personal friends, the high bureaucracy, the military and so on. The Reichstag could obstruct and delay, but it could never give direction or leadership. In a formal sense the clashes between Prussia and the Reichstag were, again according to the constitution, conflicts, so to speak, between two states, in reality it was of course a social conflict. The citizens of Prussia were not less progressively minded than the citizens of Bavaria, in fact rather more so. After all, the two most important industrial centres were now developing in Prussia, in the Rhineland and in Silesia. Prussian cities from Cologne to Königsberg were admirably and democratically administered, American mayors in those days came all the way across the Atlantic to study the achievements of their Prussian colleagues. Yet in the State of Prussia, in the central and provincial administration, and in the policies of Prussia the conservative and anti-democratic agrarians remained the strongest force. Max Weber pointed out in 1895 that they were an economically doomed class, but it did not make this anachronism any less harmful. In his study on Bethmann Hollweg as Reich Chancellor, Professor Zmarzlik has shown the incredible difficulties with which that highest official of the Reich had to contend, especially if he was a conscientious and rather honest man like Bethmann. He was balancing between or caught between the Reichstag and the Prussian Landtag, between the Prussian Ministers and the chiefs of the newly created departments of the Reich, Navy, Treasury and so on, between the Kaiser and the Kaiser's three Cabinets, the Civilian, Military and Naval Cabinets. There were also the Federal Council, the *Bundesrat,* whose more important members like Bavaria had, after all, to be considered, there were the Prussian General Staff and powerful interest lobbies like the Agrarian League, the Association of German Industrialists, influential political bodies like the Navy League, the Colonial League, the Pan-Germans, the *Alldeutscher Bund,* and so forth. It was an almost impossible position and task.

More recently, Professor John Röhl, in his book *Germany without*

Bismarck, went so far as to justify the Kaiser's so-called personal rule, *persönliches Regiment*, the beginning of which he seeks in the year 1897. The Kaiser, he thinks, had to exercise his personal influence increasingly, because the Bismarckian system without Bismarck simply ceased to function. The over-complicated and chaotic conditions of leadership need not have been fatal, had the Reich been a Reich in the old sense of the term, a vast and loose confederation, undynamic, essentially inactive towards the outside world, such as the Holy Roman Empire. But as Henry Adams observed in the 1890s, Germany was immensely strong and concentrated, strong economically, strong in the military field, and accordingly ambitious and restless. In such a country the lack of constitutional, concerted leadership was infinitely more dangerous than in the days of the Holy Roman Emperors and the six Prince Electors and the 2,000 estates, Princes, Dukes, Margraves, and villages of the Empire.

The fact is that Bismarck never thought of an immensely strong and concentrated new Germany. His conception, inasmuch as this severely practical statesman ever had conceptions, was the continuing existence of the Kingdom of Prussia, plus an annex of lesser states, with a degree of interior autonomy neutralised by the external alliance with Prussia. There would be some increase in Prussian military power and some concessions to the new middle class, a minimum of what they had been claiming during the preceding decades. In the European power game the new Reich inevitably carried more weight than Prussia had done, but Bismarck strove to keep his foreign policy as Prussian as he could : he scoffed at quarrels over some minor Balkan country, and one of his golden words was that Bulgaria was not worth the bones of a single Prussian grenadier. He believed in the ancient Prusso-Russian friendship, as the former kings of Prussia had done; the Pact of the three Emperors seemed to renew the Holy Alliance; his alliance with Austria could be interpreted as the resurrection of the old Metternich *Bund* with some changes. He did not believe in a great navy and in battleships, as late as 1897, when Admiral Tirpitz tried to win the old man over to his naval programme. He acquired colonies in Africa, because German merchants and adventurers had started the game and public opinion got a passion for it. He himself did not care at all. 'This is all very well,' he once remarked to a German enthusiast for colonies, 'but', pointing to a map of Europe, 'there is my Africa, there is France, there is Germany, there is Russia, there is my Africa.' In short, having helped to destroy the old European balance of power and the German Confederation as a pivot of this balance, Bismarck tried to restore it and stick to the ancient, modest *raison d'état* of Prussia.

In this, he could not succeed in the long run, in spite of all his skill, much less could his successors. When he kept on repeating that Germany was saturated, he wanted time to stand still, with peace abroad, the upper classes of Prussia ruling at home and he himself in command as long as he lived. A society becoming increasingly industrialised and urbanised could not accept such a situation forever. An essentially new power could not forever be guided by the ancient Prussian *raison d'état*. The annexation of Alsace Lorraine was only one symptom of this : it was a German not a Prussian annexation, German Nationalism not Prussian Conservatism dominated the newly founded University of Strasbourg. Prussia and France had been collaborating frequently in the past and Bismarck himself had insisted in his early days that this option must be kept open, but it was no longer open now. Franco-German hereditary enmity, *Erbfeindschaft*, a pernicious nonsense, quite new and utterly unhistorical, took the place of the rich and fertile relations which had existed between the two nations in the past, between France and Prussia as well as between South Germany and France. Max Weber, in the lecture given in 1895 and mentioned earlier, remarked : 'It was the tragedy of Bismarck that his own work, the new Germany, changed in his very hands, so that it had to demand at home new forms of government, abroad new policies which were utterly strange to the founder and to which he could not adapt himself.' By new forms of government Weber meant democracy, and by foreign policies, he meant imperialism, colonialism, a big navy, and that was the combination he advocated. Only peoples who ruled themselves at home, as the British did, could rule over lesser breeds. Only a government which did not fear its own people or a great part of it, could lead an active, expansive and proud foreign policy.

It has often been observed that Bismarck corrupted the German political mind, that the nation was politically far more mature in 1860 than in 1890 and that he did not allow them to learn and practise the art of self-government. Already his first successor, the gentle and politically innocent Caprivi, hinted at this in polite words. Later on Max Weber, to mention only him, elevated it into a doctrine—the horrible destruction of all political and personal integrity and independence through Bismarck's work. To which I am tempted to answer : If you have allowed one single man, and at that a man who was after all not a bloodthirsty tyrant, but a civilised gentleman, to destroy your integrity and to deprive you of all independent political intitiative, tact and wisdom, then you must be a strange people indeed. Besides, if political wisdom had weakened and steadily declined in the years before Bismarck vanished into retirement in 1890, the Germans still had twenty-four years from 1890 until the outbreak of the war to get their house in order, yet they failed to do so. When in 1908 public opinion exploded against the Kaiser because of his *Daily Telegraph* interview—what harmless times these were : the interview given by the Kaiser to an English journalist in itself was utterly innocent and incidentally rather pacific and by no means warlike in tone— the Social Democrat Ledebour cried out in the Reichstag : 'Genuine ministerial responsibility and the appointment of ministers by Parliament is the demand of the hour. You, Gentlemen, have the opportunity, because of the general discontent of the nation, to achieve real democratic parliamentary government and since you have this opportunity you must use it. If only you had the courage at last to acquire the self-confidence of free men.'

The opportunity was lost once more : The defence was too tenacious, the liberal or democratic attackers too weak, too accustomed to meek opposition only without responsibility, too quarrelsome and distrustful of each other. The 1890s, long since fully explored in their foreign political aspects, have recently been examined in two interesting studies, one constitutional and political, John Röhl's *Germany without Bismarck*, already mentioned, and in a study by Kenneth D. Barking, *The Controversy over German Industrialization 1890–1902*. Politics and economics interacted : Caprivi believed in industry and free trade, the Agrarians and the Junkers did not and contributed to his downfall. The debates over tariffs protecting East German agriculture, a central issue in the late nineties, were crude and violent, as in America before 1862. While still boasting of German idealism and our great philosopher Immanuel Kant, the old-established classes had become utterly materialistic in their outlook. This made the alleged contrast between German *Kultur* and British commercialism or mamonism, *Krämergeist*, all the more absurd. Naturally, some romantic sugar coating was never lacking on the part of the Agarians, extolling the virtue, morality, health of the village and the earth against the vices of the great cities and the greed of the capitalists. Industrialisation could not be prevented by such propaganda. A compromise was reached in 1902, protection for agriculture and for heavy industry as well : thus a new alliance came into being between coal and steel on the one side, and the old Prussian nobility on the other, the much quoted pluto-aristocracy of the last decades of the Empire.

The anti-capitalist arguments, the anti-modern demagogy used at that time by the Conservatives, often mixed with anti-Semitism, never entirely vanished from the German political scene and had, as we know, a monstrous revival thirty years later. At the same time, around 1900, its character marked by the Kaiser's personal régime, by Tirpitz at the head of the Admiralty, and by Bülow's Chancellorship, the decision was made for a bold policy, *Weltpolitik*, a great navy, imperialism. In all this there was no doubt the motive to lure the nation away from domestic conflicts, to reconcile the people and parties to the anachronistic establishment, ruled by King, Caste and Upper Classes, but how conscious a motive is difficult to say. I have remarked earlier that Bismarck's wars were not much more immoral than the wars of Napoleon III. In the same way one could say that German imperialism was no more immoral than French or British or Russian imperialism. It was, however, more awkward and less successful. German imperialism was more disturbing and dangerous, again because the whole rapidly growing enterprise of the German Reich was new, because Germany had a poor and confused internal political set-up, because her imperial policies, like her continental policies, were bare of any tradition or pre-established direction, such as French imperial policies had, at any rate in North Africa. The new Imperialism was not invented in Germany; it was an international fashion both in its optimistic, glorious or vainglorious form, the white man's burden, Cecil Rhodes, Kipling, Teddy Roosevelt; and in its pessimistic form social Darwinism, survival of the fittest, decreasing resources to feed an ever-increasing population, *homo homini lupus*, how every state must evolve into a larger state, Brooks Adams or Homer Lea in America, Mackinder in England.

For my part I consider Lenin's famous theory, the rational, economic, dialectical theory, imperialism as a last phase of capitalism, as simply false, not only in the form in which Lenin stated it, but also as more liberal minds have developed it. Imperialism, European imperialism is dead, European capitalism is still going pretty strong. Imperialism was a spiritual attitude, a fashion, and as we know in retrospect, a short-lived illusion. This could be proved easily by facts and figures, and for no country more clearly than for Germany. It was purely a craze : German prosperity came from international free trade with other industrial nations, from investments in North and South America, it did not come from her colonies, which cost a lot of money and yielded next to nothing. Eager students as they were in so many fields, the Germans studied Admiral Mahon's and McKinder's writings, more in bitter earnest than other nations did. And what do I mean when I say the Germans? The Kaiser himself, of course, whose imperialism was rather of the sunny, vainglorious variety; the great university professors, I am sorry to have to say this, the great professors of History and Economics, a highly influential and respected group. It is a strange fact that even Max Weber, that penetrating, independent, powerful thinker, fell in with the prevailing fashion and became a social Darwinist like the others. There are pages in the writings and lectures of this great writer dating from this period which read almost like *Mein Kampf*. The fashion became a deep-seated spiritual disease. Owing to Germany's political and spiritual past it assumed a special character although picked up from other nations. German imperialism had to be exclusively, aggressively German, not part of a universal trend nor having anything to do with general human progress. Germany had to win her share of the planet, her place in the sun, as the expression went, not in order to spread the rights of man or the ideas of the American or French Revolutions. A German tradition going back to the early nineteenth century was still at work here : the anti-universalist, anti-revolutionary outlook of German historians ever since Napoleon. German historicism, as I want to define it here, means the cult of the nation and of the state as something individual, specific, organically grown under more general human law, the state as a kind of god on earth. This German philosophical tradition gradually became a force which tended to separate Germany from the main stream of Western political thought, from thinkers such as John Stuart Mill or Herbert Spencer. It now came together with the new imperialism and the term for it was Realpolitik. It is a meaningless word in itself and Bismarck would have been too intelligent to use it. If politics is not a permanent adaptation to changing realities what else is it? But we the Germans, so it was thought, had been dreamy ideologues far too long; we must now become realists at long last, consistently and brutally. Alas, this realism was not very realistic, as the events proved, and they exaggerated the game, not in deeds but in words. A Frenchman of that period is supposed to have said : 'When a German wants to move gracefully he jumps out of the window', an apt description of the manoeuvres of those years.

Under the influence of the professors and the major part of the press, the bourgeoisie right down to the so-called lower middle classes, worshipped the new message, teachers, especially of physical education, parsons, doctors, dentists, small business men, minor employers and so on. They were the members of those great associations like the *Kolonialverein*, or the *Alldeutscher Verband*, who drove the Foreign Office into imperialistic adventures even when the more intelligent Secretary of State wanted to put the brake on. A great hysteria was rationalised into judgements and foreboding of this kind : 'Immense changes are under way. Centres of power are shifting from London to Washington, from Paris to Berlin, from St. Petersburg to Peking. The planet is definitely being divided up for the last time. The nation which does not participate forcefully is doomed—*Weltmacht oder Untergang*, World Power or decline into insignificance. We are late in this race, we missed centuries when other people were helping themselves to whole sub-continents, this last battle we must fight or perish.' There was indeed something democratic in this folly—radical democrats like Max Weber, moderate democrats like Hans Delbrück were leading imperialists and big navy men and even a social democrat leader like Scheidemann was enthusiastic about the Baghdad Railway, a much overrated but not unconstructive and incidentally by no means entirely German enterprise. My thesis then would be that German Imperialism was irrational, governed by politics and psychology, not by rational economic interest. Psychology is not something accidental which one just adds to the real true and important substance, economic development. Psychology is itself the main substance : it deals with human beings as they are, not as the abstraction of *homo economicus* would make them. Psychology is part of economics itself, once the most elementary needs are satisfied. This approach is not irrational, bourgeois, idealistic or romantic, as our neo-Marxists would have it today, it is a realistic approach, it takes people as they really are.

Today, when Germany's economy is ten times as productive as it was in 1900, there is no need for battleships or colonies or coaling stations or strategic outposts in the seven seas, and there was no need for it in 1900. But people talked themselves into the belief that all that nonsense was vitally necessary, and this had its effect. To illustrate further what I mean here, we have today the belief that in order to remain a world power one must be in the game of conquering outer space and getting one's share of outer space, so to speak. Once that decision is taken, all kind of rationalisations follow : it is for the sake of science, it brings strategic advantages, although I cannot help suspecting that the earth could be destroyed efficiently enough from the earth itself. In a book written by a team of Russian scientists on mankind in the year 2000 I have even read that by that time Russia will plant vegetables in hothouses on the moon. I for one can't help thinking that hard as the climate in Siberia is, it is still more favourable to humans and vegetables than the climate on the moon and it would be far less expensive to make the Gobi Desert blossom than the planet Mars. But one must do it all the same, because it is fun or because the other boys do it, one must do it—period : the reasons come later. Thus there were variations for the reasons given for German overseas imperialism. Admiral Tirpitz and his big navy friends were no warmongers; a big navy must, in their view, make Germany *ebenbürtig*, equal to other Great Powers in every respect, and if necessary capable of finding allies wherever she wanted. A big navy must protect German trade in peace and in war, but in peace no protection was needed for German trade, and when war came, although Tirpitz needed battleships, they did not help in the slightest in feeding the blockaded homeland. The Generals were not overseas imperialists at all; their task was to prepare continental war, the coming of which they thought inevitable sooner or later, and sooner the longer the peace of 1871 lasted. In that coming war they hoped to win better strategic frontiers or bases for the next war, and when that second war came then they would once more win even better bases for the war after that. Such, literally, was the outlook of General Ludendorff. Apart from this, the Generals were not out to increase the size of the army considerably and the fact is that in peacetime the German army was smaller in numbers than the French, in spite of Germany's much larger population. The more the army increased the less Prussian and the more democratic and eventually proletarian it would become, led by a vast majority of officers from the lower middle class, and that was not to the taste of the Prussian General Staff. In September 1914 Admiral Tirpitz observed : 'Victory or defeat, we shall soon have complete democracy, an army of millions upon millions of working men and women in the armament factories will take care of that.' The navy was more democratic than the army, far more demagogic in organising political and literary propaganda in the new style.

The Prussian Conservatives could not be overseas imperialists as long as they remained consistent with themselves. They voted for the naval budgets only in return for advantages they received. To sum up, German Imperialism was the product of new energies which did not know how to find an outlet, or a meaning for themselves, partly crazy, partly idealistic and romantic, but never rational. When war came it did not come over colonies or over the German Navy; Britain had after all accepted, even though

reluctantly, the German Navy. It was a continental war and nobody
doubts today that it was a German preventive war. Preventive not
only during the last twenty-four hours, when Russian mobilisation
became the final issue, but from the beginning of the crisis over the
Serajevo incident. This is generally accepted today, it seems to me,
and I am not even sure whether we needed Professor Fritz Fischer's
now famous books to prove it. Just as A. J. P. Taylor, for the fun
of it, made 1939 into a second 1914, so Professor Fischer made 1914
into a third 1939. The deliberate impudence of 1939, and the acute
awareness of it, was completely lacking in 1914. The 'iron' leadership of 1939 was dismally absent in 1914. The Western democracies
proved to be in much better shape and much better prepared for
the ordeal than Germany; in spite of the so called *Burgfrieden*,
the pretence of a truce between the political parties, domestic strife
was raging all through the war years. One cannot deny, alas, that
Germany was in good shape for war in 1939; there was no domestic
strife or political struggle during the Second World War—Hitler
had seen to that. Hitler had won the political game in 1939 and
started his war when and because he had won it, and because he
thought he had the world in his pocket. In 1914 the almost non-
existent German leadership had lost the political game and went
to war almost in despair because they had lost it. They had missed
the chance to go to war under far more auspicious circumstances
in 1904–1905. Now, they felt, was the last moment, time was
working against them—that was the psychological state articulated
most strongly and decisively by the military. This is not disproved
by the fact that the nation was happy in August 1914—it was a
kind of masochistic happiness. They were fighting against a world
of enemies, without ever asking why the world was full of enemies,
and they were happy at last to find unity at home—in the Kaiser's
word, 'I no longer know parties, only Germans'. This, too, did not
last long, for very soon there were parties and social classes again,
quarrelling as bitterly as before.

The gradually emerging lunatic war aims, fabricated by irresponsible associations like the *Zentralverband der Deutschen Industrie*,
were never officially accepted or refuted by the civil Government,
such as it was, and were more or less officially accepted by the High
Command. These lunacies I for one consider as a product of war
not as its cause. These war aims did not make the war, but the
war made the war aims. There are connections, of course, between
these aims and certain follies at work before 1914, *Weltmacht oder
Untergang*. What I deny is that there was such a clear-cut con-

tinuity, such a simple sequence of cause and effect as Professor Fischer and his acolytes would have us believe. As to the consequences of the war and the tragedy of the years 1917 and 1918 for Germany, they are indeed of overwhelming weight and once more they are in the main psychological and moral. When Bertrand Russell travelled to Berlin in 1895 he came back with gloomy forebodings: 'If the German rulers do not cease political persecution and do not allow complete democracy, war and extinction of the national life are the almost inevitable doom of the German Empire.' Half a century later the same Bertrand Russell had very different things to say of the Germany of the *fin de siècle*. Here I must quote from memory: 'The Germany of the Kaiser', he now wrote, 'was only swash-buckling and a little absurd. I lived in the Kaiser's Germany, I saw the forces of progress at work there, and they had every chance of succeeding. There was more freedom in the Kaiser's Germany than there is today anywhere on earth outside Britain and Scandinavia.' These are the words of Bertrand Russell.

I am not blaming this great philosopher for any contradiction here—both statements were true and remain true. The Germany of the Kaiser, of the Admiralty, of the General Staff, of Krupp, of selfrighteously nationalist Professors, snarling bemonocled lieutenants was also the Germany of the *Simplizissimus*, that wonderful satirical paper attacking all these individuals and trends with a freedom and wit which one can only study with nostalgia today, for that kind of serene and solemn humour seems to have gone forever. It was the Germany of the great Social Democratic Party of Bebel and his friends, of Einstein and Planck, of Gerhart Hauptmann, and two other men I don't want to mention here, of Max Reinhardt's theatre, which contributed so much to the success of Ibsen and Bernard Shaw, perhaps more than their own nations did at the time. In any case, the Germany of the Kaiser must have been a country pleasant to live in and many foreigners chose to live there, in Munich or Dresden and elsewhere. Why it did not last, why the end was so miserable and so miserably stupid, for this one would have to go back to the beginning for an explanation, to the original sin of 1871 of founding the new union in the French neighbour's royal palace instead of peacefully and democratically at home, to the feeble Bismarckian compromise between the old authority by the grace of God and the liberal bourgeoisie—the bourgeoisie who betrayed their ideals in order to get a small share of power from the monarchy, the feudal aristocracy and the military, who in their turn remained in command and excluded the democrats and the Social Democrats from national responsibility. That was the law under which the new Reich began, *das Gesetz wonach du angetreten*, as Goethe says. They could have broken away from that law, one always can, but as it happens they did not.

The Absolutism of the Hohenzollern State and the Rise of the Social Democratic Party

by WOLFGANG ABENDROTH

The rise of Prussia to dominion over the later German Reich and the success of Bismarck's bonapartist policy began with the Prussian constitutional conflict of 1862. The bourgeoisie became the servant of a state, first in the largest North German member of the German Confederation and then in all German-speaking territories with the exception of Austria and Switzerland. Yet this state withheld from the bourgeoisie, constitutionally at least until 1918, the right to determine the practical direction of policy. As Ferdinand Lassalle immediately recognised, the liberal majority in the Prussian Chamber of Deputies had lost the fight for the prerogatives of Parliament because their opposition to the King's military budget was only half-hearted. They had already lost the fight even while they still clung to these prerogatives, objectively for appearances' sake, subjectively to salve their own consciences, until they finally surrendered by accepting the Indemnity Law of 3 September 1866. Thus the way was opened up for the foundation of the North German Confederation by the Prussian victory over Austria in 1866 and its enlargement into the German Reich by the victory over France in 1871. The majority of the German middle classes had already been committed, since the inauguration of the *Nationalverein* in 1859, to the *kleindeutsch* solution of the German question, namely to the transformation of the *Zollverein* into a federal state. Most of the Liberals therefore felt that their most immediate and important aim had now been realised. They had, however, not achieved it by their own struggles, but had attained it as a gift from the very state which still granted their erstwhile opponents, the Prussian Junkers, all the privileges in the army and the administration they had held before the abortive Revolution of 1848. The capitulation of the German bourgeoisie in the face of Bismarck's quasi-bonapartist solution of the German question became for many decades the most important basis of German politics. From now on a strongly personal factor, represented at first by Bismarck and later by William II, himself the wearer of the Crown, legitimised this capitulation in the view of the educated classes. The characteristic feature of this situation was that the key positions in the executive apparatus of Prussia, the most important country in the German federal state, and in the Reich administration were held by the feudal classes; they in turn had, however, to seek continuous accommodation with the great capitalist pressure groups. This was the basic situation and thus the struggle for democracy and for a parliamentary régime, and against this power combine, became increasingly the monopoly of the working class movement. This movement was, however, itself constantly exposed to the consequences of the total political situation reacting upon the perceptions, education and views of its own adherents, members and full-time officers in the Reichstag, the trade unions and social insurance institutions. This was particularly the case during periods, when the social-economic position appeared stable owing to the rising prosperity engendered by a highly centralised capitalist system, but when at the same time the illusion of a foreign menace seemed to threaten this stability.

From this perspective it is possible to comprehend the bonapartist authoritarian tendencies in the rise of the first workers' movement from 1848 onwards, through Lassalle's programme of 1862, and from the founding of the 'General German Workers' Association' in 1863 to the end of Schweitzer's ascendancy. It also explains the persistence of Lassallean ideas amongst the membership, in spite of the anti-Prussian, federalist and *grossdeutsch* elements in the genesis of the Social Democratic Workers' Party of Bebel and Liebknecht, which was founded at Eisenach.

Personal differences between leaders and members of the two social democratic parties remained acute. The *Arbeiterschaften*, workers' groups with a centralised authoritarian structure, the product of the inevitable concessions made by the Lassallians to the trade union concept, still differed profoundly from the democratic ideas which August Bebel enshrined in his model constitution for German trade union co-operatives. Nevertheless, the parliamentary work of the two parties united them in common opposition to the Government, just as the Liberals on the other hand gave up any real defence of democratic principles. The outbreak of the Franco-Prussian war in 1870 still kept the two social-democratic groups apart. The Lassallians voted for war credits right up to the capitulation of Sedan, holding the view, which was also then shared by Marx, that it was a war of national self-defence. The Eisenach group, on the other hand, abstained, probably in defiance of the views of their own members.

But the transformation, after the capitulation of Sedan, of the war against the empire of Napoleon III into an annexationist war against the French Republic brought the two social-democratic parties together. In common they resisted the disastrous policy of separating Alsace-Lorraine from France, which perpetuated the antagonism between the two nations. This consequence was foreseen in the manifesto of the General Council of the International Workers' Association and Engels himself predicted that it would provoke a Franco-Russian alliance in the future. Both parties now opposed the patriotic orgy which gripped the middle classes and the bourgeois parties; they preferred to do their democratic duty by swimming against the tide of public opinion, in so far as it put a pseudo-patriotic emotionalism in place of concern for the real national interest; they refused to descend to comfortable acceptance of a mistaken mood. They did not allow themselves to be deflected by pressure on the part of the authorities. The Brunswick Committee of the Eisenach Group, which was effectively the party's executive but could not for legal reasons openly admit it, was arrested, yet they voted henceforth against war credits. The trial of August Bebel and Wilhelm Liebknecht at Leipzig in March 1872 amounted to a misuse of the charge of high treason and started the process by which legal maxims were undermined in order to suppress any critical thought. It foreshadowed the reinterpretation, by the supreme court of the German Reich, and again much later by the Federal Constitutional Court, of the crime of preparing a specific act of high treason into a crime of treasonable thought. Before this trial, jurisprudence, committed as it was to the rule of law, held with unanimity that the crime of preparing a treasonable undertaking presupposed the actual planning of a concrete act of violence designed to abolish properly constituted authority. Now for the first time a penalty was imposed for 'preparing high treason' merely on the general assumption that possibly in an indeterminate future situation a revolution might break out. These repressive acts by the authorities could not, however, prevent the declaration of solidarity with the Paris Commune contained in Bebel's speech in the Reichstag on 25 March 1871. Nor could they undo the responsible policy towards the international movement as well as towards the nation which had been adopted by the Social Democrats during the Franco-Prussian war.

Although the struggle between the two Social Democratic parties flared up again, the split had become an anachronism and after

Schweitzer's inglorious resignation it was only a question of time before it was healed. The way was open to the unity congress of Gotha on 14 and 15 February 1875 and the formation, out of hitherto warring groups, of the Socialist Workers' Party. The last psychological obstacles to unity were removed by the chicaneries imposed upon both parties by the police and the judiciary following the Reichstag elections of 10 January 1874. In these elections both parties secured about 3 per cent of the votes cast and together they obtained nine seats. Clarity of doctrine was certainly not one of the virtues of the party unified at Gotha; the criticism which Karl Marx directed from London against its programme was in this respect correct in all essentials. Marx and Engels were, however, mistaken in their belief that the Eisenach wing had already adopted and digested their own scientific methods and had thereby overtaken the earlier Lassallians. The popular literature of both the earlier parties and soon also of the united party was still dominated by the writings of Lassalle, which were most immediately comprehensible to the progressive German workers, even if these workers had in practice and on many questions advanced beyond Lassalle. Even August Bebel, that most talented and clear-sighted leader of the Eisenach wing, was only able to study the first volume of *Das Kapital* and Engels' *Condition of the Working Classes in England* during his long imprisonment after the high treason verdict.

The unity of the two parties increased their influence : in the Reichstag elections of 10 January 1877 the Social Democrats gained more than 9 per cent of the vote. Earlier the Socialists had given proof, even to the Liberals, of their reliability in the defence of the rule of law by their conduct in the *Kulturkampf* and on the Jesuit Law. Now they earned the fruits of their energetic and shrewd parliamentary tactics which August Bebel had maintained against the ultra-radical views of Wilhelm Liebknecht; the self-confidence of the workers was strengthened through the unity of the party. The mental confusion of all too many of its functionaries was gradually being cleared up from the beginning of 1877 by Friedrich Engels' public dispute with Eugen Dühring in the columns of *Vorwärts*.

The series of articles by Engels continued to be published, in spite of initial opposition at the party congress of 1877, in the central party organ even though they were banished to the literary supplement. They helped party members, thirsting for instruction and knowledge, to acquire Marxist ideas during the ensuing period of persecution. Socialists were, however, still handicapped by their own low level of education and by the prevailing modes of thought in the rest of society.

It was not long before Bismarck hit back against the rapid progress of a party which was aiming to develop the self-consciousness of the working class in the struggle for democracy and socialism. Adolf Stöcker's attempt to win back the workers to the 'christian-nationalist' objectives of the authoritarian state by anti-semitic slogans and the offer of minor social reforms was clearly failing. Thus the two assassination attempts on William I, which had no connection whatever with the Social Democratic Party or with any socialist worker, had to serve as an excuse for unleashing a wild monarchist and anti-socialist hysteria. The Reichstag elections which were held under these auspices in 1878 only reduced the party to 8 per cent of the vote. The shameful surrender by the majority of National-'Liberals' of their own principles in the same Reichstag, which also brought the turn towards Protectionism, forced the Social Democrats into illegal existence, at first for two and a half years, but then, through the extension of the emergency law, in practice for twelve years. For exactly the same length of time the party was to be outside the law under Hitler.

Certainly Bismarck's Socialist Law seems today harmless enough, compared with the sufferings inflicted by the Nazi terror upon the followers of democracy, socialism and humanitarianism, particularly upon the underground cadres of the old working class movement. The penalties threatened under this law were substantially less than the penal norms until recently in use against Communists in the Federal German Republic. It looked very different to the citizens of those days, when even the educated classes thought in terms of the rule of law, however undemocratic the conditions enshrined by it. But the wave of persecution could not break the party. Social Democratic candidates could still fight elections and Socialists take part in parliamentary debates. Socialist associations were, however, not allowed to function. But in those days the candidate in a constituency was on paper not standing for a party, even if this was in fact usually the case, but was nominated by an electoral committee set up specifically for the purpose of the election. The illiberal and anti-democratic perfectionism, which deprives members of prohibited parties of their parliamentary seats and prevents former members from taking part in elections, was not conceded to Bismarck by the Reichstag. It was put into practice in the Federal German Republic between the proscription of the Communist Party in 1956 and the readmission of the German Communist Party in 1969. On the other hand, the climate of opinion among the middle classes, which in many parts of the country still influenced the majority of industrial workers now tempted Höchberg, Schramm and for the time being Bernstein as well into tactics of assimilation and resignation; this amounted to a surrender of the high intellectual level and the ideas of class war which had been attained by the party. On the other hand the harsh repression gave rise to several waves of anarchism, to which the two former Lassallians Johann Most with his London journal *Freedom*, and then Hasselmann succumbed. Nevertheless, the foundation of the newspaper *Sozialdemokrat* created not only an organisational link between the socialist groups operating locally, but also an intellectual centre. After 28 September 1879 this paper was being distributed illegally in Germany from Switzerland. Karl Marx and Friedrich Engels gradually gained influence with its editors through a slow process of education and hard struggle; there was also systematic collaboration and mutual criticism between the editors of this illegal party organ and the best minds in the parliamentary group in the Reichstag. The periodical *Die Neue Zeit* (The New Age), appearing legally in Germany since 1883, also contributed as a literary-theoretical journal under the leadership of Karl Kautsky to the advance of marxist ideas among the cadres of the socialdemocratic movement. Thus the key elements in the party acquired that coherence of view which in turn produced the vital feeling of solidarity, discipline and sacrifice, courage and devotion to the aims of the workers' movement. Without these qualities it would have been unthinkable that the activists and the movement could have survived the loss of livelihood, the dispersal of families through expulsion from the areas of 'lesser martial law', and the prison sentences. On the other hand the strength of the Socialdemocratic party, which on 27 October 1881 lost only a quarter of its votes and thanks to the electoral system retained twelve seats, was undoubtedly the reason for the inauguration of the new social policy in the imperial message of 17 November 1881, which ushered in the development of welfare statism in Germany.

During this illegal phase the party held three congresses; at Castle Wyden from 20 to 23 August 1880, where the self-limitation to legal methods was cut out of the party programme; at Copenhagen from 28 March to 2 April 1887, where the editorial policy of the *Sozialdemokrat* was approved in principle and opportunist criticism coming from the ranks of the parliamentary party in the Reichstag was dismissed; and at St. Gallen from 2 to 6 October 1887, where the rebirth of the International, and thus the formation of the 2nd International was decided upon and the revision of the party programme was initiated. These three party congresses on the one hand confirmed the strategy of forcing concessions to the working class by determined opposition against the monarchical authoritarian state, using all available parliamentary means; on the other hand the adoption of marxist ways of thinking began to reveal itself more and more clearly.

August Bebel's book *Woman—Past, Present and Future,* appearing in new editions ever since 1879, was certainly not free of shortcomings in the application of marxist methods; but for a self-taught man it was an astonishing achievement. It showed that social democracy was able to produce leaders from the working class, whose academic achievement put that of most official professors of social science well in the shade. In this way it was possible to master a problem which baffled the bourgeois parties until the victory of the revolution in 1918 forced them to face it. The Social Democrats remained, thanks to Bebel's book, the only party until the Revolution demanding political equality for women. As late as August 1918 all the other parties in the Reichstag rejected votes for women!

With the elections of 1884, in which the Social Democrats were able to gain 9.7 per cent of the vote and twenty-four seats, all the losses incurred during the period of repression had been made good. A renewed economic boom strengthened the trade union movement, the party's proposals for industrial accident and injury insurance reinforced the influence of social democracy among industrial workers. Anti-trade union discussions soon started again and there was a new wave of trials against secret societies. Patriotic fervour was whipped up for the new colonial policy and for the elections of 21 February 1887, in which the 'Septennat', the grant of the army's peacetime strength and the military budget for seven years, was the chief issue. All this could not prevent the Social Democrats from raising their share of the vote to 10.1 per cent. The wide acclaim given to the International Socialist Congress, which met in Paris for the centenary of the storming of the Bastille; above all the great wave of strikes, running parallel to the economic boom and culminating in the spontaneous mass strike of miners in the Ruhr in 1889, which brought in the general unionisation of miners, these events would in any case have led to the collapse of Bismarck's anti-socialist cartel policy, even if there had been no crisis of confidence between Emperor and Chancellor. Controversy about the extension of the Socialist law broke up the coalition between National Liberals and Conservatives: the Liberals wanted to reduce the duration and harshness of the law, the Conservatives in contrast wished to sharpen its severity. On 25 January 1890 the law was rejected in its more lenient form, because no compromise could be reached between National Liberals and Conservatives, and on 30 September 1890 it therefore ceased to be in force. On 20 February 1890 the Social Democrats experienced an astonishing access of strength : they obtained 1,427,000 votes against 763,000 in 1887. The Chancellor's plans for a renewal of the repressive law or for a constitutional coup, which he had been hatching in the last few weeks before his fall, were now seen to be illusions. Even the *haute bourgeoisie* and the Junkers now had to acknowledge that in the face of such a popular movement it was too risky to try and govern according to Bismarck's senseless speculations without Parliament and Constitution and with the Reich reduced to an aristocracy of princes.

Thus the party regained its legality, but it was now a different movement from what it had been before prohibition struck it. From a relatively small group it had grown into the political mass party of the German worker. The state and capitalism, the party's real social antagonist, confronted it with as much hostility as ever. Nevertheless only a great historical crisis, and no longer the more or less haphazard machinations of the state bureaucracy, could now crush it or alter its essential character. The party now had a clearer conception of its historical role, and therefore of its strategy and tactics, than had been generally the case with its leaders and functionaries before the emergency law. They knew from experience that their political pressure on the state and trade union pressure on the owners of capital could bring substantial concessions to the working class they represented. They also knew that they could not thereby achieve the goal of their struggles, namely a democratic republic which could be used by a self-conscious proletariat, united under their leadership, for the transformation of a capitalist class society into a classless society. But they were convinced that by this struggle for social reforms they were not only fighting for the interests of the proletariat and, in addition, of those other broad strata of society who did not belong to the ruling classes, but were also developing the class consciousness of the workers and winning over those groups from the middle classes that were capable of becoming allies. Thus they hoped to create the conditions for the victory of Social democracy over the authoritarian state and the ruling classes in the inevitable economic and social crises which they expected would shake capitalist society. They knew that with the concentration and centralisation of capital the proportion of the total population tied to the ruling classes by their real and objective interest was diminishing to the same extent that the power

of corporations and companies was growing. They realised clearly
that within the capitalist economic system ever widening strata of
society were being turned into wage-slaves and employees, deprived
of their formal independence and subjected to the requirements of
the large capitalist concerns, whose only production rationale was
their own profit and the extension of their power.

In these circumstances the Social Democrats believed that they
had to avoid all policies of premature action and adventurist
revolution-mongering in order to safeguard their basic strategic
concept, the legality of party and trade unions, long enough to
turn the defensive struggle against every attack on this legality into
an offensive for the conquest of political power. The establishment
of a democratic republic under these conditions would subordinate
the state to the rule of the proletariat, representing the great
majority of society. The state would then expropriate the great
concentrations of capital and land in order to organise a socialist
economy in which the satisfaction of the needs of all members of
society and their cultural fulfilment would be the incentive for
production, and no longer the profit of individual capitalist corporations. Scientific Marxism would serve the Social Democrats as a
means of analysing the situation, as a strategic point of departure
and as a method of determining the objective. The Social Democrats
were therefore anxious to spread Marxist knowledge as widely as
possible among the working classes who were to be organised in
party and trade unions. The politicisation of the largest possible
groups of workers and employees became one of the main tasks of
the party. The authority of the leaders rested for the time being
solely on this concept and on their proven reliability and loyalty
during the period of the emergency law; the leaders still conformed
essentially to the type of the tribune of the people—whether they
were nationally recognised, like August Bebel, Wilhelm Liebknecht
and Paul Singer, or whether they were respected functionaries in
a region, like George von Vollmar or Ignaz von Auerum, or whether
they represented a special group like the women's movement, as in
the case of Clara Zetkin. The type of the party bureaucrat, the
professional politician seeking his personal advancement through
adaptation to the existing political-social system, had not yet
appeared.

The politicisation of the working masses was seen as an educational task to prepare them for the take-over of power in the state
and for self-government of the economy in a socialist producers'
community. To stimulate the desire for education among the lower
classes in a class society, which still deprived them of equal

educational opportunities and above all of the leisure essential for education, this still appeared to be the *sine qua non* even of the political fight for power and of social emancipation. Trade union activity seemed to be of exceptional importance in maintaining and expanding the share of the workers in the social product, and in reducing the hours of work. But trade union work was regarded as only a part, albeit of central significance, in the total process of developing proletarian class consciousness, in which the independent world of the sports clubs and the educational associations of the socialist workers equally played their role.

The preservation of the restored legality of the party seemed to be a condition for the proper functioning of the whole movement. This inevitably led to temporary difficulties with some sections of the party who did not understand the significance of legality. In their mood they were still under the sway of illegality, the previous phase of the movement, and were unable to discard the mental habits of that phase. This was the basic reason for the controversy with the Young Socialists at the party congress at Halle from 12 to 18 October 1890, which continued at the Erfurt party congress in 1891, but was soon to be resolved. On the other hand the need to remain within the bounds of what was considered legal, and the judiciary had restricted this through their concept of 'preparing' a treasonable enterprise, limited the extent of the acceptance of Marxism, or at least its public expression. This did not, however, change the acceptance of Marxism in principle. Karl Marx was in touch with the leaders of his party until his death on 14 March 1883; it is typical of the party in our own day that the 80th anniversary of his death received so little attention. After Marx's death Friedrich Engels discharged the task of ultimate doctrinal authority, whatever the tactical differences between him and individual members of the party leadership on specific questions.

The formal acceptance of this total design was signified by the party programme which the Erfurt Congress, meeting from 14 to 20 October 1891, adopted unanimously. At this congress the proposals made by the commission appointed at St. Gallen, including Auer, Bebel and Liebknecht and also those of the Magdeburg Opposition which included Paul Kampffmeyer and was 'Young Socialist' in character, were turned down in favour of Karl Kautsky's draft; as far as immediate political demands were concerned Eduard Bernstein's points were in part accepted. The Erfurt Programme became the basis of ideological education as well as theoretical discussion in the party until the outbreak of the First World War. Even the Revisionists questioned it only in matters of detail and not as a whole; in particular they did not for the moment reject the aim of transferring the large economic units into social ownership. Only a decade later did the Revisionists begin to stress an abstract polarisation of reform against revolution and to take over the legend, commonly accepted among bourgeois academics, that the second part of the programme, directed towards actual, realistically obtainable reforms, stood in contradiction to the theoretical first part. This legend is obviously unhistorical yet all the more accepted by professional historians. It runs thus : the first and theoretical part of the programme lays down the aims of the revolutionary process and the transformation of capitalist private ownership of the means of production into social ownership, the demand for a change from production for profit to socialist production for the benefit of the community; the achievement of these objectives depends on the possession of political power by the proletariat. The second part of the programme, so the legend says, names the 'realistic' aims of reform. In fact no important reform has ever been conceded by a ruling class to the classes under its domination, except when that ruling class has stood in fear of the determination of the subordinate classes to challenge the *status quo*. Moreover, the achievement of significant reforms in the long run strengthens rather than weakens the will to power of the class which has struggled for these reforms, certainly for the future and often for the present, provided this class remains conscious of the fact that it owes these concessions by its opponents to its own will to fight. For this reason it is perfectly possible to accommodate reformist aims and struggles in a movement dedicated to the overthrow of a whole society and its power structure. Reform is part and parcel of the strategy of such a movement, provided it never loses sight of its final aim. But the movement of a suppressed class for democratic liberation will, on the other hand, lose its momentum, if it fails to incorporate its various partial objectives into a general and coherent concept for the total transformation of society.

Thus the two parts of the programme formed a dialectical unity and there was no inner contradiction between them. For 'it is not the desire for social reform, but the deliberate limitation to reform which distinguishes the social reformer from the social revolutionary'. The theoretical part of the programme was the counterweight which, within the unity of the total programme, gave party members the awareness of their whole political activity by guiding their doctrinal education. On the one hand the doctrine protected them from the temptation of confining themselves to mere quantitative changes in existing society without altering its class character, but on the other hand it gave them the strength to pursue with energy the struggle for their immediate demands, in advance of the qualitative change in the situation through the conquest of political power and before there was an objective possibility of immediate revolutionary action. The practical part of the programme in turn had the function to preserve the theoretical part from becoming an abstract declaration of mere expectations, a Sunday creed of a political community of the faithful; for the masses the practical part formulated immediately intelligible demands which could be realised with a prospect of rapid success.

The Social Democratic Party had through its struggle against the emergency law and its unambiguous fight against the monarchical authoritarian state become a magnet not only for the industrial workers, but also for that part of the bourgeois intelligentsia which, in spite of the assimilation of the once liberal democratic middle class parties into the Hohenzollern Monarchy that had become the German Reich, wanted to hold fast to their democratic ways of thinking. The SPD was now strong enough to incorporate such groups and to bring them into its own world of ideas. Franz Mehring was once a left-liberal opponent of socialism and made the first serious attempt to try to get to grips with the problems of the new party in a historical context. After prolonged intellectual controversy he joined the party of the working class. He became not only its historian, but one of the most independent and best theoreticians of Marxism. George Ledebour came from the same group of left-liberal intellectuals. He became one of the Social Democrats' best parliamentary speakers and gave a good account of himself in all the later political controversies. The protestant parson Christoph Blumhardt made his intellectual way to Socialism from his originally pietist position. He also remained a convinced Protestant Christian, notwithstanding the reprimand he received from the Lutheran Church of Württemberg. Thus he was involved in many clashes within a party which, although nominally not atheist, contained a vast majority of functionaries and members who through their own views gave it a decidedly atheist slant. This was due not least to the anti-democratic attitude of the churches which were so closely tied to the state. In spite of this Blumhardt always remained committed to the social and political conceptions of the party and firmly rejected the rising Revisionism.

Friedrich Naumann's national-social movement for a time seemed to hold out the hope that it could persuade the upper classes of the need for a social policy and for progress towards political democracy. The activities of this movement in actual practice soon made it evident that it was bent on a narrow rationalisation of German domestic policy in a modestly liberal direction, for the purpose of 'integrating' the working class into the aggressive imperialism ever more openly pursued by the upper classes. Thus it was doomed to frustration and the more critical elements among the educated public, who had passed through Naumann's movement, soon felt again the attractive power of Social Democratic ideas. Rudolf Breitscheid was converted to Social-democracy after a lengthy engagement with German liberalism and its renewed failure; the theologian Paul Göhre also joined the party.

Under the aegis of the Frankfurt programme and with a sound basis for the tactics to be followed during this period the party now increased its size constantly: its proportion of the vote rose in the Reichstag elections of 1893 to 23.3 per cent; in 1898 to 27.2 per cent; in 1903 to 31.7 per cent; in 1907 in the so-called Hottentot elections, held amid the 'patriotic' hysteria aroused by colonial war, the party's share fell back to 28.9 per cent, but no concessions had been made to the prevailing atmosphere even though the Revisionists had wanted it; in 1912, however, the share rose again to 34.8 per cent of the vote and 27.7 per cent of the seats and the SPD had thus become by far the largest party in the Reichstag.

At the same time the number of members grew and inevitably the full-time apparatus of the party also. In 1899 the party had in matters of organisation been freed from legal restrictions by the repeal of the ban on political associations in Prussia. In 1905 a new party statute created the first typical example in Germany of a party based on a broad membership and with rationally arranged party regulations. The party congress, composed of delegates elected by local organisations, determined the party's political direction and the parliamentary party had since 1890 felt itself bound by its edicts. The organisation and its administrative tasks grew. The number of parliamentary seats and deputies increased and with the introduction of parliamentary salaries and expenses the deputies began to become full-time professionals. Amid the pressure of parliamentary business they tended to forget all too easily the social realities outside the Reichstag. The growth of a party press produced a wide-spread system of local newspapers with large editorial staffs. Taken together all this led to the rise of a numerous class of professional politicians and party employees. Thus the whole range of problems connected with bureaucratic institutionalisation and its consequences became a matter of the first importance. Oligarchical tendencies as against party democracy, first described but not sociologically analysed by Robert Michels, steadily rose in strength.

The real carrier of the ideology of integration was now born, a new
social class, consisting of the bureaucracy of the party including its
parliamentary representatives, and of the working class associations,
including trade unions and co-operatives. This class was concerned
for the administrative continuity of the party in its current mode of
existence and thought conservatively within the framework of this
task. It could not and would not think beyond its own present situation. It was only natural that this class of functionaries began to
consider the institution itself more important than its original
purpose, not from subjective egotistical motives but out of a sense
of responsibility. On the other hand this class was bound to acquire
the power to determine the parameters of democratic discussion in
the organisation.

The consequences of this situation were for a long time limited
by the existence of many party newspapers, politically divergent
and not centrally controlled, transmitting a discussion of issues
which was locally coloured and close to the ordinary member. Above
all, the possible dangers were kept within bounds because at the
head of the party there was, until the death of August Bebel in
1913, a tribune of the people of great authority, who was no party
bureaucrat and who had risen to his eminence in quite different
circumstances. Nevertheless, the growth of this new broad social
stratum of a working class bureaucracy and of full-time professional
working class parliamentarians created the basis for the erosion of
the will to action in a future revolutionary situation for which the
party was making the intellectual preparations. This 'voluntarism'
had previously existed among the leadership and among many of
the honorary non-professional officers and it now gave way to a
passive waiting for developments. This had in any case always been
advocated in the official pronouncements of the party in order to
keep within the law.

This process had several phases and took place in the various
parallel organisations of the working class movement in different
ways and at different speeds. Among the free trade unions the initial
phase was formed by the economic boom of the mid-1890s, during
which there was a controversy between the victorious 'centralists'
and the 'localists' similar to the debate between Bebel's majority
and the Young Socialists in the party. The 'centralists' believed in
unions organised for the whole Reich, in which the power to decide
about disputes with capital was to be vested in the central authority.
The 'localists' wanted the power of decision to remain with the
local groups, which had inevitably been the custom during the
period of the Socialist Law when trade union groups were constantly

under threat of being outlawed. The centralised craft unions became firmly established and were linked together in the General Commission of Karl Legien. Only a few unions were able to organise themselves for the whole of an industry. During the existing boom, which was, however, again followed by a down turn in the early years of the new century, the unions were able to achieve considerable successes, strengthen their membership and organisation and build up a sizeable network of insurance societies to supplement the public social insurance system. Thus the organisational financial responsibilities of the professional officials increased, but so did their power in the unions and in relation to the party. Their lack of interest in theory was understandable, in view of the heavy work load they had to shoulder in their special trade union functions, and it was therefore hardly surprising that they felt disinclined to take risks which might endanger their legal existence. This is the explanation for the strange but only apparent contradiction, that in 1905 the unions were slow and reluctant in following the mass strike of the miners which, as in 1889, had started spontaneously, and they tried to end it quickly, while the SPD, thanks to its revolutionary doctrine, analysed the situation correctly. In spite of the considerable successes achieved by this strike the trade union congress of the same year treated the mass strike basically as an illusion. For the same reasons Karl Legien and the General Commission anticipated, by the decision of the chairmen's conference of 1 and 2 August 1914, the capitulation of the parliamentary party in the face of the first imperialist world war and the turn towards the *Burgfrieden,* the cessation of party warfare for the duration.

The first attempts to assimilate the party to the existing political system and society can already be discerned in George v. Vollmar's speech in Munich on 1 June 1891; but v. Vollmar did not as yet wish to question the party doctrine. At the Erfurt Congress he fully approved the party programme. In South Germany, where more liberal conditions prevailed than in the North, the problems of assimilation were continually being raised in practical form in connection with regional policy. The systematic doctrinal attack on the Erfurt programme, on the expectation of revolution and on the policy of combining the fight for reform with the preparation of revolution in a way that made sense in the awareness of the party leadership, this attack was mounted by Eduard Bernstein. He saw in the hope of revolution a liability for the reformist struggle and soon became the spokesman of the revisionist wing of the party. From the theoretical point of view his enterprise was an inadequate attempt to construct a social liberal system of ideas.

Bernstein's arguments, in so far as they imputed to Marx an abstract thesis of capitalist collapse, failed to come to terms with the real Marx; in that they denied the centralisation and concentration of capital, and foretold the absence of economic crisis, they followed the then as now fashionable views of academic social science, but were soon enough contradicted by the course of history. Only with regard to the uneven development of agriculture and industry did revisionism for the time being accord with the facts. It is only in our own time that the structure of agricultural property has become so uneconomic from the technical point of view that all major industrial nations have been driven to grant considerable agrarian subsidies or to adopt other forms of intervention; and yet this cannot prevent the constant diminution in the number of farms. Bernstein's hopes of uninterrupted evolution towards democracy by means of 'legal' reforms were even more out of tune with the historical facts and available possibilities. It required the catastrophe of the 1914 war and of the November Revolution of 1918 to abolish the authoritarian state. One simply cannot grasp the course of history with theories of evolutionary progress and with mere hopes. This revisionism was, apart from the agrarian problem, from the theoretical point of view weak. On the agrarian questions Karl Kautsky did not have the courage to analyse the problem accurately and to consider that there was a transposition in the phasing of developments. He tried rather pettifoging reinterpretations of statistics and dubious prognostications in order to defeat Eduard Bernstein and Eduard David. The increase of peasant indebtedness which frequently produced considerable waves of rural discontent was, however, an indication of changes to come. In these circumstances the defeat of Revisionism at the Dresden party congress in 1903 came as no surprise. Franz Mehring made the apt remark that at bottom the content of Revisionism was a constant oscillation between eclecticism and scepticism and that its real substance was lack of substance.

The problem which I outlined earlier was, however, not removed by the victory in the field of theory of the Marxist adherents of the Erfurt programme. It kept on reappearing. The mass organisations of the SPD and of the trade unions were, according to theory, the negation of the existing socio-economic order in which advancing organised capitalism was living side by side with the remnants of feudal landownership. But the proletarian organisations had their existence within that order and their bureaucracy, like every other, accustomed to its routine, was less and less able to imagine the overthrow of that order. The party bureaucrats were certainly disinclined to risk the existence of the organisations for which they were responsible in mass actions designed to achieve or prepare the overthrow of the existing order. Thus all these questions were reopened when the Russo-Japanese war and the Russian Revolution of 1905 raised the problems of imperialist war and revolution in acute form. The party congress at Jena in 1905 still seemed to give the answer in accordance with the original concept. But the rejection of the mass strike by the trade union leadership produced in 1906 a compromise between the General Commission of the unions and the party's executive, which in substance amounted to the capitulation of the party to the union leadership and which was confirmed by the party congress at Mannheim. The so-called Marxist centre of the party thus ultimately revealed itself, at a time when imperialist war and mass struggles were in the offing, as merely the instrument of a policy of immobilism radical only in its language. The term 'Marxist centre' arose from the discussions of those years and was applied to the wing of the party which was led by the executive and the majority of Reichstag members and was politically represented by August Bebel and doctrinally by Karl Kautsky. The left wing of the party, under such outstanding though frequently differing leaders as Rosa Luxemburg, Karl Liebknecht, Franz Mehring, Georg Ledebour and Clara Zetkin, began to go its own way. In the fight over the Prussian three-tier electoral system it started to attack the immobilist policy of the leadership, in common with some revisionists who were hardly conscious of the consequences of their attitude. The 'Marxist centre' still remained consistent, at least in its position on the problems of imperialism and fought against the official colonial policy, though Eduard Bernstein was already prepared to retreat even on this front. The Stuttgart Congress of the 2nd International in 1907, after lengthy debate on the best methods of combating imperialism and the danger of war, agreed unanimously to a resolution drafted by Rosa Luxemburg, Lenin and Martow. This resolution, while realistic enough to leave the tactics of the various member parties to their national leaders, dependent as they were on the realities of mass opinion, left on the other hand no doubt about the unconditional rejection of any imperialist war by social-democratic parties all over the world. This resolution, to which the leaders of the German Social Democrats agreed, imposed the duty on all member parties of the International to use the outbreak of a war as a means of hastening the fall of the capitalist order by rousing the people against the crimes of war. The whole party still agreed to the manifesto of the International Social Congress held at Basle on

24-29 November 1912 which reminded all governments that the Franco-Prussian war had given rise to the Commune, the Russo-Japanese war to the Russian Revolution of 1905.

The SPD and the International, however, failed to pass the test at the outbreak of the First World War. On 28 July 1914, the day Austria declared war on Serbia, hundreds of thousands of German workers were still demonstrating against the war in all major cities; on 2 August 1914 British workers were still taking to the streets for the same reason. But in the meantime, the patriotic hysteria of national and European suicide had gripped the German masses, and unfortunately not only the lower middle classes.

There were sections of the party whose rejection of any kind of adaptation to the existing power structure was beyond doubt. They recognised this power structure as a reality, but only for the purpose of producing out of its contradictions the concrete possibilities of changing and overthrowing it. They had no intention, as was the case with many of the revisionists, of accepting the status quo against minor concessions or of coming to terms with it. Yet even they did not foresee that it would be possible to exploit pseudo-national emotion with such explosive force against any vestige of reason. They could not believe that all rational thought would be extinguished among the masses, once they had been brainwashed into believing that the 'nation' was threatened. Today's equivalents would be 'Freedom', 'Europe', 'The West'. It had been the hope of revolutionary Social Democrats that the proletariat would, in a revolutionary upsurge, prevent the war, regarded as inevitable in the late capitalist order, and thus avoid mass slaughter. The revolutionary Socialists expected revolution before war, but revolution proved possible only after the bitter experience of war. The manipulation of public opinion by the government, and by the vested interests of imperialism extended its grip to the proletariat, and the working class bureaucracy became its instrument. The mass hysteria of early August 1914 in Germany, which was followed within days in other countries, still awaits socio-psychological analysis. In Germany there was a recurrence of the same hysteria in March and early summer of 1933 among the middle classes, but not among the workers; it did not recur in any country at the outbreak of the Second World War.

In 1914 the SPD faced the choice of either remaining true to its origins and its traditional tasks by swimming against the tide as it had done in September 1870, thereby sacrificing its legal existence but winning the chance of seizing the inheritance after the hysteria subsided; alternatively it could adapt itself and discard its former ideas, however much modified. The generation of popular tribunes had departed with the death of August Bebel in 1913 and the professional politicians and bureaucrats had taken over. The capitulation of the trade unions under Legien's leadership had already occurred; thus the surrender of the parliamentary party and of the party executive was only the logical consequence of the situation. The old policy of the 'Marxist centre' had become impossible. With only fourteen dissenting votes the parliamentary party decided to agree to the war credits and to accept the domestic political truce. The unions refrained from labour disputes of any kind for the duration of the war. The party supported the war and by agreeing to the war credits without conditions gave up any attempt to control the government. The Emperor could in his speech from the throne state without fear of contradiction that 'he no longer recognised any parties', because the solemn undertaking of the Social Democrats objectively signified the surrender of their role as a political party. The party organisation was by virtue of the political truce to a certain extent accepted by the ruling classes, but it was by no means taking a share in political decisions; for the Reichstag itself had in practice totally given up any participation in decision-making when it failed even to debate the gross violation of international law implied by the attack on neutral Belgium. Thus the SPD had declined into an 'integrated' part of the prevailing pluralist system. Therefore it was no longer able in its new role to develop the self-consciousness and the political awareness of the masses. The party leaders could now only react to and follow the mood of the masses. They had to go further and make sure that their own surrender to the holders of power was permanently imposed on the masses, in case these latter should become restive again. The mentality of discipline was so strong in the SPD that for the moment even the minority in the parliamentary party fully accepted the surrender. One of those who had been outvoted in the parliamentary party over the rejection of the war credits, Hugo Haasek, was even prepared to signify his subsequent agreement in full plenary session of the Reichstag on 4 August 1914.

A small group of party intellectuals and a few radical union leaders, however, immediately took up the systematic fight against this policy of surrender. Among them was Rosa Luxemburg, Franz Mehring, August Thalheimer, Heinrich Brandler and Julian Karski, from the beginning in alliance with Clara Zetkin and soon with Karl Liebknecht as well. They fought without regard to official party discipline, and they all knew that the fight must soon force them into complete illegality. The party organisation was no longer at their disposal and at most served them for a while longer as an arena for battle.

Thus it was only when the masses took a hand that matters came to a head. Then the Revolution, not desired at all by the Majority Social Democrats, desired but not actively advanced by the Independent Social Democrats, created the democratic Republic. In this way the work of the old prewar social democracy triumphed once more and defeated not only the monarchical authoritarian state but also its own organisations, whose 'leaders' had become totally alienated from their earlier ideas. The working masses had been educated to act with self-confident solidarity and class-consciousness, to struggle for democracy, by the SPD as it was before 4 August 1914. This now enabled them, having lost their illusions about the nature of the war, to smash, even without effective leaders, the monarchy, itself exhausted by the war. It gave them the strength to force their organisations against the will of the leadership to accept their independent and democratic action. The first German Republic was born in face of the resistance of the Majority Social Democrats and without any initiative from the executive of the Independent Social Democrats; but the Republic was created on the basis of the achievements and the educational work of the SPD which had been accomplished before 1914 in the time of the Socialist Law and during the gestation and effectiveness of the Erfurt Programme. Without the example of democracy vouchsafed by this first Republic the democratic reconstruction after 1945 could not have been initiated.

The Classical Tradition in Germany—
Grandeur and Decay

by WALTER JENS

On 10 November 1837 a nineteen-year-old student gave his anxious
father an account of his studies in a long letter: '... having arrived
in Berlin, I broke off all my previous connections ... and tried to
immerse myself in the arts and the sciences ... I acquired the habit
of making extracts from all the books I read, thus from Lessing's
Laócoon ... Winckelmann's *History of Art*, Luden's *German
History*[1] and to scribble down my thoughts as I went along. At the
same time I translated Tacitus' *Germania*, Ovid's *Libri tristium* and
started to learn English and Italian privately, i.e. from grammar
books. ... Then I translated parts of Aristotle's *Rhetoric*, read the
de augmentis scientiarum of the famous Bacon of Verulam and
occupied myself intensively with Reimarus, on whose book *Of the
acquired instincts of animals* I reflected with great pleasure': this
was the scheme of work of a student of law round about 1830, two
years after taking the abitur at a classical grammar school
(Humanistisches Gymnasium), these were his attainments in the
field of belles letters and the humane arts!

And let us quote now, as a tailpiece to the letter of a son to an
anxious father the letter of a troubled father to his son, the letters
of a man enduring considerable suffering, who shows himself concerned, because his son, evidently not convinced of the value of the
classics, is not succeeding too well in his studies of the ancients:
'Herodotus Xenophon, Thucydides, Demosthenes and the divine
Plato', so reads this letter of 11 February 1917, 'Homer, Cornelius
Nepos, Caesar, Livius, Sallustus, Tacitus, Ovid, Virgil, Catullus,
Horace—take any history of civilisation, knowledge, art or litera-
ture ... these names will be enshrined in it in letters of gold. If you
do not get to know them now—you will never learn to know them.
You will be immeasurably the poorer for the whole of your life.
How much I would love to have my Virgil, Horace, Homer,
Sophocles, Plato here. How vividly many of the odes of Horace
have come back to me, they come during the night—in the long,

long nights and keep me company—how happy I would be if my store of such knowledge were ten-fold, as large as Lessing's.'

Is there a philologist whose heart would not beat faster when reading such sentiments? To annotate Aristotle's *Rhetoric*—a text which nowadays has its difficulties even for experienced Greek scholars—to translate Tacitus and Ovid, to celebrate the divine Plato, to invoke these glorious names, to swear by this whole classical canon, and to do it with an emphasis, compared with which Hofmannsthal's famous speech, delivered in 1926 on the occasion of the Gathering of the Friends of the *Humanistisches Gymnasium*, sounds like a halting testimony . . . could one ask for more? A crown of laurels for these letter writers, a crown of laurels . . . but for whom? A crown for the man who said of himself 'I am no Marxist . . .' but only because his name was Karl Marx. His was the letter written in 1837. A crown also for that prisoner facing multiple charges who from his prison enlarges on the exemplary quality of the Greeks and Romans. The letter to his son was written from a prison of Kaiser Wilhelm II by Karl Liebknecht.

At first sight this is a strange spectacle : revolutionaries are talking as if they were peaceful grammar school masters of the type of Serenus Zeitblom, accustomed to close acquaintance with the classics. On second thoughts this must appear as no more than a matter of course, when one considers that well into our century education and culture were identical with mastery of the classical humanities. Friedrich Nietzsche, pupil of Ritschl,[2] and Karl Marx, who as a student was initiated by the great Welcker[3] into the mythology of the Greeks and Romans and who studied the elegies of Propertius under the aegis of August Wilhelm Schlegel : if these two, Nietzsche and Marx, had met, they would have found common ground in the ideal nature of the classics, which neither of them ever questioned, and as for their conversation, the dispute between a classical philologist who had obtained his doctorate and one who did not (the one who did not was Nietzsche; Marx obtained his doctorate with a dissertation on the Greek philosophy of nature)— this conversation, one may imagine, might have been conducted in Latin; for Marx's leaving certificate certified 'that he is able to translate expeditiously and carefully the less difficult passages from the classical authors read at the *Gymnasium* and even the more difficult passages after due preparation and with some help' and that 'on the linguistic side he had given proof of much practice and effort for genuine Latin feeling and had acquired a satisfactory capacity for speaking Latin' . . . these abilities, we may assume, would have allowed Marx to bandy words with his opposite number, that other classical philologist, who had already at the age of fifteen confessed : 'I make a note in Latin, if I have nothing else to do, of things I have heard or read somewhere, and in doing so I try, following the precepts of Kater Murr, to think in Latin.'

Thus we have the apparently strange, but in fact plausible notion : the Pantheon of the nineteenth century, populated by men who have nothing in common in the political sphere (at any rate after the end of their school years : even Bismarck, having had a sound classical education, took the *Abitur* as a rabid Republican), this Pantheon populated by men whose doctrines are diametrically opposed ... yet all had enjoyed exactly the same texts : this gave them the possibility of a common basis of understanding in the midst of the most profound antagonism. The spirit of a classical education had been a truly formative influence with them, it had not been merely drummed into them—all of them, G. E. Lessing, pupil of the electoral school at Kamenz, as well as Nietzsche, native of Rökken, alumnus of Pforta, where summer holidays happened only every second year and where otherwise there were six free days a year, all of them underwent a remorseless discipline by virtue of which they knew, like Lessing, how to translate Euclid at the age of fifteen, or like Nietzsche at eighteen had learnt to form their German style on the example of a classical author (Sallustus) and all of them could be found in a small number of schools or lecture rooms between Leipzig, Bonn and Tübingen.

Let us imagine it : A. W. Schlegel was lecturing, Marx sat at his feet ! And above all the lecture rooms of Hegel and Schelling, where Kierkegaard sat next to Engels, who had come, eighteen years of age, on his bicycle from Lichterfelde and had written in those days : 'If you ask anybody in Berlin, who has even the slightest inkling of the power of the spirit in this world, where the battle ground was on which the fight for German public opinion on politics and religion, that is to say the fight for the control of Germany, was being fought out, you will get the answer that the battle ground was in the University, namely in Lecture Room 6, where Schelling is giving his lectures on the philosophy of Revelation.'

It was the Pantheon of the Classics : let us think of it, and the historian of German education, Friedrich Paulsen,[4] has described it forcefully, in the heyday of the nineteenth century there was no one in any institution of higher learning who was unable to read Plato or Homer. In fact, the utopia of the sixteenth century, a world of Latin-speaking dentists, Homer-reading lawyers and Sophocles-quoting merchants, had become a reality around 1850.

All of them, those who were learning and those who were teaching, like the grammar school headmaster Hegel, were so much formed by the spirit of classical antiquity, that it was no accident that for many of them the work of the schoolroom proved the practicability of revolution. Hegel measured the polity created by the French Revolution by the yardstick of that free polis of antiquity, under whose sway, transposed into the Christian context, the separation between the subjective private sphere of the bourgeois and the substantive realm of the community, the citizen's field of action, would vanish. Nietzsche flung down the challenge to Christianity in the name of the Greek moral code of the master, Marx pointed the difference between human work and the capability of animals by introducing that category of beauty, which German idealism from Winckelmann to Hegel had applied to Greek institutions; thereby he gave to work that was aesthetic the true dignity of a human function. The *Economic-Philosophical Manuscripts of 1844* mark the moment when the theories of classical German literature proved their political fertility. It is the capitalist relations of production, the private acquisition of the social product, the degradation of work, which prevent man from 'producing according to the laws of beauty'. From this perspective classical education was a political fact. On the one hand it served as a means of communication and exemplification for a few individuals with revolutionary views. On the other hand it was an instrument for a class, the bourgeoisie, which was excluded from immediate political participation and which sought to realise in the realm of the spirit the autonomy denied to it in reality. For the bourgeoisie classical education was a means of compensation therefore, in the sense of a prestige-substitute for a socially frustrated group. It served to bolster the self-confidence and to advance the self-awareness of the liberal German middle class in its 'heroic phase'; this class defined the image of the *homo vere humanus* as an image apparently utterly remote from contemporary issues and of purely aesthetic significance. But it was also this middle class, whose leading aim was the abolition of feudal barriers, guild regulations and state-imposed limitations, that had a very concrete interest in legitimising the concept of the individual who is master of his own affairs, above all his economic affairs. In securing a basis for this legitimisation the Greeks were useful helpers in need and the classical image of man became a political as well as aesthetic fact. The liberation from feudal traditions may have succeeded only in the field of ideas, the ruling class may have conceded this liberation with relative ease, because they saw through it as an act less designed to change real conditions than the perceptions of those conditions and therefore an act without any apparent consequences in reality; nevertheless it was a liberation and there can be no doubt of the progressive and politically negotiable intentions of classical humanism, at the moment of its organisation as an educational and cultural force after 1800.

Schiller and Humboldt, Hölderlin and Hegel measured the inadequacies of existing reality against the ideal nature of perfection and confronted the servitude of the present with the freedom of the past. Indirectly they highlighted the need to change social conditions; they did not draw a veil of harmony over the intolerable nature of reality; instead they adopted a strict separation of the sphere of reality and the realm of beauty, for example Schiller in his essay on The Aesthetic Education of Man, and in this way they were able by implication to denounce the degradation of the real world and to continue the work of enlightenment. It was not by accident that the concept of freedom, made concrete in the example of Athens, formed the centrepiece of classical culture during its liberal phase. The freedom of the individual was defined by Hegel in the aristotelian manner as man's ability to be himself— in the Metaphysic he says "That man is free who exists for his own sake and not for the sake of another". The freedom of the state— and here Athens, not Sparta is the ideal—the freedom of the Greek polis was contrasted by the young Marx with the Christian monarchy, the free community with the byzantine state. Marx, like Schiller before and Nietzsche after him, thus affirmed the existence of outright hostility between classical antiquity and the present; on the other hand he tirelessly stressed that the Greek republican constitution could not be revived; and hence his invitation to the Germans to create in their own land the conditions which would allow man to become fully himself.

The freedom of the individual, the freedom of the Republic, and finally the freedom of the state, which is identical with the freedom of the individual : on these facets Hegel, describing the classical polis, but with the community of the French Revolution in mind, writes : 'The Greeks, if we regard the forms of their realized life immediately presented us, lived in that happy middle sphere of self-conscious and subjective freedom and substantive ethical life. They did not persist, on the one hand, in the unfree Oriental unity, which is necessarily bound up with a religious and political despotism for the reason that the individuality of the subject is overwhelmed in the universal substance ... because it has essentially as personality no right ...; neither, on the other, did

they pass beyond to that subjective penetration, in which the particular subject separates itself from the whole and the universal,
in order to make itself more explicit in its ideality. The universal
of morality and the abstract freedom of personality, both in its ideal
and external aspect, remains in accordance with the principle of
Greek life in undisturbed harmony ... the substance of political
life was so far merged in the individual, as he on his part sought
his own liberty absolutely in the universal ends of the entire civic
life.'[5]

These sentences from the *Aesthetic* show how Hegel seeks to
answer the question raised by the Revolution about the realisation
of freedom, by harking back to Greek models. These sentences
point in exemplary fashion to those elements in the first phase of
the new humanism capable of producing a progressive tradition.
Looked at in this light it has to be emphasised that the elimination
of classical studies in our country—and this is to be feared at a
time when capitalist society no longer requires ideologues to
educate the bourgeoisie but an operationally orientated élite of
functionaries—the elimination of these studies, regarded as obsolete
and no longer capable of being an instrument for the maximisation
of efficiency, would weaken the memory of an epoch formed by
the spirit of bourgeois enlightenment. For this very reason it is
important to stress the jacobinical, republican, bourgeois-progressive
elements of the neo-humanist movement, both before and after its
organisation by Humboldt. Admittedly if these elements were today
carried on without reflection and without critical ideological recon-
sideration, it would amount to making a farce out of a heroic
tragedy, according to the theory of the *Eighteenth Brumaire;* what
really matters is the transformation of the bourgeois model of
freedom towards the real humanism postulated by Marx.

Under the aegis of the Greeks the attempt was made to cast off
the Latin-French predominance across the whole spectrum of
cultural life—witness Winckelmann's and Lessing's fight against the
Latin-French tradition! Greekomania indirectly served the purpose
of becoming conscious of one's own values and of advancing the
idea of national unity. With the aid of the ancients the bourgeoisie,
gradually becoming stronger, opposed feudal as well as clerical
tutelage. Let us remember the enthusiasm with which Humboldt,
in the twenty-seventh paragraph of his programme for the study
of antiquity, refers to the 'only truly legal constitution in Greece',
the republican; let us recall that it was not least Humboldt's liberal
attitude, which gave to classical education, even though it was
organised by the state, the character of a critical discipline, which

could not be enlisted to serve some specific purpose; let us finally remember that Hölderlin's last vision before insanity overwhelmed him was, as Pierre Bertaux[6] has emphasised, concerned with the theme of patriotic conversion, with that revolution which he characterised in his notes on the *Antigone* as the 'reversal of all ideas and forms'. Hölderlin perceived a touch of rebellion in the *Antigone* and regarded the republican Sophocles as an advocate of such a revolution. The example of Hölderlin the Jacobin and classicist shows to what extent classical models were politicised around 1800. It illustrates the determination with which the bourgeoisie, constituting itself the representative of society as a whole in the fight against feudalism, gave Greek ideas an ideological content, with the help of which conservative traditions could be overcome and their own cultural world could be inaugurated.

This radicalism of middle class humanists of the year 1800 was, however, not translated into practice. It remained an aesthetic radicalism and a rebellion of ideas, because the republican imagination lacked the real social force that would have enabled it to make its expectations concrete. The creations of philosophy and literature were apparently backward-looking in their frequent reversion to classical antiquity, in fact, however, they were progressive in intention, using classical examples to advance the common good against obsolete private interests. These appeals to the past, spurred on by the impatient desire to see the democratic republic in being, could not be translated into reality; on the contrary the discrepancy between a classical culture which transcended the paltry purposes of a philistine society and the *Obrigkeitsstaat* with its persisting feudal order was made even more manifest by Heine's own vision. Heine dreamt of synthesis between the political French Revolution and the philosophical German revolution, to be achieved in an uprising of the future which would change the whole social structure fundamentally, but this dream proved to be a mere fantasy. What had long been seen in outline, an expression of the miseries of Germany, now became brute fact: the social débâcle of this liberal bourgeoisie which, intent only on the preservation of its property, gave up its social objectives. It began to elevate the Prussian element of unity above the jacobinical element of freedom (not to speak of equality) and to raise national above social aims. In the end Versailles was conquered, but the Bastille remained intact. There now began what one could call the fall from grace of the humanities, or more dramatically, the descent into hell of that classical culture, which had at first been in league with the latent progressive tendencies of the times and now made its peace with the potent reactionary forces of the period.

Thus the links with bourgeois liberal thinking were cut, as Robert Minder[7] has impressively demonstrated; the Jacobinical tradition broke, the spirit of classical culture no longer created counter-images, ceased to expose appearances and illusion by a strict separation of reality and artifice and, as mere ideology and legitimation of authority, became an accomplice of the ruling powers; in place of revolutionary patriotism there was chauvinistic bragging—a telling example of this is the declaration of a group of distinguished classical philologists on the occasion of the *Reichsgründung* in 1871, published under the title *Hellas and Germany*. Criticism became acclaim; what had once been objectivity turned into consensus; in place of the struggles of an under-privileged class against feudal cultural habits there was a declaration of war by the frondeurs of cultivation and property against the proletariat ('education', 'culture', 'Bildung', was around 1800 regarded as a personality-forming process; by 1850 it had become, as Frolinde Balser has shown,[8] socially foreshortened, the characteristic quality of a ruling class; official Prussian statistics are therefore logical in calling the highest social stratum in the middle of the century 'the prosperous and cultivated class'). Elitist traits, foreshadowed earlier, became increasingly dominant. Later on Gustav Roethe[9] wrote : 'Let us send these ruffians, for whom Greece and Rome means nothing, into the vocational secondary schools; but let us step out gaily and take a smaller group up onto the heights, undisturbed by the stumbling of the weak who may get on as best they can.'

Not until the second half of the nineteenth century is it possible to speak of classical culture becoming the preserve of the apolitical aesthete; only now does the view of classical antiquity as non-literary and based on the visual arts, whose normative function had been proclaimed by Winckelmann, become a dangerous tradition. In the same way, on the question of the relationship between art and reality, the triumph of Kant's subjectivist interpretation over Hegel's more socially orientated explanation had fatal consequences. It is only now that culture and politics, still regarded as identical by Goethe, become separate spheres. Of those separate spheres, however, each has its validity : the one lends the other an ideological aura, in imprinting the hallmark of Weimar upon the empire of Bismarck, while the other secures to the first the maintenance of its privileges. Here was the 'pure' spirit, which had renounced all attempts to penetrate and change the world, the spirit of profundity and inwardness, the silent spirit purified of 'rhetorical dross', of 'babble of civilization' and of 'literary jacobinism', the spirit which Thomas Mann, a later apologist for reformism, described in his *Meditations of a Non-political Man* (the same Thomas Mann who a few years later saw in the separation of Marx and Hölderlin a symbol of the German catastrophe) . . . We have all experienced how well this selfconsciously-sublime spirit was compatible with the starkest terror. We know too well how the concept of the 'autonomous personality', complete with its inner freedom, takes on the nature of an alibi, when it becomes a matter of bringing to bear against the horrors of this world the dignity of such a cultivated personality, whose value resides allegedly in its extra-territoriality. How differently Hegel saw it, when he pointed to achievement within the bourgeois world as the sole measure of a man's cultivation!

The macabre connection between aestheticism and terror, the way in which the escapist element which is just as much inherent in the cry for the self-sufficiency of the individual as the revolutionary ingredient, in the end became an absolute value—these are matters on which, after Auschwitz, we need waste no words. But it must make us ponder that it was so easy to interpret the maxims of a classical education in an anti-democratic sense—the theories of the Stefan George Circle serve as an example of this. And again the message of neo-humanism, which for the sake of the freedom of the individual, proclaimed the need for a critical detachment from power, could so easily descend to the level of an ideology which advocated indifference to the powerless—a sign of elitist hero-worship.

Disengagement from the crude factual structure of history, whose provisional and changeable character was highlighted by the counter-images of idealism, was turned into total rejection of certain phenomena of the modern world which did not fit in with conservative concepts: the press, public opinion, democracy, the masses. 'The masses as masses are without judgement and fanatical' says Werner Jaeger;[10] the parliamentary system—'the parliamentary rule of parties and patronage had the result of opening the doors to mediocrity' says Ernst Robert Curtius;[11] big business and the rule of money were attacked with weapons from the current arsenal of middle class cultural critique—Jaeger very logically names big business and the proletariat in one breath as the enemies of humane civilisation! The pride of aristocracy as the shield of a middle class threatened by proletarianisation: all this is a compensatory ideology but now, in contrast to a century earlier, regressive and reactionary, looking down upon the class below! Clearly the catalogue of anachronistic cultural critiques is long, the elitist and irrational tenor of the pronouncement speaks for itself.

And so they were conservative under the Kaiser, spoke of a 'general staff of the intellect', trained in 'the Schools of Hellas and Rome' and proved through this martial orchestration how completely Humboldt's ideal of education had been degraded in the course of the century. How unbridgeable the gap between an anti-utilitarian ideology and an education purposely aimed at 'entry into the higher echelons of state and church'! And so they remained conservative after 1918 under Weimar, in happy agreement with the enemies of the Republic and in every case it was not the minor practitioners but the masters of the craft who were to the fore when it was a matter of giving imperialism the necessary self-confidence... those masters who never tired after the end of the First World War of pillorying wherever possible democratic forces, in flagrant disregard of an illustrious liberal tradition going back to Mommsen.

Eduard Schwartz,[12] by no means an extremist, said in a speech to German students in 1920, 'Anybody who is able to wander through the old town of Weimar, forgetting the revolting memory of the so called National Assembly, feels in every fibre the link with the Potsdam of the great Prussian king and remembers that Karl August had no higher ambition than to be an officer in the Prussian army.' This sentence was spoken more than a century after the days when the humanists of the classical bourgeois enlightenment, from Schiller to Hölderlin, from Lessing to Hegel, had extolled the free polis and the free individual as an autonomous subject, yet related to his social context, and had proclaimed their defiance of all tyranny. This sentence was formulated barely a decade and a half before fascism finally usurped what the representatives of a higher education, which had labelled itself 'elitist, idealist, heroic and consciously national', had so willingly offered up. The apotheosis of the West proclaimed by Hitler and Goebbels —the summoning up of Holy Europe, formed by Greeks, Romans and Germans, the Europe that was to be preserved against the hordes from the steppes of Asia—this was only a brutally redoubled echo of such sentiments.

Was Thomas Mann right therefore in saying that classical culture had perished with that bourgeois society which had supported it? In that case the hour would have struck in which Hegel's dictum had come true : 'It is always a vain undertaking to maintain forms of culture when the substantive forms of the spirit have been restructured. They are like withered leaves that are pushed away by the fresh shoots emerging from their roots.'

Withered leaves : how much obsolete baggage is still being purveyed in the schools of the Federal Republic, handed on from class to class, only because that is what tradition and the curriculum demand ! Generations of pupils bored by Ovid's *Metamorphoses*, Latin lessons started with Caesar, Greek lessons with Xenophon; 'war is the father of all things' is the motto, *enteuthen exelaunei stathmous treis, parasangas pente*, in comparison Asterix is the true Homer; but in fact the meaning matters not when Caesar is throwing his bridges across rivers, for what is at stake is the gerund and gerundive, and when Xenophon's soldier has his entrails hanging out of his abdomen (an unforgettable moment in the lower fifth) they are saying 'what matter the entrails? the pupils are practising the verbs ending in -mi'. (And they are doing it with the routine application that may have distinguished the *Humanistische Gymnasien* of the year 1900, in which all the teaching staff, with the exception of the mathematician, were classical philologists !)

It will be seen that we have our backs to the wall; we have to decide what is to be jettisoned as ballast and what must be maintained at all costs. To be jettisoned in the first place is that western ideology, which on the pretext of preserving historical continuity, is only concerned with legitimising the status quo, with maintaining the established structure of authority, with protecting rotten reality from being shown up by the spectre of a better future. Further to be jettisoned, to be exposed as irrational, is the habit of thinking in terms of a history of Salvation : namely viewing classical antiquity as a phenomenon transcending history, the idea of the sanctity and universality of the Greco-Roman heritage and with it the tendency to make absolute certain patterns of thought which had relevance only in a specific situation.

This view, which adopts the ideas of the German classical age without reflection and celebrates the perfection of antiquity in the vocabulary of Goethe's time (but reduced to the level of an ornament in the gallery of bourgeois cultivation) has indeed outlasted all catastrophes and wars. A quotation illustrates this : 'The Acropolis in Athens and the Capitol in Rome were for us spiritual symbols of freedom and order. The rights of the individual, the dignity of man, the idea of justice, a sense of proportion, an understanding for the cosmos as a spiritual structure, anxious fear of chaos—to these ideas I owe many essentials of my being.'

Thus Konrad Adenauer, replying to an address in 1964, recaptured in simple language the appeal to the spirit of antiquity which Hofmannsthal had sought to raise in solemn speech in the year 1926. An expression of sentiment, which could with no effort be supplemented with an anthology of similar effusions; strangely enough the equation 'Greek equals humanist' and 'classical equals canonical' can be found especially among academic pronouncements in the DDR—how slow to change this whole incubus is!—the very theme of the working conference held at Jena from 23–25 January 1969, 'The place of classical antiquity in socialist culture' shows that Marx's categorization of Greek art as 'the norm and unattainable model' was here apostrophised in a very unhistorical and unmarxist manner. The same goes for the entirely bourgeois interpretation of the maxim 'Why should not society in the childhood phase of mankind, in the place where it reached its most beautiful development, exercise an eternal charm?' In addition there is the danger that the concept of 'the harmonious personality' derived from these perceptions of the ideal will lose the dialectical element which in the age of Goethe gave it that factor of 'antagonism', in the sense of *hen diapheron heauto*. (On the other hand we must emphasise that in the DDR, in contrast to the Federal Republic, there have been attempts to undertake an analysis, based on an ideological critique, of the classical system of culture, education and its social implications; Johannes Irmscher's exemplary investigations into 'classical antiquity in the educational system of the Weimar Period and the Age of Fascism' need to be pursued further.)

In the face of so much mythologising, giving 'classical' antiquity a canonical status, as if there had never been any historical relativity concerning antiquity, it is time to point out the entirely realistic fashion in which, as Irmscher has shown, the early neo-humanists subordinated classical studies to the needs of bourgeois society. Quite soberly the analogy was drawn between the ideal of the free polis in antiquity, as a social model, and the vision of equality in contemporary society, and this goes for Humboldt as well as for Gesner and Heyne.[13] Humboldt was only too well aware of having idealised antiquity beyond what reality warranted. The same is true of Schiller who in his essay on the legislation of Lycurgus and Sollon was concerned to describe hellenic despotism, a point of view later taken up by Goethe. It is true of Matthias Claudius— 'the Greeks, too, were born with only one nose' he writes—and of the great philologist Friedrich August Wolf,[14] who—let us hear and marvel—declared it superfluous that a medical student should learn

Latin. (The demands of the school curriculum, we should mention in passing, were not excessive in the neo-humanist age : Thucydides was, in contrast with modern usage, declared too difficult for the sixth form in many school regulations.)

At a time when the 'classical heritage' has become part of the bourgeois household gods (or—and this is a paradox—a species of materialist marching rations after the style of Alfred Kurella : 'I cannot imagine a Socialist, who fails to understand that the world of ideas and images, concepts and figures, myths and theories produced by European antiquity belong not only to the rarely touched iron ration but to the daily diet of a socialist personality') ... at such a time it should be our task to take to heart the maxim of T. S. Eliot which says : the past undergoes as profound a transformation through the present as the present receives guide lines from the past : 'Every new work of art, every new idea changes the whole previous system of rank and order.' Taking Eliot's maxim further we may add that the metamorphosis of old masterpieces, often in turn derivative, is the more striking, the bolder it is. The greatness of artistic masterpieces is identical with their lack of finality which is in the nature of a promise and of which the essence is an invitation to try once more, or twice or a hundred times, and to explore ever new contradictions : Odysseus King and proletarian, son of hell and Christian knight, stoic sage and epicurean gourmand, conscientious objector and militarist, Lutheran and Jesuit, fascist and Jew!

Theodor Fontane, after attending a performance of 'Oedipus Rex', felt it as the special problem of this work that everybody could see in it what he would. It is this ambivalence and multiplicity, this great promise, which Brecht in his cycle of poems 'Of the Construction of Enduring Works' has highlighted as the hallmark of all lasting creation, that gives to so many documents of antiquity their high rank.

> Impermanent still
> Like a machine, which is needed
> But which is inadequate
> But foreshadows an improved version
> In the same way is built
> The work that lasts, like
> The machine full of faults.

From this perspective the significance of the 'classical' creative works lies not in their integrity, but in their capacity to evoke debate through a constant process of self-transformation. It is not

the perfection, but the provisional nature, not the classical character, but the element of insufficiency at the highest level, which
posterity finds unacceptable and which it therefore seeks to supplement (this, the insufficient, literally takes on the nature of requiring
to be made sufficient) : the element of fragility and changeability
... the finite nature, these are the qualities which give to the
phenomena of antiquity their enduring quality. How differently we
view the episode of the sirens in the Odyssey after the interpretation
of Kafka (*The Silence of the Sirens*), Brecht (*Rectification of
Ancient Myths: Odysseus and the Sirens*) and Horkheimer-Adorno
(*Odysseus or Myth and Enlightenment*)! How differently Greek
tragedy looks after the appearance of Brecht's dramatic theories!
Suddenly one perceives elements which had been overlooked for
centuries : the epic flow, there is no drama, the action goes on
behind the scenes and is transposed on to the stage through the
reports of messengers; the alienation effect is also being used :
stylisation on the one hand—men impersonating women—the
corresponding directness of naturalism on the other; tragedy and
comedy supplement each other; form is free, none of the 'stabbed,
followed by applause' of Lessing, dramas end with reflections on
their wider implications ... all this is clarified, of a sudden, through
the theory of the epic theatre, its revelations and misinterpretations.
    Let us listen once more to Brecht.

> How long do works last?
> Until they are completed.
> As long as they cause trouble
> They will not perish.
> Inviting to take trouble
> Rewarding participation
> This is the secret of endurance
> As long as they invite and reward.

    To accept this invitation means to take away from the classical
texts their status as classics, to give them back their historical
relativity and thereby that power of contradiction, which refuses
to be domesticated and thus, as an antagonistic force in a world of
total functionalism, points to a counter-sphere the essence of which
is to be not disposable.
    In this perspective the very distance in time, the element
of strangeness stressed by Hegel in his end of school speech (on
28 September 1809) and more recently by Uvo Hölscher and
Manfred Fuhrmann,[15] which gives classical education and culture
with its lack of contemporaneity the possibility of achieving critical

distance. 'Experience through contrast' and 'Insight through the
quality of strangeness' prevent an overhasty identification with the
urge of the moment; the obsolete quality, freed from necessity and
purpose, points to 'a substratum of opposition' and in its strangeness
puts in question the prevailing positivism; the historical potential
—progressively interpreted and critically assessed—achieves, to
quote Adorno, the character of an antidote to the 'tyranny of
immediacy' which, imposed on knowledge for reasons of efficiency,
'prevents men from recognising the mechanism which maims them'.

In this light the curse of being a museum piece becomes for
classical culture identical with the chance of being able to safeguard
its autonomy. At least partially absolved from utilitarian considerations, detached from society, it can constitute itself into a meta-
science, which can maintain 'the intellectual manoeuvring space, in
which critical transgression, opposition and rejection can flourish'.
Thus Herbert Marcuse who, in the course of his reflections on the
non-operational (or rather transcendental) dimensions of a non-
scientific culture particularly mentions classical philologists as well
as writers among its potential administrators, and this not just by
accident ... indeed who would be more suitable to confront
established reality, in Marcuse's meaning, with that humanizing
ethos which has never been translated into reality yet is designed
to be historically realised, who would be more suitable to undertake
such a confrontation than the advocates of a discipline whose
history is a history of magnificent anticipations and modest achievement, great promise and laborious denials, bold ideas and seering
frustrations, a history of rational enlightenment, born with the
Greeks, and of relapse into romanticising myths, a history of
endless attempts; a Sisyphus-story, determined by rebellion and
escapism, marked by the revolutionary hope of bourgeois enlightenment and the betrayal of this hope in the course of the last century
... a history whose significance may be measured by whether and in
what way the human values enshrined in it can transcend the status
quo.

The possibilities are great, the hope that they might be put to use
is slight. The conservative tradition is dominant; false allies, it must
be feared, will soon extinguish the faint light of humanism, whose
ideology they have, intent upon short-term gains, long declared
obsolete. Only a few, for the most part adherents of critical theory,
have recognised, that in order to preserve and extend the intellectual
room for manoeuvre there is no way other than to continue and,
in Hegel's sense, to overcome the tradition which, using classical
culture for the promotion of republican consciousness, began with

Lessing and did not end with Marx ... a tradition which reaches from the limited humanism of the bourgeoisie to the genuine humanism that guarantees the freedom of equals, the realisation of which remains our task today as much as it was in the days when the nineteen year old student from Berlin was justifying himself to his father.

NOTES

1. Winckelmann's *Geschichte der Kunst des Altherthums*, first published in 1764; *Geschichte des teutschen Volkes* by Heinrich Luden (1780–1847) a twelve volume history of Germany up to the thirteenth century, which the author left unfinished.
2. Friedrich Wilhelm Ritschl (1806–1876), great classical philologist, to whom Nietzsche owed his first appointment at the University of Basel.
3. Friedrich Gottlieb Welcker (1784–1868), classical philologist and friend of W. von Humboldt, taught Marx at the University of Bonn.
4. Friedrich Paulsen (1846–1908), *Geschichte des gelehrten Unterrichts auf den deutschen Schulen und Universitäten von Ausgang des Mittelalters bis zur Gegenwart*, 1885.
5. Hegel, *Aesthetik*, 2. Band; English translation by F. P. B. Osmaston, *The Philosophy of Fine Arts*, London 1910, vol. ii, p. 181/2.
6. Pierre Bertaux, *Hölderlin. Essai de biographie intérieure*, Paris 1936.
7. Robert Minder, *Kultur und Literatur in Deutschland und Frankreich: Fünf Essays*, Frankfurt, M. 1962.
8. Frolinde Balser, *Die Anfänge der Erwachsenenbildung in Deutschland in der ersten Hälfte des 19. Jahrhunderts*. Eine Kultursoziologische Deutung, Stuttgart, 1954.
9. Gustav Roethe (1859–1926), German philologist and literary scholar, author of books on Goethe, Luther, Brentano, etc. Professor at Göttingen and Berlin.
10. Werner Jaeger (b. 1888), classical philologist, went into exile in the 1930s.
11. Ernst Robert Curtius (1886–1956), Romance philologist and literary critic, friend of Stefan George, André Gide and T. S. Eliot, translator of Proust.
12. Eduard Schwartz (1858–1940), classical philologist, author of books on Emperor Constantine and the Church, the Odyssey and Thucydides.
13. Johann Mathias Gesner (1691–1761), classical philologist, educationist, Professor of Rhetoric at Göttingen; Christian Gottlob Heyne (1729–1812), classical philologist, Gesner's successor at Göttingen.
14. Matthias Claudius (1740–1815), poet and editor of the 'Wandsbecker Bothe'; Friedrich August Wolf (1759–1824), classical philologist, friend of Goethe and W. von Humboldt, Professor at Berlin University from its foundation in 1810.
15. Uvo Hölscher (b. 1914), classical philologist, Heidelberg, and Manfred Fuhrmann (b. 1925), classical philologist, Constance.

German and English Intellectuals: Contrasts and Comparisons

by R. HINTON THOMAS

When I began to consider how to compare German and English intellectuals, I soon realised that there is an initial problem of definition[1]. What is an intellectual? I turned for help to the *Encyclopaedia Britannica* (1968), but in vain. There is no entry under 'intellectual'. In *The Oxford English Dictionary* the nearest I could get was to be told, not very helpfully, that an 'intellectual being' is 'a person possessing or supposed to possess superior powers of intellect'. The idea of an intellectual can be, and often is, more distinctive in Germany. Compare, for example, the silence of the *Encyclopaedia Britannica* on the subject with the extensive and differentiated treatment of the question in the *Brockhaus Enzyklopädie*. The reason for this is clear. It is, partly at least, because in Germany over the years the image of the intellectual has polarised into extremes, and extremes always expose characteristics in their most clear-cut form. Where, as in England in the case of the intellectual, the extremes are missing, the image is necessarily more nondescript.

The one extreme is abuse of the intellectual, with its own specific vocabulary, ranging from 'Literat' und 'Zivilisationsliterat' to 'Asphaltliterat' and, indeed, 'Intellektueller'. The other extreme is a correspondingly affirmative view of the intellectual. In this sense 'Intellektueller' signifies a superior type of man, to be sharply distinguished from the notion of a merely learned or cultured person. Two quotations from a well-known contemporary German writer on cultural affairs, Heinrich Vormweg, can serve as illustrations. The first, 'the intellectual sets his experience of reality ... in opposition to the generally prevailing awareness, which necessarily stagnates under the pressure of institutionalization, compromise and conformism ...'. The other, 'all so-called cultured people are without doubt potential intellectuals ... It is only in the moment a person claims authority for his insight and formulates it that he is an intellectual'.[2]

Such a conception of the intellectual would be difficult to apply, say, to Lessing and other representatives of the German Enlightenment in the eighteenth century. It is, in fact, a feature of my argument that the discussion of the intellectual requires a distinction between the situation before Germany felt the impact of industrial capitalism—for the first time around the period of Romanticism— and the situation thereafter. Any generalisations about the German intellectual disregarding this important break in development are bound to be problematical, which is why in the present paper I limit my concern to the intellectual in what I refer to as the modern sense. The necessity for this distinction becomes immediately apparent if we inquire into the reasons for, at the one extreme, the denigration of the intellectual in Germany.

To understand the reasons, we have to bear in mind the slowness of development in Germany towards industrialisation and the shock to traditional modes of thought and feeling of the rapid shift to advanced industrialisation, when this at last happened around 1880. The type of society threatened by the new and alien element of rationality (understood by none better than Max Weber), was identified by Tönnies as 'Gemeinschaft'. Near-synonyms were 'Nation', as used by Lagarde, and 'Kultur'. These were idealised in resistance to 'Gesellschaft' and 'Zivilisation', by which was understood modern urban society, breeding the disreputable 'Zivilisationsliterat', with his lack of 'Gemüt', 'Innerlichkeit', 'Seele'—the villain in Thomas Mann's *Betrachtungen eines Unpolitischen*. At the same time the idea of 'Heimat, gained in significance, as the place where one feels most intimately at home, cosily protected against the alien and unfamiliar and therefore the uncanny (*das Unheimliche*). Towards the beginning of his famous book *Gemeinschaft und Gesellschaft* (1887) Tönnies plays with the reassuring nuances of 'Heimat', and Rilke lovingly evokes its implications in his review of Frennsen's *Jörn Uhl* (1901). This is a novel in the category of the then familiar 'Heimatkunst', and, when the intellectual figures in such novels, it is predictably in a cold and bleak light. 'On the surface of the new Reich', thus Lagarde in 1878, 'swims the intellectual (*Literat*) ... This poisonous weed must be extirpated from our streams and seas ... Then the clean mirror will reflect the flowers of the shore and the stars of heaven, the ancient gods will re-emerge from the depths ...'.[3] The sequence, of course, does not stop there. Thus Eugen Diesel in 1926 : 'We no longer have a unifying spirit of piety. All we have is intellectuals stringing formulae together and hovering over everything like an evil spirit over chaos'.[4] Most obviously it was left to National Socialism, playing off the organic state against disruptive materialism, to enlist the 'organic philosophy of our age' against what Rosenberg called 'the whole lifeless intellectual rubble of purely schematic abstractions'.[5] What has been said about anti-intellectualism in Wilhelminian Germany is confirmed by a parallel elsewhere. Thus seeking the sources of an anti-intellectualism which he discerns at the roots of American consciousness, Richard Hofstadter, in a chapter entitled 'On the Unpopularity of the Intellect', stresses the importance in this connection of 'the escape from civilization to Arcadia, from Europe to nature ... from the settled world to the frontier. Again and again the American mind turned fretfully against the encroachments of organized society, which were felt to be an effort to reimpose what had once been thrown off; for civilization, though it could hardly be repudiated in its entirety, was still believed to have something pernicious about it'.[6]

England has never to this extent abused its intellectuals, nor for that matter has it wished to pay them, even in intellectual circles, such respect as became the case in Germany. It has always respected scholars, but the intellectual as such—and by modern German standards, to take some obvious names, men like Mill, Darwin and Keynes are very borderline cases—has been in England too indeterminate a notion to attract particular abuse or praise.

The question now to be answered is why in Germany the image of the intellectual polarised in this way. One factor above all is paramount. Dominant forces representing an archaic and rigid conservatism found it in their interest to make the intellectual appear disreputable; liberal and radical opinion, working for progressive change, was correspondingly motivated to give him a place of esteem, to attribute to him a necessary and responsible function. There were signs of this, as Heinrich Mann's Zola essay shows, in Wilhelminian Germany, and also in the Weimar Republic. The Nazi régime having outlawed its intellectuals, it was a matter of honour thereafter to be regarded as such. It was in the backwash of National Socialism that in the Federal Republic, and above all in the nineteen-sixties, authority acquired, above all in intellectual circles, associations with evil, and critical resistance to it—in the person of the 'Intellektueller'—the aura of a noble purpose.

If we ask in what writer the 'Intellektueller' in this modern sense —yielding in the end to the figure of the 'Linksintellektueller'—is most significantly pre-figured, the answer must surely be Heine. The enemy for him, both within himself and without, was a reactionary romanticism, supported by a powerfully institutionalised conservatism. So he reveals many of the features present in those whom, in the way in which the term came to be used above all in Germany, one would most naturally categorise as 'Intellektuelle'. The spirit (*Geist*), he said provocatively, has its everlasting rights and, as he returned to religion, he confessed that he had surrendered to all the orgies of the intellect. His very self-conscious kind of critical awareness was nurtured by an alienated relationship to the society about which he wrote so many true and bitter things. The reason why he would not return to Germany, he told Laube, was that exile was the price he had to pay in the interests of thought. There was for him an inherent and inevitable discrepancy between any reality, once institutionalised, and his expectations. Preoccupied with how things ideally might be, he had to laugh, he said, at the crude, vulgar and foolish way in which such ideas were commonly understood by ordinary people within the limits of everyday life. With whom in England at the time is he to be compared? His contemporaries included Byron and Shelley. Like him they were both rebels, but, if we call them intellectuals, we are using the word in a different tonality, and I doubt whether many Englishmen would naturally so refer to them. This makes Heine's impressions of England, as recorded in the *Englische Fragmente*, of rather special significance. It is an interesting fact that so 'intellectual' a person—and possibly for this reason—so misunderstood what had happened and was happening in English history. The gradualness of the development towards constitutional progress baffled him, as did the part played by the aristocracy, and why in a country so obviously valuing liberty it could be treated with such tolerance. The Church too seemed to him ripe for demolition, but he found people surprisingly unconcerned to get rid of it. English parliamentary debates depressed him. Instead of enunciating principles, people were too much concerned with practical advantages and disadvantages and were too much obsessed with facts.

As an observer of English life Heine invites comparison with two of his contemporaries or near-contemporaries, Johann Georg Forster and Georg Gottfried Gervinus. That Forster was at least as revolutionary a type of man as Heine is shown from his involvement in Jacobin ideas around the time of the French Revolution, but he had a much keener interest in empirical inquiry. The son of a scientist (also a clergyman) he took part, for example, in Cook's voyage round the world, and he viewed the social and economic realities in a less blinkered way, as we can see from his impressions of England in his *Ansichten vom Niederrhein*. What struck him, relative to Germany, was above all the progress of industrial production, exemplified, for instance, in the many little factories he saw scattered round Birmingham. If by an intellectual one means no more than a man who, in the public arena, brings a progressive mind to bear on social and political problems. Forster can safely be so described. The same applies to Gervinus who, differently from Heine, was practically involved in day-to-day politics, as co-founder of the *Deutsche Zeitung* and a member of the Frankfurt National Parliament. If, he wrote, 'German life is not to stand still we must attract talents, which now have no goal, to the real world and the state, where new spirit has to be infused into new matter'.[7] Hence his admiration for Shakespearian England, with its combination, as he saw it, of a healthy political life with pragmatic thinking, and for the 'instinctive assurance' of English life, made possible, so he believed, by a genuine and effective forum of public debate, 'where there is created a great practical activity (*eine große Praxis*) and little theory, a productive life (*ein schaffendes Leben*) and little reflection'.[8] He would have agreed with Forster's analysis : 'in Germany there is no "Gemeingeist" and no public forum of debate (*Öffentlichkeit*). The very words are so new and strange to us that they have to be explained and defined, whereas every Englishman knows what is meant by *public spirit*, every Frenchman by *opinion publique*.'[9]

Thus, Forster and Gervinus, unlike Heine, recognised the greater strength, stability and breadth of the English middle class. Referring already to the seventeenth century, Habermas has been able to speak of 'the predominant role of the "town" ' and a 'politically functioning "Öffentlichkeit" '.[10] Men of ideas were, more than in Germany, in a position to find themselves close to the areas of political decision and government, as Milton to Cromwell, Hobbes to Charles II. Burke springs to mind in the eighteenth century, and then, to quote Habermas again, we get that 'peculiar combination of literature and politics'[11] represented by men like Pope, Gay and Swift. In the seventeenth and eighteenth century, Golo Mann writes, 'English society was so healthily practical that even its intellectual representatives were characterised by a sober practicality, which guarded them against radical excess'.[12] The foundation of the Royal Society reflected this and contributed to it. Thus Thomas Sprat, in his famous history of the Royal Society, wrote : 'While the old philosophy could only bestow on us some barren terms and notions, the new shall impart to us the uses of all the creatures and shall enrich us with all the benefits of fruitfulness and plenty.'[13] It is an interesting fact that Sprat was a bishop of that Church which Heine would have liked to see overthrown as a barrier to social progress, that the new foundation thus had the Church's blessing, and that its early members were men of firm religious conviction, the enemies of scepticism of whatever kind. It is reasonable to say that 'the strength of institutionalized science was such in seventeenth-century England that the foundation of the Royal Society immediately after the Restoration ... and its subsequent vigor and influence, may have helped to give English philosophy its two hundred years of empirical if not downright utilitarian cast. A potentially dissenting profession was thus pulled into the orbit of scientific particularism and academic institutionalization ...'[14] To this we have to add, built up over the years to come, that tradition of public service which English middle-class society, so much more broadly based and broadly structured than was long the case in Germany, seems to have generated and which found expression in the history of families. In this connection one recalls Noel Annan's phrase about the 'English intellectual aristocracy'. Elaborating this, it has been remarked, 'this tangle of Macaulays, Trevelyans, Huxleys and Darwins intermarried, bred dynasties and —perhaps most important—held academic and administrative posts. Some were heads of colleges, daughters took pioneering firsts in classics, cousins ran the British Museum, uncles were great headmasters, wives produced a whole new constellation of scholarly and established relatives'. But he goes on, 'this situation did not turn every thinking man into a supporter of the status quo. Thomas Arnold, Mill, George Eliot, Tennyson and others may be placed within some great spectrum where liberal faith and conservative strictness meet, but hardly William Morris, Ruskin, Carlyle, or Matthew Arnold. And it was precisely the descendants of Mr. Annan's aristocracy—Haldanes, Stracheys, Cornfords, Bells—who formed the nearest England ever had to a formal radical intelligentsia.'[15] One should also take account of the sectarian development, over a wide social spectrum, of English protestantism in nonconformist directions. This provided the basis on which social energy combined with austerely moralising forms of religious involvement. This did not by any means preclude social and political dissent, but in providing for it, even motivating it, it pre-empted the field and, to the displeasure of Marx and Engels, left it less open to revolutionary initiative.

Let us, however, return to the fundamental fact that, long before Germany knew what it meant to have a significant degree of industry in its midst, in England this was part of life In Germany, on the other hand, a cultural tradition, with values derived from a society of a different order, acquired such aura and authority that, when the new industrial reality materialised towards the end of the nineteenth century, this was not easily absorbed into the intellectual context. One consequence was a romantic anti-capitalism, apparent already in a man like Lagarde, the expression 'of a sense of discomfort in modern life, of an attitude which on the one hand wanted the advantages of industry and capitalism, on the other however wished to preserve the accustomed social conditions of the pre-industrial era'.[16] There is expressed in literary and intellectual circles a dislike of urban conditions so insistent as not to be lightly disregarded. The writers associated with 'Heimatkunst', to take an extreme example, saw the city, meaning primarily Berlin, as the source of all evil. More significant, since the Naturalist movement was declaredly so concerned about social injustice in modern urban life, are the cases of writers like Johannes Schlaf and Wilhelm Bölsche, who were outspoken in their contempt for the industrial metropolis. Then to Georg Heym, for instance, the city becomes a central image of decay. The early Döblin fits into this context, though later he was to write one of the great novels of city life, *Berlin Alexanderplatz*. But even then he makes Franz Biberkopf the victim in a struggle, as is said on the opening page, 'with something that comes from outside . . . and appears as fate'. His forward position on the German Left did not prevent Tucholsky regarding Berlin with contempt. His dislike of capitalist materialism might be regarded as sufficient reason, but his talk of 'a wild over-valuation of the economic factor', in conjunction with the idea of the 'solidarity of the intellectuals' against the 'solidarity of all the money-earners'[17] suggests an antipathy of a deeper kind, especially in view of his portrayal of more idyllic and withdrawn situations, and his love of Schopenhauer and Raabe. Karl Kraus's criticism of some of the cultural consequences of modern life, justified though it might be on the evidence he chooses, shades over into an idealisation of what had preceded it. Enzensberger might be instanced in the same connection. When in German culture modern industrial life is at issue, one senses sometimes a rather self-conscious coming to terms with it—even in the case, on the contemporary scene, of Gruppe 61. If one looks at the English industrial novel already around the middle of the nineteenth century, as Raymond William does in *Culture and Society*, the contrast is obvious enough. In England anti-industrial attitudes—which is a different thing from the not infrequently expressed distrust of men of commerce—are hardly more than occasional and episodic, as with D. H. Lawrence and Huxley, and they figure later anyhow. England has known no 'Heimatkunst' as such, but it has had a Thomas Hardy, who loves the countryside but knows it to be subject to the laws of change—the contrast is plain enough.

What made Expressionism, strikingly absent in England, possible, if not inevitable, in Germany was that a single generation, born around 1890, heirs of a cultural tradition enthroning ideals of harmony and totality, found itself confronted, as its parents had not been and so without effective transition, with a society under the pressure of radical transformation by advanced industrialisation. The result was a high degree of intellectuality, the outcome of so sudden and challenging an exposure to all the new and varied stimuli of a society under the impact of advanced industrialisation. This gave rise to a very modern kind of awareness, to what Kurt Hiller called the 'analytical feeling (*analytische Sensation*)' of the 'intellectual city-dweller'.[18] What this heightened intellectualised awareness signified is also epitomised in a statement of Hiller who, though older than most of the Expressionists, was often a significant spokesman of their problems and intentions : 'Only such minds are respectable and acceptable in which intellectuality (*das Geistige*) is ceaselessly on the move ... Intellectuality as a flame continuously fired by the soul ...'[19] A sentence or two of Gottfried Benn beautifully illustrates the correlation : 'Earlier in my village everything was linked with God or death, never with finite and material things (*mit einer Irdischkeit*). Then things stood firm in their places and reached down into the heart of the earth. Until the plague of knowledge (*Erkenntnis*) struck me'. Then 'everything happens only in my brain'.[20]

The point at issue is the emergence in Germany of a radical and very self-conscious intellectualisation of awareness, to which nothing in England can properly be said to correspond. Benn is only one example. Nietzsche is another. In Nietzsche's philosophy, be it noted, there is also the counterbalance of more instinctive values, and Benn in his way exemplifies the fascination of the negation of extreme intellectuality in terms of primitive and unifying experience. A 'brain-animal (*Gehirntier*)', a 'wretched brain-dog (*armer Hirnhund*)', 'so weary of his head (*der Stirn so satt*)', he yearns already in his early poetry for regression to the 'silent sap (*stumme Säfte*)' of a less conscious state. Thomas Mann comes into the picture too. Tonio Kröger, a self-confessed 'Literat'—or intellectual—marked by 'scepticism', 'freezing of feeling' and 'weary irony', turns against himself his criticism of the coldness of 'analysis' and 'formulation' and knows the seductions of the warmer 'joys of ordinary life', represented by those who do not need 'Geist'.

It can therefore hardly be insignificant that at the same time a type of philosophy comes to flourish—irrationalist, it is sometimes called—in which the emphasis is placed on the dynamism of inward areas of consciousness. Here too England, for better or for worse, offers no real comparison, least of all as regards the way, most conspicuously around the time of Expressionism and thereafter, the two extremes—intellectualisation and irrationalism—interlock and interplay, complimenting each other all along the line, and generating the richness and depth that makes so much modern German literature so endlessly fascinating and rewarding.

The difference between England and Germany is so striking in this respect that it calls for an explanatiaon. One part of this has to be related to the unbalance thus created between intellect and feeling, another to an aspect in connection with which it is useful to recall some remarks of Lukács in conversation with Leo Kofler. In England (and France), Lukács pointed out, the 'integration of a nation into a political unity is closely connected with the coming into existence of modern society'. The situation in Germany, before and particularly after 1848, was that of people who might recognise the problematicalness of the society to which they belonged without having the means to make their misgivings politically effective. A conflict, that is to say, arose 'as it were from the inner feelings of the true German, who still stood on the ground of the old reality, and, if he was sensible, had nevertheless seen the untenability of this reality'. The insight, however, 'did not permit a political realization'. Thus was created 'the irrationalist illusion of something external being brought to the inside and of something inner which is really external'. Examples used by Lukács are Heidegger and Klages, the latter with his theory of 'Geist' as the enemy of 'Seele'—and, comments Lukács, 'Hitler did nothing but turn this into a solid demagogy, in which the true-bred German is made the bearer of this "inwardness" '.[21]

It is from the last decade or two of the nineteenth century that these divergent, but complementary extremes, move into the foreground of German intellectual life, often accompanied by a harking back to what presented itself as a more intact, pre-industrial past. We find evidence of this sometimes where one would least expect it, as in Naturalism. Its antipathy to the city has already been noted, and a recent book on Naturalism has rightly stressed its attitude of 'withdrawal from social involvement'.[22] Its language is surprisingly often of a kind that by implication goes some way towards idealising the 'poetic' and the 'beautiful', as in a statement like this : 'The theatre opens to us ... the pure world of ideas free from the fortuitous and the finite. It shows us man in his essence (*Wesenheit*)'.[23]

Naturalism's occasional links with 'Heimatkunst' are not unimport-
ant in this connection, nor is the fact that its social energy proved
so short-lived. By comparison with England's greater familiarity
through longer experience with the social problems of industrialised
society, it is furthermore a matter worth commenting on that the
label of 'modernity (*die Moderne*)' should have been so self-
consciously attached to a movement at this late stage, by English
standards, making it its business to come to grips with them. In
Expressionism the reference back, often in the guise of a utopian
future, to a state of pre-industrial happiness is much in evidence.
Edschmid, for example, visualises a 'great divine garden', a 'paradise
behind the world of material things', and the simple and happy life,
which Hiller describes with such enthusiasm and likewise christens
'Paradise', has only the most superficial trimmings of modern
civilisation.[24] He might sing the praises of a new intellectualism, but
his conception of 'Geist' was not without its ambiguities. He was
insistent that he and his friends were not to be insulted by being
called intellectuals : 'Let people not brand us "Intellektuelle".' We
want to be called men of will (*Willentliche*)',[25] and to what he called
'die Geistigen' he tended to attribute the quasi-religious role of
saviour.

The comparison between the intellectual and the religious thinker,
noted by some sociologists, is particularly revealing when applied
to German intellectuals, more so than to English, despite maybe
figures like Carlyle, William Morris, Kingsley and Havelock Ellis.
In this respect too Heine, whose intellectuality strove towards the
compensation of religious synthesis, is a strikingly modern figure in
the German context. An analysis, for example, of Marcuse's language—and nowadays it is easy to forget that, as a German, his
formative years coincided with Expressionism—would reveal a disguised, secularised religious tonality, increasingly so as his thoughts
turned more and more towards return to inwardness, innocence, and
the 'recovery of nature' as the utopia towards which man has to
strive. Or take the case of Carl Einstein, the central figure of whose
Bebuquin (published in 1912) knows more than most about the
experience of alienation and fragmentation, and the implications
of that kind of intellectual awareness. Einstein is an intellectual if
ever there was one. He was also at heart a man of religious, not to
say mystical, yearnings, an aspect to which a recent study[26] of his
posthumous papers has given added significance. *Bebuquin* 'culmin-
ates essentially in a lament on the loss of God and the loss of self',[27]
and of Bebuquin's ultimate development in the uncompleted part
of the book Einstein said that 'until his death he always found con-

solation in secret images of Paradise'.[28] Einstein's high degree of intellectual awareness brought him to the point at which, echoing Nietzsche, he became the critic of the intellectualism he himself so conspicuously embodied : 'The weakling, aesthete, intellectual, murderer of life', 'theoretical knowledge, helplessness in practical affairs'.[29] As if to give symbolic expression to the direction in which his thought and feeling pointed, in his last days, fleeing from the Nazis in occupied France, he took refuge in a monastery; immediately before his death he assisted at the mass, describing himself then to his closest confidant among the monks as 'happy as never before'.[30]

Einstein was born in 1885, the same year as Ernst Bloch. Both men therefore were young at the start of the Expressionist movement, and both owe something to its climate of thought and feeling. Characteristic of this was a religious type of experience, most obvious in its visions of salvation and of man's rebirth to purity and wholeness. Marx's thought, originating in the context of the German classical debate about the overcoming of 'specialisation (*Einseitigkeit*)'—in modern parlance the division of labour—through 'totality', pointed from the beginning in the same direction, and it was to Marx that Bloch became most particularly indebted. His conception of existence, as notably in *Prinzip Hoffnung*, has been of man as impelled by a utopian motivation towards ultimate fulfilment, subject to the consideration of a force of imperfection in social life and human nature operating against it—the parallel in religious doctrine is obvious enough. Meanwhile the utopianism latent in Marx's ideas has left its mark on the German New Left, where his theory of economic and social change comes to be combined with speculation about the bliss to come in a world redeemed from the sins of alienation.

In fact, Jaspers singles out 'the delight in programmes of salvation (*die Lust an Heilsprogrammen*)'[31] as a distinguishing feature of the German tradition. The contrast with England can be measured in terms of the smaller part played by the messianic element in Marxism. There are various reasons for this. One is the role played by that peculiarly English interplay of sectarian protestantism and social energy, to which I have referred. Another is the more prominent and more distinctive role of Jewish intellectuals in Germany, and recent research has served to underline the extent to which the Jewish contribution has helped to steer social and political thinking in Germany into messianic directions. This can be seen, for example, in important sectors of German socialist thought. If in *Die Weltbühne* 'socialism is represented as a movement for

Man's redemption',[32] this is part of the explanation. Other reasons include England's more pragmatic tradition over a long period and, in the modern context, the different circumstances in which, as we have noted, English culture entered its relationship to advanced industrial society—circumstances less tempting to the imagination to indulge itself in romantic and utopian alternatives to what is possible within the given reality of the moment. This may not have been all to the good, and it might be right to criticise English intellectual life on this account. At all events, the result has been some very characteristic English institutions, among which I want in the first place to single out the Fabian Society—a good example, it seems to me, of what Tucholsky, lamenting its relative absence in Germany, called 'intellectuality which has assumed concrete form (*konkret gewordene Geistigkeit*)'.[33]

It is true that the beginnings of the Fabian Society were in the shadow of a quasi-mystical idea, Thomas Davidson's notion of the 'fellowship of the New Life', and the 'Basis', which for some time every member had to sign as a kind of pledge, had vaguely religious sounding associations. But what Laski called the 'ethereal qualities of its origins' faded into the background. The Society developed a 'zest for facts and figures', devoting its energy to the 'careful analysis of actual problems', to concrete results within the limits of the possible and through practical political activity. The Fabians 'did not even confuse the public mind by some transcendental world-outlook', but rather 'did a creative and cleansing job by persuasion and intelligence in a sober and practical way'.[34] They parted company with Marx early on, disapproving above all of the way he seemed to confuse the 'intuition of passion of prophecy with orderly inference from fact'. Beyond this, and equally important in the present context, the Fabian Society served as an intellectual forum, and as such the Fabian Executive, to which, for example, Shaw belonged, can be described. Through the Fabian Society—like earlier the Royal Society without parallel in Germany—the energies of powerful minds became focused on practical tasks, on the job of social reform according to a philosophy which—too materialistically maybe, and with too much regard for monetary and economic advantage—envisaged progress not in grandly utopian terms, but of what in the light of experience seemed possible in the circumstances.

The last point can be illustrated by reference to G. D. H. Cole, writer, scholar, academic, politician—a representative English intellectual. He went to a public school (and sent his son to another, one of the most superior). Thence he went to Oxford, to one of the most prestigious of its colleges, and took the course most associated with preparation for high office in the civil service, the Foreign Office and the Church. Later he was to hold a distinguished professorship at Oxford and a Fellowship at the most élitist of colleges. As a young man he had developed an interest in Guild Socialism, but was to become a leading figure in the Fabian Society, and in the First World War a Trade Union Official. Having in his student days at Oxford come into contact with the world of adult education through the Workers Educational Association, in the early 1920's he became Director of Tutorial Classes in the University of London, founded the Tutor's Association and was its chairman for some while, and played a major role in linking the adult education movement with the Trade Unions.[35]

Cole's biography thus brings into the picture another feature of English life and society which I want briefly to refer to, namely adult education. This has also played an important part in Germany, mainly through the 'Volkshochschulen', but there are two important points of difference as regards the Worker's Educational Association. The first concerns the origins of the 'Volkshochschulen', which go back through the pioneering Robert von Erdberg to the Danish residential colleges around the turn of the century. These appealed to Erdberg as being founded within a culture in close touch with the soil, and he saw the task of the German 'Volkshochschulen' above all as an aid to the dissemination and deepening of spirituality and inwardness. When in 1919 he became the first head of a special department for adult education in the Prussian Ministry of Education, he issued a memorandum in which he declared the aim of the 'Volkshochschule' to be to 'redeem' the nation 'from the one-sidedness of a barren intellectual culture',[36] and the director of one 'Volkshochschule' said that the task was to 'awaken and make available for right use the many spiritual forces that still lie fallow in the rural population, for this is the real source of the nation's strength'.[37]

English culture, we said, faced the impact of advancing industrialisation from a position of greater and more longstanding familiarity. In Germany—as the history of the 'Volkshochschule' movement reflects—it too easily generated a nostalgia, concealed or overt, for an intact, deeper, truer order of affairs. In England the response in intellectual circles to modern industrial society was more practical, more day-to-day, more in terms of everyday social justice. It was thus that the Workers Educational Association came into existence, sharing with the Fabian Society belief in the importance of facts and seeing its job as that of enlightening about them people who through no fault of their own were educationally under-privileged. Like the Fabian Society too, the Workers Educational Association channelled high intellectual energies to social aims and practical objectives within the limits of the possible. The history of the Workers Educational Association, like the Fabian Society, offers a long list of names of people associated with it—R. H. Tawney, for instance, A. D. Lindsay, Raymond Williams, Richard Hoggart, to name but a few—for whom 'intellectual', except in a very general sense, would be too narrow a classification. Hugh Gaitskell's first job, for example, after a public school education and a distinguished record at Oxford, was as a Workers Educational Association tutor.

So did perhaps Heinrich Mann have a point when he spoke of German intellectuality as 'jamais vraiment assouvie par la vie réelle'?[38] If so, may it help to explain why a specific contribution of German intellectuals has been to devote so much theory to the theoretical problem of theoretically combining theory and practice, why the species of intellectual is more prolific in Germany than in England, how it came about that a well-known contemporary German writer, asked on a visit to England what he thought of English intellectuals, is said to have replied that he had not found any—and why England's contribution in the area of abstract think-ing and theoretical systems has, notable exceptions apart, been so much less exciting than Germany's?

In *Culture and Anarchy* Matthew Arnold, the enemy of 'Phili-stines' and 'Barbarians' and taking Socrates as a model, urged the value of 'that power of a disinterested play of consciousness' on 'stock notions and habits' : 'And he who leads men to call forth and exercise in themselves this power, and who busily calls it forth and exercises it in himself, is at the present moment . . . more in concert with the vital working of men's minds, and more effectually signifi-cant than any House of Commons' orator, or practical orator in politics'.[39] That is not a bad description of the role of what came to be known as the intellectual, both in England and Germany. But in the case of Germany we have to take account of a further factor, not entirely absent in the English tradition, but in Germany playing a much more crucial role. For there would seem to be a connection between a heightened and radicalised self-awareness of the intellec-tual, and a tradition of power narrowly based and harshly exercised. A bad history of power makes all power seem bad to the intellec-tual, and he can turn this to his advantage. The more easily can he identify himself and his role, and in a liberal society the more important are then its occasional misdemeanours as enabling him to prove himself to himself. The *Spiegel* Affair was decisive for the self-awareness of German intellectuals in the Adenauer era; it would have been much less of an 'affair' against a different historical background. Significantly, the stage at which, applied to men like Auden, Isherwood and Spender, the idea of the intellectual did for the moment, but ephemerally, acquire a sharper profile in England was when, in the 1930s, power intruded brutally from outside, as fascism in Spain and Germany.

This is to make the point that at least in Germany it is the phenomenon of power—and power specifically within the framework of industrial society—that creates the phenomenon of the intellectual, in the sense in which Germany has become familiar with it and England lags behind. If Heine so strikingly prefigures the intellectual thus regarded, it is by virtue of an intellectuality generated by an inflexibly institutionalised conservatism at the point at which Germany was coming to feel the first real, if as yet limited, effects of industrial production with its social consequences and implications. A catchword current in Wilhelminian Germany embodied the conflict of 'Geist' *versus* 'Macht', 'spirit' *versus* 'power'. This tension, in which each of the extremes heightens the self-awareness of the other, continued in Weimar Germany—which is why Thomas Mann was put to such pains to argue his way towards a synthesis. It has been paramount in the Federal Republic —read Günter Eich's Büchner Prize speech, for example, of 1959.

The tension—a constant theme of intellectual discussion in Germany, never so in England to this extent—is, however, in the final analysis more complex. We have rather to speak of a dialectic. One part of it comprises the effect of the rationality claimed by the intellectual, as a spur to representatives of practical life, with whom power resides, to defend this by appeals at the other extreme to irrationality. This, as we have seen, was true of Wilhelminian Germany. It is still true today, as is well illustrated in F. C. Delius's rearrangement in literary form of the CDU/CSU economic congress of 1965 :

> Der Intellektuelle kommt vom Rationalen her,
> Die Sphäre der Wirtschaft ist
> im hohen Maße
> irrational
>
> . . .
>
> . . .
> Der Herrschaft der Intellektuellen
>
> . . .
> kann nur begegnet werden, wenn wir

in unserer modernen Welt wieder
die Kraft zum Idealen aufbringen.[40]

The other part of the dialectic, anticipated early in the century, consists of this turned round, the inversion being able to appear all the more plausible against the background of an idealism so intensely inward-directed as to let the social and political reality the more easily appear as inherently the enemy of the heart's desire. Under the influence particularly of the Frankfurt School, and with an additional push from the German New Left, Marx comes to be reinterpreted in such a way as at least severely to relativise his own belief in science and industry. In the name of nothing more precise than the creative principle—which intellectuals have customarily branded as a hallmark of reactionary philosophies—the intellectual comes to spearhead the attack on technological society. This is on the basis of a neo-Marxism viewing modern industrial society as a conglomeration of alienating forces and institutions which have all the time to be challenged in the name of the recovery of self, whatever in real terms that may now mean. A 'vitalist attack on intellect and causality' is thus 'passed off behind a pathetic critique of modern capitalist mass society'.[41] The irony is that such attitudes—increasingly now at work also outside Germany, but essentially of German origin, mediated by Marcuse—bear a suspicious family resemblance to ones which in earlier phases German intellectuals commonly thought of as progressive were vociferous in condemning.

Whether or not we find this a matter of concern will depend on one's point of view, and also perhaps on the extent to which by hindsight earlier situations are allowed to colour one's judgement. At all events, this establishes one final point of difference. As Heine did not seem to want to know, but as Gervinus recognised, in England an adequate forum of public debate has long been taken more or less for granted. The result has been to give minimal encouragement to anything deserving of the name of 'extra-parliamentary opposition', with all the opportunities it offers to intellectuals to identify themselves and stake their claim. This generalisation, however, may well be in the process of becoming less true than it was only a few years ago, and in that case a future lecture on the theme of mine today might they well turn out to be less in terms of contrasts than comparisons.

At all events, by standards long prevailing in the more empirical English tradition German intellectuals will frequently seem characterised by too theoretical a disposition, by a utopianism too often and too easily remote from real life, and a reluctance to live in peace with the practical world. The other way round, however, the qualities thus highlighted in Germany might perhaps be turned into a criticism of English intellectuals, as too practically orientated, too tolerant of the real world, too uncritical of power and institutions, ready to go too far in accepting things as they find them. This amounts to the simple and happy conclusion that in this respect, as in others, German and English culture are productively complementary.

NOTES

1. Shared interests in the Department of German Studies at Warwick, and the constant discussion arising from them, means that the ideas of others have crept into this paper as if my own. I am grateful to my colleagues for their otherwise unacknowledged contributions.
2. Heinrich Vormweg, *Die Wörter und die Welt*, Neuwied and Berlin, 1968, p. 116.
3. *Deutsche Schriften*, 3rd ed., Munich, 1937, p. 276, quoted in Fritz Stern, *The Politics of Cultural Despair*, Anchor ed., 1965, p. 55n.
4. 4th revised ed., Stuttgart and Berlin, 1932, p. 197.
5. Munich, 1934 ed., p. 697, 698.
6. Richard Hofstadter, *Anti-Intellectualism in American Life*, London, 1964, p. 49.
7. *Geschichte der deutschen Dichtung* (1871 ed.), IV, p. v.
8. *Die preußische Verfassung und das Patent vom 3. February 1847*, Mannheim, 1847, p. 104.
9. 'Uber die öffentliche Meinung (Fragment eines Briefes)', in *Georg Forsters sämmtliche Schriften*, Leipzig, 1843, V, p. 249.
10. Jürgen Habermas, *Strukturwandel der Öffentlichkeit*, 2nd ed., Neuwied and Berlin, 1965, p. 54.
11. Ibid., p. 71.
12. 'Der Auftritt des Intellektuellen in der Geschichte', in Karl Hoffmann (ed.), *Macht und Ohnmacht der Intellektuellen*, 1968, p. 11.
13. Quoted in G. M. Trevelyan, *English Social History*, 2nd ed., London, 1946, p. 258.
14. J. P. Nettl, 'Ideas, Intellectuals and Structures of Dissent', in P. Rieff (ed.), *On Intellectuals. Theoretical Case Studies*, New York, 1969, p. 74.
15. Gerald Kaufmann (ed.), *The Left*, London, 1966, p. 105-6.
16. Hans-Hellmuth Knütter, *Die Juden und die deutsche Linke in der Weimarer Republik*, Düsseldorf, 1971, p. 40.
17. 'Wir Negativen' (1919).
18. These aspects are worked out more fully in my essay 'Das Ich und die Welt. Expressionismus und Gesellschaft', in W. Rothe (ed.), *Expressionismus als Literatur*, Berne & Munich, 1969.
19. Kurt Hiller, *Die Weisheit der Lange-Weile*, Leipzig, 1913, I, pp. 237 seq.
20. 'Heinrich Mann. Ein Untergang', in Benn's *Gesammelte Werke*, Limes Verlag, 1959, II, p. 9.

21. Georg Lukács-Leo Kofler, 'Society and the Individual', in *Karl Marx 1818/1868, Bad Godesberg*, 1968, pp. 59 seq.
22. John Osborne, *The Naturalist Drama in Germany*, Manchester, 1971, p. 71.
23. *Kritische Waffengänge*, 4, p. 20.
24. Quoted in my essay in Rothe (ed.), op. cit.
25. Quoted in ibid.
26. Cf. Sibylle Penkert, *Carl Einstein. Beiträge zu einer Monographie*, Göttingen, 1969.
27. Ibid., p. 66.
28. Quoted in ibid., p. 40
29. Quoted in ibid., p. 106.
30. Quoted in ibid., p. 129
31. Karl Jaspers, *Wohin treibt die Bundesrepublik?*, Munich, 1966 p. 199.
32. Knütter, op. cit., p. 59.
33. Op. cit.
34. H. J. Laski, 'Fabian Socialism', in *Ideas and Beliefs of the Victorians*, London, n/d, pp. 78 seq.
35. Cf. Margaret Cole, *The Life of G. D. H. Cole*, London, 1971.
36. The memorandum is quoted more fully in R. H. Samuel and R. Hinton Thomas, *Education and Society in Modern Germany*, London, 1949 (reprint 1971), p. 141.
37. Quoted in ibid., p. 139.
38. Quoted in David Roberts, *Artistic Consciousness and Political Conscience. The Novels of Heinrich Mann 1900–1938*, Berne and Frankfurt am Main, 1971, p. 135.
39. Matthew Arnold, *Culture and Anarchy*, London, 1869, p. 271.
40. F. C. Delius, *Wir Unternehmer*, Berlin, 1966, p 54.
41. Neil McInnes, 'The Young Marx and the New Leaf', in the *Journal of Contemporary History*, VI, 4, 1971.

The Weimar Republic—Failure and Prospects of German Democracy

by KURT SONTHEIMER

The year 1919 saw the beginning of an adventure that was to last fourteen years—the first parliamentary democracy in Germany. It ended in failure and, taking all the historical factors into account, perhaps it was bound to do so. How can democracy, a form of government that implies the rule of the people, be maintained if the people do not want it? How can a democracy exist without democrats?

But if it is the case that a democracy which suffers from a lack of democrats has small chance of survival and stability beyond a fleeting moment, how could it come about in the first place that a democratic constitution was adopted in Germany in 1919?

A glance at German history during the disturbed winter of 1918–19 shows that the Weimar Republic was not a mere product of chance. It promised—albeit only for a moment—a reasonable solution of the problems arising from Germany's defeat in the First World War. It is often said that the two German democratic régimes, Bonn as well as Weimar, were forced upon the German people by its enemies. This is not true. It is true that the Americans under President Wilson entered the First World War with the slogan of making the world safe for democracy and the President's 14 Points, which influenced the German leaders to put a speedy end to the War, did include demands of a similar kind. But there can be no question of a democratic constitution having been imposed by the victors. This might be more true, but only in a technical sense, of the origins of the constitution of the Federal Republic, which required the explicit consent of the Occupying Powers. In both cases, however, in 1919 as well as in 1949, the establishment of a democratic political system was also the aim of the German constitution makers. The majority of the members of the Weimar National Assembly as well as of the Parliamentary Council in Bonn fully desired a democratic, pluralist constitution and were not under any pressure to adopt a constitution they did not want. It would be quite wrong, therefore, to explain the failure of the first German democracy by claiming that it had been forced on the country from without. To cling to such a view is to perpetuate a legend. It is more nearly true to say that the German democracy of Weimar was a product of defeat and always, even if unjustly, associated with defeat.

At the moment of the armistice on 9 November 1918 the imperial régime was not only militarily, but also in its domestic policies, at the end of the line. The Kaiser had, by delaying his abdication too long, lost the chance of saving the Monarchy; the Army, the strongest bastion of the Empire, withdrew in good order but beaten into a Germany shaken by domestic upheavals; the bureaucrats at their desks awaited in fear and trembling the shape of things to come. The rapidly spreading November revolution petrified the traditional ruling classes, the aristocracy and the *haute bourgeoisie*, with fear of bolshevisation, the spectre of which appeared everywhere in the establishment of so-called Workers' and Soldiers' Councils.

Thomas Mann once said, looking back on those weeks and months, that the ruling circles of the old Reich had become 'soft as pulp' in those days. It is the intriguing paradox of that historical moment, that the very groups who had for decades fought against the advent of democracy because they wanted to preserve their privileges, now took refuge in a system of bourgeois democracy. They, as it were, embraced the democratic régime as their shield and protection in order to save at least a portion of their former pre-eminence under the new system. They were ready to make their peace with bourgeois democracy. When, however, the conditions favourable to democracy, arising from its revolutionary origins, began to change, a succession of crises in the Weimar Republic became inevitable, for the old enemies of liberal democracy now rose again from within its fold.

The liberal democratic republic was thus supported by a majority of the German people in 1919. But it was significant for the developing fortunes of the Republic that the party coalition which had upheld the Weimar State in its first few months, namely a grouping of Majority Social Democrats, the Centre Party and the German Democratic Party, was unable to obtain a majority in the first regular Reichstag elections of 1920. From now on the opponents of democracy, inside and outside the parties, increased steadily in numbers, and even if the decision of the German National Assembly in favour of democracy was genuine, it nevertheless proved to be the product of an ephemeral historical situation.

The Revolution of 1918–19 did not bring about the rule of the German working class. By this time the SPD had long ceased to be a revolutionary party. The Majority Social Democrats under Friedrich Ebert did not want to further the Revolution, but to bring it under control and to establish security and order in the country as quickly as possible. But for this purpose they needed help against their own more radical comrades, who were determined to erect, instead of a democratic Republic, a Soviet Republic based on the dictatorship of the proletariat. Only the Supreme Command of the Army could effectively give this help. Thus arose the politically curious alliance between the SPD leader Ebert and the Chief of the Supreme Command of the Army, General Gröner, which was basic to the establishment of the Weimar Republic. In this way the Government succeeded in mastering the Revolution, in formally initiating the election of a National Assembly and in finally completing the constitution of Weimar, but this democratic order, open to friend and foe alike, was flawed from the beginning. With a degree of self-deception one might suppose that the opponents of bourgeois democracy were to begin with so few in number because there was genuine acceptance of such a democratic system; in fact this was due only to the realisation that a democratic republic was the sole practical alternative to the threatening danger of bolshevism.

Ernst Troeltsch, the famous liberal historian and sociologist of religion, presents in his 'Spectator letters' an excellent contemporary view of that period : 'To understand the developments that are to come one must be aware that this democracy was in essence an anti-revolutionary system, dedicated to the maintenance of order and opposed to the dictatorship of the proletariat. It would be shortsighted to celebrate a triumph and to assume that the goals of 1848 had been attained. No, what had been in 1848 a bold, progressive venture was now a conservative slowing-up and reining in of the Revolution, a way of legalising the activities of the opponents of the Revolution and securing their growing influence. At least to begin with there was no Treaty of Versailles. It was therefore still possible to hope that if all went well abroad, that is, if the peace treaty, in spite of heavy burdens, were to open the possibility of recovery and reconstruction.... But all went far from well. In fact it went about as badly as possible, at home and abroad. From without there came the Treaty of Versailles, with its all-devouring exploitation, its new chicaneries and ceaseless threats.... At the same time at home the conservative parties, under cover of the more stable conditions developed by the demo-

cratic régime, turned with growing vehemence and passion against
the coalition of the moderate parties on which the Reich was based.
Responsibility for the defeat and all the humiliation of Versailles
was now pinned on this coalition of the centre, the destruction of
which was to break the rule of social democracy.'

These lines of Ernst Troeltsch, written in these early years of the
Republic, reflect its illusory promises, and its sad failures. The
Weimar Republic was the result of improvisation, almost of in-
decision, not the product of a far-reaching and decisive political
will. For example, Friedrich Ebert asked the liberal constitutional
lawyer Hugo Preuss late in 1918 to prepare a draft constitution,
since he had the confidence of the Social Democrats, and they
themselves were not in a position to draft a constitution. So he
took on the job because the leading men of that moment did not
quite know how to set about it. Thus the organisational scheme of
the Republic, the Constitution, was put together in Weimar; it
arose from a momentary pause for breath between imperial authori-
tarianism and social revolution, and was not the product of popular
energies and passions. Once the threat of revolution had passed
and a sufficient number of peoples had recovered from the numb-
ness of defeat, the enemies of this democracy were present in all
quarters and did not pull their punches.

The signature of the Versailles treaty rapidly aroused the fiercest
hostility of many groups, which had up to then maintained a waiting attitude towards the Republic. By 1920 an observer like
Troeltsch could discern the spectre of counter-revolution :

'This is the latest turn in the ebb and flow of events. The
Deutschnationale Partei thinks it safe to reappear as the party of
the old Conservatives and as the old *Vaterlandspartei*. It is dropping the cautious mannerism of a "people's party", which earlier
on it felt was needed in the new situation and which is now confined to a daily more virulent antisemitism. Some of the universities
are electing their rectors from amongst the most militant of war
propagandists and the majority of students are returning to their
old associations and their ideologies. The Protestant Church of
Prussia is preparing to become the counter-bastion to the revolutionary states. In short, the foundations of counter-revolution, in part
carefully planned, in part instinctively adopted, are becoming
apparent.'

After the move to the left which engulfed Germany in the revolutionary winter of 1918/19, there followed, after the signature of the
Treaty of Versailles, a swing to the right. Occasionally it proved
possible to contain it momentarily, for example after the murders

of Erzberger and Rathenau, but on the whole the rightward movement advanced inexorably and drove the Reich, after the mis-
guided episode of the Kapp-Putsch, into the crisis year of 1923.
Only Stresemann's deliberate policy of reason and stabilisation
managed temporarily to rescue the country. The years 1924–9 were,
as is well known, the most stable in the history of the Weimar
Republic; but linked with the great economic crisis of 1929 the
destructive forces of fascist revolution, aided and abetted by the
traditional enemies of democracy, bore down with redoubled violence upon the fragile Republic and in the end overwhelmed it
with an appearance of legality.

One can attribute the downfall of the Republic to a variety of
causes, which were for the most part inherent in the circumstances
of its origins. The Weimar Republic arose from a number of com-
promises which, in the main did not, even after a short lapse of
time, prove viable. In contrast to constitutional development in
Britain which, if I judge it correctly, has usually known how to
combine constructively the old and the new, the Weimar Republic,
to quote Karl Dietrich Bracher in his new book *The German
Dilemma*, 'rested in its power structure on a series of incomplete
and precipitately contrived pseudo-compromises between the old
and the new; between the imperial army and the revolutionary
Government, between employers dedicated to the status quo and
trade unions conscious of increased strength, between federalist
and centralising tendencies, between inflexible political parties
deeply separated by tradition and ideology. A majority of the
population accepted this fragile emergency structure only reluctantly and through force of circumstances, as was clearly revealed
in the first elections after the adoption of the constitution. In the
formation of the new state and power structure the rulers entered
into bargains which had little durability and their anti-republican
enemies to the Right and to the Left were able, after only a few
weeks, to transform their attitude of obstruction in principle into
open defiance of the state. The Weimar Republic was from the beginning forced on to the defensive; subsequently it was weakened
by an almost incomprehensible indulgence towards its declared
enemies, but even more by the fact that democracy was not able
to satisfy the craving for authority and order fostered by centuries
of authoritarian rule in Germany.'

The Weimar Constitution was not able, as its Founding Fathers
had hoped, to accomplish the necessary function of integrating
divergent political and social forces; on the contrary it became the
springboard for the subversion and overthrow of democracy. The

weakness of the Weimar Constitution intensely preoccupied the Parliamentary Council, the makers of the Basic Law of Bonn, but however busily they might search for weak spots the decisive factor was that in the Weimar period the general conditions for the success of democracy simply did not exist. Above all the political parties no less than the bulk of the German people, lacked a positive attitude towards the values and virtues of liberal democracy.

Theodor Heuss, the first president of the Federal German Republic, used telling arguments in the Bonn Parliamentary Council to rebut the view that the failure of the Weimar Republic was due to its constitution; for example, primarily to the excessive powers of the President, or to proportional representation, or to the ambiguous relationship between Reich and *Länder*. Heuss said : 'It is now fashionable, and we have had echoes of it here, to denigrate the Weimar Constitution. It is now customary to say that because Hitler's turn came and the provisions of the Weimar Constitution did not stop him, therefore this constitution was bad. The historical process does not work in quite so primitive a manner.

'The Democracy of Weimar was so slow in getting off the ground and never got properly into gear because Germany never conquered democracy for herself. Democracy came to Germany—and this has become almost banal by now—in the wake of defeat. But because it was not taken by storm it could not develop its own myth nor acquire its own know-how. Thus it happened that the further evolution of democracy took place in an atmosphere of nationalist Romanticism and monarchical restoration and in the shadow of the wretched crime of the stab-in-the-back myth. These things were much more decisive in governing the operation of the Weimar Constitution than the technical formulation of this or that constitutional paragraph, even if we may today consider some of them less than perfect.'

One can only agree with Theodor Heuss. The reason why the Republic of Bonn has become a more stable and virile régime is not primarily because the Basic Law is so much better than the Weimar Constitution, but because in Bonn the political, economic and social conditions and what is now often called the 'political culture' are so much more favourable to a proper functioning of democracy than they were in Weimar. This can be shown very clearly by an analysis of the intellectual opposition to the Weimar régime. I would like to devote some attention to this aspect of the Weimar situation, particularly as it has been the subject of some of my own researches.

Intellectuals of the Left, men like René Schickele or Heinrich

Mann, welcomed the great change as the dawn of a new and more humane era for Germany. Neo-conservative groups, on the other hand, though they did not want the Wilhelmine past brought back, hoped for a repetition of the climax of August 1914, which they saw as a crowning experience of German renewal, welding all classes together into a national *völkisch* unity. But all too quickly they reached the opinion that the spirit of the new Republic was not national, that the constitution that had been devised could not guarantee a genuine concentration of the nation into a tight union and they turned away from the Republic in anger. They began a ceaseless campaign against the Weimar system, against the policy of fulfilment, against parliamentary government and liberal democracy. They conjured up before the eyes of their readers visions of the unity, power and honour of the Reich, which had been shamelessly surrendered by liberal politicians for the sake of personal advantages; they swore by the community of the people, and believed to have found in a hierarchical order of society the true answer to the disintegration, pluralism and class war of Weimar democracy. They flirted with the notion of the dictatorship of a charismatic leader, whom they awaited longingly, so that he would put an end to the alleged chaos inside Germany and give back to the stunted structure of the state its former power and glory.

In the democracy of Weimar they despised the 'system', by which they meant a murky mechanism moved by the selfish interests of political parties, who in their partisanship had lost all sense of national responsibility.

The promise which a political writer like Moeller van den Bruck held out to his readers was that of the Third Reich, an empire of shining splendour, in which all Germans were united into an indivisible nation. But in order to reach that goal it was first necessary to do away with parties, parliaments and with the democratic form of government of the western type. And all this was written in order to advance, at least through the written and spoken word, this kind of development. It was the aim of Moeller and his collaborators to *politicise* the German people, and in practice that meant to *mobilise* it against the régime of Weimar. An understanding, a reconciliation wtih the Republic was impossible for them. Only its supersession could usher in the New Era of which they dreamed.

There were many intellectual and militant groups of this kind; some were decidely conspiratorial; they called for the national revolution and put their trust in the dynamic power of a small number of revolutionary cadres which would pave the way for the new era. They advocated with Ernst Jünger a revolutionary nationalism, despised effeminate humanitarianism and the politics of compromise, and brooded ceaselessly on the chances of over-throwing the rotten democratic state through *action directe*, by force.

In his great political novel *Dr Faustus*, Thomas Mann sketched retrospectively the atmosphere among intellectual circles cultivating such ideologies. Let us listen for a moment to the conversation among a group of academics in Munich in the years after the First World War:

'It is probably superfluous to state that not for a moment did they recognise the form of government which we got as a result of defeat, the freedom that fell in our laps, in a word the democratic republic, as anything to be taken seriously as the legitimised frame of the new situation. With one accord they treated it as ephemeral, as meaningless from the start, yes, as a bad joke to be dismissed with a shrug.

'It was an old-new world of revolutionary reaction, in which the values bound up with the idea of the individual—shall we say truth, freedom, law, reason?—were entirely rejected and shorn of power, or else had taken on a meaning quite different from that given them for centuries. Wrenched away from the washed-out rheoretic, based on the relative and pumped full of fresh blood, they were referred to the far higher court of violence, authority, the dictator-ship of belief—not, let me say, in a reactionary, anachronistic way as of yesterday or the day before, but so that it was like the most novel setting back of humanity into mediaevally theocratic conditions and situations. That was as little reactionary as though one were to describe as regression the track round a sphere, which of course leads back to where it started. There it was: progress and reaction, the old and the new, the past and the future became one; the political right more and more coincided with the Left. That thought was free, that research worked without assumptions: these were conceptions which, far from representing progress belonged to a superseded and uninteresting world. Freedom was given to thought that it might justify force; just as seven hundred years ago reason had been free to discuss faith and demonstrate dogma; for that she was there, and for that today thinking was there, or would be there tomorrow.'

This kind of mental attitude was not confined to esoteric circles of intellectuals. In the programmes of many patriotic organisations and associations this hostility towards liberal democracy of the Weimar type was only too clearly to be seen, and National-socialism was only the most primitive, if also the most potent variant. One can only stand amazed that the democratic state allowed all manner of organisations, finally even political parties and their associated para-military formations, to strut across the scene without so much as an attempt to conceal their aim of subverting democracy. How was it possible that a democracy should do so little against those who were encompassing its imminent downfall?

This striking weakness of the Weimar Republic had, so it seems to me, two main causes : first, the assumption that an open society arose from an intermingling of widely changing political attitudes and groups and that, if whole sections of the people were not to be excluded from political participation, it was necessary for the sake of democracy not to deprive even the anti-democratic groups of their voice. Secondly, there was no accepted consensus in the Government or in Parliament about the principles of democracy. If one looks closely at the attitudes of the political parties which willy-nilly supported the parliamentary system, one is forced to the conclusion that apart from the dwindling adherents of the German Democratic Party, the Liberals, there was no one who could raise much enthusiasm for democracy à la Weimar. The ideological position of the various groups went far beyond that compromise formula by which it was just possible to operate democracy in the particular political circumstances right at the beginning of the post-war period. For the Social Democrats it was galling that their aim of a popular socialist régime remained entirely theoretical and that they were thus losing part of the working class to the Communists. The Centre Party was orientated more towards the cultural and religious rather than the purely political sphere and was not particularly interested, as Brüning's policy was to show, in the maintenance of parliamentary forms as such; further to the Right the German People's Party had to be painfully forced by Stresemann to collaborate meaningfully with the parliamentary régime and moved after Stresemann's death even more to the Right. The Conservatives never did anything but compare the Weimar Republic with the splendour of the Bismarckian Reich and therefore regarded democracy as a form of government inseparable from national impotence and popular decadence. In short : there was hardly anybody who could wholly identify with the existing régime. The Republic was not merely short of democrats, the democratic groups in the country were themselves insecure and disunited. The fact that after his rise to power Hitler was able to abolish all remaining democratic institutions without much ado and in short order, arises from the democrats' lack of confidence in their own ideals. Those who do not believe in democracy cannot defend the system when it is under attack. The opponents of the Weimar Republic were in the end able to triumph so mightily over the democrats because the latter ducked the blows aimed at them instead of mounting a large-scale defensive operation. A historically important example of this attitude is the coup d'état against Prussia on 20 July 1932. Braun and Severing, dismissed from their offices in Prussia by Chancellor Papen, contented themselves with verbal and written protests and awaited a favourable verdict from the Leipzig Constitutional Court against Papen's breach of the constitution. When, months later, the verdict came it was a judgement of Solomon giving both parties some of their case. By then the facts of political power had long moved against the democratic position in social-democratic Prussia and that was what really mattered. The Prussian Social Democrats had failed to defend themselves vigorously and had thus surrendered an important bastion of the Republic.

If one attempts to classify the opponents of the Weimar republic into their various camps a threefold grouping becomes apparent. There was, from the time of the battles of the November revolution, a section of radical workers who began to gather round the banner of the Communist Party, founded in Germany in 1919. Their hostility towards the moderate Social Democrats was indestructible, for the SPD was in the eyes of the Communists an instrument of the ruling bourgeoisie for the suppression of the Proletariat. The Communists gained in numerical strength in the last few years of the Republic, but the cleavage which had arisen, in the bloody encounters during the Revolution, between the revisionist and the revolutionary camps remained unbridgeable even in the face of the serious threat to the Republic posed by the National-socialists. The Communists preferred to see the Republic succumb to the Nazis rather than help the Social Democrats defend it. For the Communists the Social Democrats became in the end the Social Fascists.

The mass of the opponents of democracy were, however, to be found in the nationalist camp. Here a clear divergence was soon discernible between the old, conservative Nationalists looking back to imperial times and the Neo-nationalists, Young Conservatives or whatever they might call themselves. For the Old Conservatives, who were represented by the *Deutschnationale* People's Party, the Weimar State was nothing but a miserable decline from the peak of Wilhelmine splendour. They swore by the old imperial glory, in which they could see nothing but greatness and purity and despised a state in which a saddler's apprentice like Friedrich Ebert could become a President.

Behind the *Deutschnationale* a growing number of increasingly vocal younger people were coming up, nationalists like their elders, and often more bitter and militant in their struggle against the Republic. Their view of the Wilhelmine era before 1914 was almost as merciless as their opinion of the Régime of 1918–19. Although they professed allegiance to permanent Revolution, they were unwilling to acknowledge the half-hearted Revolution of 1918, but wanted to bring it to its true conclusion. They dreamed of a genuine German people's republic, a fraternally united nation under strong and determined leadership—and thus saw in the political system of Weimar nothing but gross pursuit of vested interest and fiercest fratricidal strife. Many of them had returned from the war with a feeling that they had not been defeated and so they waxed indignant about the allied policies of Versailles and for simplicity's sake blamed the democratic parties for having caused the whole misfortune. When at the end of the twenties the Nazis under Hitler mobilised the dissatisfied masses against the Weimar Republic and the system, it became quickly obvious that they had a large part of nationalistically inclined youth on their side. 'German youth', so one could read, 'supports Hitler'. Even if this was not entirely true, it was the case that Hitler's swastika was not only the flag of the discontented and the disappointed, of the irredeemable Jew-haters and the fanatics of the Teutonic cult, but also the banner of youth. What was it that drove the young especially into hostility towards the democratic state?

The question is difficult to answer. The common explanation is that Weimar democracy was not attractive. No doubt it turned out to have little attraction, and young people, insofar as they were looking for great causes and ideals, could not find in it any inspiration towards human or institutional greatness. But is this answer, so often given, really adequate? How could there be national grandeur after a defeat which the enemy powers, especially France, tried to turn into permanent inferiority? Perhaps we should not have signed the Treaty of Versailles, but what use would that have been? To make war was no longer possible, even if many in their emotional distress pretended that it was possible at any time. In its domestic affairs the Weimar Republic did indeed present a spectacle of internecine strife and disunity. The vested interests of parties did seem at times to overwhelm the common good of the nation, but this, too, requires further explanation. Why were the parties, even the genuinely democratic ones, often so

sharply divided? Because their ideological roots committed them
to aims which could not be achieved without fundamental conflict
with the goals of the other parties. The really acute clashes arose,
however, from insufficient agreement about the constitution itself.
After 1920 the original democratic majority of the Weimar
Coalition faced a majority of basically non-democratic parties. In
this situation how could there be that unity and continuity in the
state which nationalist youth expected? It was just the obstinately
negative attitude to the parliamentary process, the growing agitation
against the Republic which paralysed democracy itself. The
nationalists contributed through their activities to the weakening of
democracy, then they accused democracy of being weak and yet
expected this Republic to develop a special attraction.

The talk about the unattractive drab democracy of Weimar is
ill-founded, not only because it rests on mistaken assumptions, but
because it takes the citizens to be an entirely passive object. It is
the particular feature of democracy that it must be as far as possible
the concern of all and that it must offer all sections of society the
chance of participation. To talk of the attractive power of a form
of government is itself a sign of an authoritarian mentality. Democracy seeks its justification not in a higher or lower degree of glory
and attraction, but in a liberal legal order for both the individual
and the community.

Attempts were not lacking to commend the virtues of the
Republic to the younger generation. Thomas Mann made many
appeals from 1922 onwards to the German middle class, and particularly to the academic youth of the country, to cast aside the
reactionary ideologies and to learn at last that this German Republic
was not to be despised and that the best German traditions could
flourish under its aegis. 'German youth and bourgeoisie', so we
read in his speech *Of the German Republic,* 'Your resistance against
the republic is only fear of words, yes, these words make you rear
and shy like unruly horses. . . . But these are only words, relative
things, forms determined by the needs of the moment, useful tools,
and it is childish to suppose that their meaning must necessarily
be some alien humbug. The Republic—of course it is still Germany.
And could not democracy be a more homely haven than some
vainglorious, sabre-rattling, gesticulating empire?'

But the persuasive tones of a writer fell on deaf ears; those to
whom this appeal was addressed, stamped their feet impatiently
and felt happier in the rush away from Weimar, so mightily
encouraged by the Nazis. The catastrophic dimensions of the Great
Depression undermined any vestige of confidence among the masses

in the parliamentary form of government and an increasing number
looked expectantly to the Leader who promised not only work and
bread but also power and glory for Germany. By the same token
an increasing sense of resignation took hold of the democrats who
took a few, but not nearly enough steps to stem the brown tide.
The opponents of democracy triumphed over the Republic which
had offered no resistance to their attacks.

The fundamental political decision taken in 1919 was in harmony
with the historical situation then prevailing, but subsequently it
did not provide a viable basis for a healthy political evolution.
One should not lay the failure at the door of the Constitution
itself—those of its provisions which proved doubtful were doubtful
only in a society that lacked and could never reach a consensus
about the basic political and economic order. But how was it that
Weimar democracy could in the end produce a numerical pre-
ponderance of anti-democrats? The many reasons which have to
be adduced here are the same as the reasons for the failure of the
Weimar Republic. We know that from many books, and only the
sum total of external, internal, economic, psychological and general
historical factors, together with the behaviour of individual politicians, produced 30 January 1933.

Numerous as were the objective causes which almost inevitably
made the Weimar Republic fall victim to its adversaries, the history
of the Republic is also the story of the sins of omission of many
individuals. To be able to see them as such is, however, the privilege
of posterity. It required the national-socialist catastrophe to con-
vince many Germans that obstinate resistance to democracy was
more disastrous in its consequences than the imperfect democracy
of Weimar could ever have been.

The trauma caused by the failure of Weimar played an important
rôle in the genesis and evolution of the Federal Republic. This is
still the case today. German politicians of all parties are very
sensitive if historical comparisons are made with the conduct of
parties in the Weimar Republic. For Weimar appears, in this view,
always as a precursor of Hitler's tyranny.

The Parliamentary Council of Bonn created a 'counter-consti-
tution' to the Weimar Constitution. It was concerned to avoid the
alleged defects of Weimar in so clear-cut a manner, that the new
basic law could never become the legal framework for an authoritarian, let alone a totalitarian form of government. The new
constitutional provisions have, in the main proved effective and
constructive, but just as one cannot ascribe the failure of Weimar
to specific constitutional shortcomings, one cannot put the political

stability of the second parliamentary Republic to the credit of the Basic Law only. Every constitution depends for its quality on the political forces at work within it and on the consent of the people. Paradoxically the Hitler régime and its catastrophic collapse at the end of a murderous world war helped decisively to create the preconditions for the success of the second German democracy. The end of the Third Reich finally dispersed the political illusions against which a policy of moderation and reason could not prevail in the Weimar period. The total defeat of the régime, the disclosure of its crimes have so completely discredited all anti-democratic prescriptions that even the present enemies of parliamentary democracy have first to pay lip-service to the parliamentary system before they can voice their criticisms.

Hitler's rule and its collapse have greatly changed the structure of German society and made it more homogeneous. The deep ideological and class differences of the Weimar period have disappeared. We are experiencing a process of far-reaching, perhaps too far-reaching, ideological and sociological levelling. Another positive feature of our situation is the successful absorption of the federal army into the structure of the Federal Republic. The Bundeswehr is not, like the Reichswehr, a state within a state, but a reliable instrument of the political leadership.

All this is not the result of a straight application of lessons which might have been learnt from the history of the Weimar Republic, but largely the result of historical processes which were unavoidable and which left little room for deliberate intellectual direction. The decisive factors in favour of the Bonn Republic and in contrast to the prevailing atmosphere of the Weimar Republic, are the real desire for democracy and the absence of sizeable, politically important anti-democratic groups, be they nationalist or Communist. The evolution of the political parties in the Federal Republic has been marked by a progressive exclusion of all radical groups. The Federal Parliament is today entirely dominated by the successor parties of the former Weimar Coalition. In the Weimar Republic the triad of Social Democrat, German Democratic and Centre parties retained its majority only till 1920. In the end the victors were the political groups of the nationalist right-wing opposition, supported in Parliament by the extreme Left, all of them in principle opposed to the parliamentary democracy which they finally succeeded in abolishing. Today the opposition in the Federal Parliament is in principle democratic and, as could be seen in 1969, a true alternative to the Government.

Let us, however, not end with the complacent statement that our

Bonn democracy is a democracy without serious antagonists. So far there have been no great crises, and the acceptance of the parliamentary system has been linked with the assurance of economic prosperity. What would happen if this assurance collapsed? In that case, would doubt about the effectiveness and virtue of the democratic system spread with equal rapidity?

Perhaps not quite so quickly, but hardly anyone could guarantee that those groups which a few decades ago formed the breeding ground for the opposition to democracy, had now been transformed into completely convinced converts to democracy. There may still be lessons for us in the sad story of the Weimar Republic as a democracy without democrats. No one could say with complete certainty that our democracy has become a genuine way of life for us, but we are making progress in this direction. Since every historical situation makes new demands and requires fresh reactions, we cannot be sure that a few lessons from the Weimar Republic will save us from all the dangers which threaten democracy. André Gide has given expression to this uncertainty which envelops the present at all times. 'Is it ever possible to recognise in advance the new dangers? Is the path ever the same and he who treads it ever the same person? Can the future ever imitate the past? Therein lies our burden that we are constantly playing a new game and we do not yet know if the cards that will be dealt to us will turn out good or bad.'

The Historical Roots of National Socialism

by F. L. CARSTEN

I do not believe that National Socialism was an 'accident' in the course of German history, or a 'strange aberration'—any more than Bolshevism was an 'accident' in the course of Russian history. Any movement able to seize and to hold power for any length of time must have roots linking it firmly with the specific historical development of the nation in question, must give expression to the aspirations and to the longings of millions of people, must be able to mobilise them for its aims and retain their active or passive allegiance. Otherwise no government, however perfect its machinery of terror, could maintain itself in power for more than a few months. The National Socialist dictatorship was not alien to the German people, nor was Germany an 'occupied country' (although this has been alleged), but National Socialism grew on German and Austrian soil. Professor Bracher is entirely right when he calls his last book : *The German Dictatorship*.[1]

On the other hand, I do not believe that National Socialism was the inevitable outcome of a long historical process which started with Martin Luther and his reliance on the authority of the German princes. Nor do I think that the Germans—preconditioned by centuries of absolute government—are fundamentally unsuited to democratic government and longing for a firm, paternal hand to guide them. After all, Germany possessed in the Hanseatic towns, the Free Imperial Cities and the Assemblies of the Estates ancient self-governing institutions able to hold their own with those of any other country, institutions, moreover, which in many cases could look back upon an unbroken tradition from medieval to modern times. Yet such views were widely held, especially in the countries allied against Germany in the last war, and were propounded with all the airs of pseudo-scientific knowledge. In the middle of the war, in 1941, Sir Robert Vansittart, the permanent under-secretary in the Foreign Office, gave a series of famous broadcasts which were published under the title 'Black Record—Germans Past and Present'. There he likened Germany to a butcher-bird 'steadily destroying all its fellows' : 'Well, by hook and by crook—especially crook—

the butcher-bird got three wars before 1914.'[2] Vansittart went back to the deeds of the Germanic tribes and of the Teutonic Order to show that 'Germany as a whole has always been hostile and unsuited to democracy'. He compared the activities of the Hanseatic League to those of the *Auslandsdeutsche* of the twentieth century; he stated boldly that the dictatorship of Hitler derived from the authoritarian system of Bismarck and the autocracy of the Kaiser, that 'No other race could have managed to idolize such people'.[3]

Vansittart thus subconsciously adopted some of the racialist theories and fantasies of the man he was fighting against. But professional historians too, in the years of the war, saw in Hitler the logical outcome of the German past, and 'the Germans' as ardent supporters of Hitler's policy of conquest. In the same year in which Vansittart was holding forth on Germany's Black Record, Mr. Rohan Butler stated in his book, *The Roots of National Socialism* :

> This achievement of national socialism is a great and original tour-de-force, but it does not alter the fact that national socialist theory is almost entirely derived from the common elements in traditional German thought during the past hundred and fifty years. For that line of thought which leads from Herder to Hitler is traditionally and typically German . . .[4]

Mr. Butler also considered that the socialism of the founder of German Social Democracy, Ferdinand Lassalle, was national socialism and that the object of his policy was dictatorship;[5] while another Oxford historian, Mr. A. J. P. Taylor, wrote at the end of the war in an attempt to show the deep roots of the German dictatorship :

> During the preceding eighty years the Germans had sacrificed to the Reich all their liberties; they demanded as reward the enslavement of others. No German recognized the Czechs or Poles as equals. Therefore every German desired the achievement which only total war could give. By no other means could the Reich be held together. It had been made by conquest and for conquest; if it ever gave up its career of conquest, it would dissolve. . . .[6]

What I object to particularly in these sweeping generalisations are the words 'every German', 'typically German', and the claims that 'no German' recognised the Slav peoples as equals : As if other European nations had not produced their racialist writers—the French, for example, Gobineau, and the English Houston Stewart Chamberlain—, as if there was no other tradition in German political thought but that leading to Hitler, as if there had not been a wave of pro-Polish thinking and writing in Germany in the first half of the nineteenth century, as if wars of conquest were only waged by Germans, as if the wave of terror unleashed by Hitler in 1933 was not for several years solely and entirely directed against Germans! It is, of course, understandable that views such as those quoted above were held during the years of the Second World War, but today saner opinions should prevail.

No one can seriously doubt that Hitler was carried to power by a colossal wave of nationalist fervour, fed by years of propaganda against the 'shame' of Versailles and by the infamous stab-in-the-back legend. As early as November 1918—only a few weeks after the revolution which caused the collapse of the German Empire and the flight of the Kaiser—a German officer wrote :

> In the most difficult moment of the war ... the revolution, prepared for a long time, has attacked us from the rear. ... I do not know of any revolution in history which has been undertaken in so cowardly a fashion and which—what is much worse still—has necessarily aggravated the dire plight which has befallen us; perhaps it will lead to a complete catastrophe ...[7]

The man who wrote this was then a junior officer; but he was destined to become the chief of the German general staff, to resign in protest against Hitler's plans of aggression against Czechoslovakia, and to die by his own hand on 20 July 1944, the day when the plot against Hitler's life miscarried. In the years after 1919 the stab-in-the-back legend became one of the most potent weapons in Hitler's armoury—and millions of Germans believed him only too willingly.

German nationalism—like most European nationalisms—came into being in the course of the nineteenth century. More precisely, it was born at the very beginning of the century, at a time when the Germans had been deeply humiliated by the victories of Napoleon and the French occupation of wide stretches of Germany. Hence German nationalism was virulently, passionately anti-French. The Corsican conqueror was hated as the scum of humanity, as the arch-fiend. The poet Heinrich von Kleist exclaimed :

> Dam the Rhine with their corpses,
> let it, jammed with bones,
> foam, flow around the Palatinate, and
> thus form the frontier !
> A pleasure hunt when the shooters
> track the woolf !

Kill him! the last judgement
will not ask you for the reasons![8]

At the same time another poet, one of the leading lights of the
Prussian Reform movement, Ernst Moritz Arndt, tried to explore
the reasons why the French had become 'such a heartless, perfidious,
sly and vain people', and he discovered the principal source of their
'depravity' in their *Mischmasch* (mixed race) and bastardisation.
In his opinion it was the greatest misfortune of the French 'that the
capital and the centre of the whole state and the entire French life
developed in the most bastardized districts of France, for this centre
was the pernicious cancer which corroded all that was healthy and
strong in the other parts of the country...' The Germans, on the
other hand, so Arndt found, had not been bastardised by other
peoples, were not of mixed origin, and had remained, to a larger
degree than many other nations, in a state of 'natural purity' : they
were blessed because they were 'an original people'.[9] Considering
that Arndt himself came from the Baltic island of Rügen, where
the descendants of Slavonic tribes formed the bulk of the local
population, a very strange assertion indeed! Such an admixture of
Germans and Slavs had taken place all over eastern Germany in
the course of the Middle Ages—in the very areas where the kingdom
of Prussia was to grow. Nothing is further removed from the
historical truth than the alleged racial 'purity' of the inhabitants of
Prussia, Brandenburg, Pomerania and Silesia—but perhaps this was
a particularly strong reason for asserting this purity in the face of
all the evidence.

Arndt also was the first to write about the 'Northern Man'—later
a famous slogan of National Socialist propaganda. He echoed
Kleist by declaiming :

Kill all the French!
Kill all knaves!

A very close associate of Arndt in the struggle against the French,
the famous founder of the German sports and gymnastics movement, Friedrich Ludwig Jahn, stated in a lapidary fashion : 'the
purer a nation, the better; the more mixed, the more like bandits'.
Even after the defeat of Napoleon he declared publicly : 'Whoever
has his children learn French ... errs, whoever persists in this, sins
against the Holy Ghost. But if he has French taught to his daughters,
this amounts to teaching them prostitution.'[10] Jahn also tried to
imitate ancient Germanic customs by sporting a colossal beard and
wearing allegedly Germanic clothes. His ideal was the Germanic

hero, Arminius or Hermann, who had defeated Varus' legions in
the year 9 in the Teutoburg forest—the hero too of a famous play
by Heinrich von Kleist. If German nationalism and racialism were
born together at the time of the War of Liberation against Napoleon,
yet another trait appeared at the same time—not so much on the
side of the Reformers and Patriots, but on the side of their conservative opponents in Prussia; for the Junker Ludwig von der
Marwitz accused the chief minister of Prussia of transforming the
kingdom into 'a Jewish state' because he favoured Jewish
emancipation.

Arndt and Jahn aimed at the creation of a Greater Germany
which was to include not only the Austrian lands, but also the
Netherlands, Denmark and Switzerland. Its new capital, so Jahn
demanded, should be built on the Elbe and be called 'Teutonia'.[11]
In Arndt and Jahn, not in the other Reformers of the early nineteenth century, all the elements are present which were to be
characteristic of National Socialist ideology more than a century
later : veneration of the *Volk*, of racial purity and all things
Germanic, extreme hatred of foreign nations, virulent nationalism,
anti-semitism, and Pan-Germanism, which aimed at uniting not
only those speaking German, but also several other 'Germanic'
nations. One may consider them cranks—and many did so then
and later—but a direct line runs from them to the *völkisch* en-
thusiasts of the later nineteenth century, and from them to Hitler;
and the youth of Germany was permeated by their ideas. It is no
accident that their selected writings were re-issued to the *Wehr-
macht* in the Second World War. This honour they shared with
another 'prophet', Paul Bötticher, who called himself Paul de
Lagarde.

Lagarde was born in 1827, the son of a teacher at a Berlin
Gymnasium, and as a teacher too the son had to earn his living
until he succeeded, at the age of forty-two, in obtaining a chair at
the University of Göttingen—by that time he was a well-known
orientalist. But side by side with his academic work he published a
series of *Deutsche Schriften* which even in his own day became the
bible of the nationalist student corporations and later exercised a
profound influence on generations of young Germans. The gospel
Lagarde preached was a fantastic combination of racialism, anti-
semitism, Pan-Germanism and expansionism. As early as 1853—
when he was only twenty-six years old and long before the unification of Germany—Lagarde demanded the incorporation in Germany
of Russian Poland, as well as Alsace and Lorraine. He considered
that Magyars, Czechs and 'similar nationalities living under the

sceptre of Austria' were 'a burden to history'; as their territories were thinly populated, German emigration was to be directed, systematically and according to a carefully worked-out plan, into Istria, Bohemia, Galicia, Posnania, Silesia and the Slovak and Magyar districts of Hungary. Simultaneously the Polish and the Austrian Jews were to be transferred to Palestine; even if they were willing to Germanise themselves they could not be suffered to remain : 'it is impossible to tolerate a nation within the nation'. Lagarde considered the Germans 'far too soft a material' to be able to withstand the Jews who were hardened by years of Talmudic training.[12]

In his later writings these schemes were worked out in greater detail. Austria's only task, Lagarde postulated in 1875, was to become a colonial state of Germany. All the nationalities of the Habsburg Empire—with the only exception of the Southern Slavs—were 'politically valueless : they are only material for new Germanic creations'.[13] A few years later he repeated that the only feat worthy of the German nation was the Germanisation of the countries bordering on Germany in the east; territory for German settlements was to be gained to the east of Poland and to extend to the Black Sea, and further German colonies were to be formed in Asia Minor : 'we suffocate from education and the liberalism of the bureacrats'.[14] Austria could only be preserved through 'ruthless Germanization' : 'we must not play up to the Czechs and similar people : they are our enemies and have to be treated accordingly'.[15] Territory was to be gained from Russia; if Russia proved unwilling to cede it, 'we will be forced to start expropriation proceedings, that means war'. But the Germans, Lagarde added, were a peaceful nation; 'yet they are convinced of their right to live, namely as Germans, and convinced that they have a mission for all the nations of the world : if they are prevented from living as Germans, prevented from carrying out their mission, then they are entitled to use force'.[16] As to the Jews, Lagarde stated in 1881 : 'The *alliance Israélite* is nothing but an international conspiracy for the promotion of Jewish world power, similar to the Freemasons, in the semitic field the same as the Jesuit Order in the catholic area. . . . Every foreign body within a living organism creates discomfort, illness, often festering sores and death.' The Jews as foreigners were 'nothing but the carriers of putrefaction'.[17] These and many other statements of the Göttingen professor could be taken straight from the pages of *Mein Kampf*. In the twentieth century the ideas of the German mission in the world, of the need to gain living space in the east became the common coinage of German nationalism.

In the later nineteenth century anti-semitism was wide-spread in Germany, partly in academic circles, partly among the lower middle classes, which were hit hard by the rapid economic changes of the time, the advance of capitalism and the severe economic crisis of 1873, due to over-production and over-speculation in the years after the Franco-Prussia war. Severely anti-semitic were the writings of the composer Richard Wagner on artistic and religious topics in which he accused the Jews of invading German cultural life and corrupting the German language : in the end no one would be able to understand his own word. 'The Jew', so Wagner alleged, had taken over German intellectual work and created 'a repulsive caricature of the German spirit' which he presented to the German people as a 'pretended reflection'.[18] To Wagner, the Jews were 'the plastic demon of the decay of humanity'; their 'triumphant security' they owed unfortunately to the favours of liberal princes.[19] In 1879 the famous historian Heinrich von Treitschke wrote in the very conservative journal *Preussische Jahrbücher* that people of the highest education, men who would indignantly repudiate any idea of religious intolerance or of national arrogance, were exclaiming 'as with one voice : the Jews are our misfortune !'[20] Treitschke's lectures at Berlin University, inspired by his fervent nationalism and Pan-Germanism, found an enthusiastic echo among a multitude of students. From the universities these slogans penetrated into the market place. An Anti-semitic Party was formed in 1886 which gained five seats in Hesse in the *Reichstag* elections of 1890; its leader was a librarian at Marburg University, Otto Böckel. In the *Reichstag* elections of 1893 the Anti-semites polled 263,000 votes and obtained sixteen seats; in 1898 their votes rose to 284,000 while the number of their deputies dropped to twelve.[21] In the elections of the early twentieth century, however, the influence of the Anti-semites declined.

Yet the decline was deceptive, for meanwhile there had come into being perhaps the most important annexationist and anti-semitic organisation of pre-war Germany, the *Alldeutscher Verband* (Pan-German League). It was founded in the 1890s and originally was chiefly preoccupied with imperialist propaganda, with Germany's need to acquire a much larger colonial empire. By 1901 it had 22,000 active members, in addition to numerous organisations which were corporate members of the League, among them a very large union of white-collar workers, the *Deutschnationale Hand-lungsgehilfenverband*. In the *Reichstag* dozens of deputies belonged to the Pan-German League, mainly from the Conservative and National Liberal parties. Officially the Pan-German League was not anti-semitic, but from 1908 onwards a new and energetic leader, Heinrich Class, a pupil of Treitschke, gave to its propaganda a much more aggressively expansionist and anti-semitic tune. In that year Class began a campaign against the Jews as the carriers of materialism : they were to be treated as foreigners, to be excluded from certain professions and to be forbidden to acquire property. Class maintained close contacts with powerful economic organisations and many influential politicians, usually preferring to work behind the scenes. The Pan-German League was one of the most influential pressure groups in Imperial Germany.[22]

Class was strongly influenced, according to his own testimony, by Lagarde and by another racialist writer, born in 1855 as the son of a British admiral, Houston Stewart Chamberlain. Chamberlain finally married a daughter of Richard Wagner, settled in Bayreuth and became the arch-priest of the Wagner cult; at the end of his life he became an equally ardent admirer of Adolf Hitler. At the very end of the nineteenth century Chamberlain published two massive volumes, *The Foundations of the Nineteenth Century*—a far more substantial exposition of racialist theory than Lagarde had ever produced. Chamberlain interpreted the whole course of European history from the moment of the appearance of the Germanic tribes 'as a struggle between Teuton and non-Teuton, between Germanic conviction and anti-Germanic sentiment'. 'Among all mankind,' he claimed, 'the Aryans stand out physically and spiritually; therefore they are by right ... the lords of the world.'[23] According to him, the Indo-Europeans had opened the doors to the Jews for idealistic reasons : 'like an enemy the Jew broke into the gap, stormed all positions and planted—I do not want to say on the ruins, but on the breach of our genuine singular character— the flag of his features which are eternally alien to us'. To achieve their domination the Jews, while remaining themselves racially pure, were infecting the Indo-Europeans with Jewish blood by putting out thousands of small sideshoots : 'if this continued for several centuries, there would be left in Europe only one racially pure people, that of the Jews; all the rest would be a herd of pseudo-Hebraic half-castes, that is beyond any doubt a people degenerate physically, mentally and morally'.[24] All these fantasies were clothed in a mass of scientific, learned jargon, not likely to appeal to the masses, but to the educated and semi-educated; as early as 1912 *The Foundations of the Nineteenth Century* went into its tenth edition.

For two decades Chamberlain lived in Vienna, and there he was in close touch with a far more successful propagandist of the Pan-

German and anti-semitic cause, Georg Ritter von Schönerer, the son of a successful railway builder who had been ennobled for his services to the Monarchy. In Vienna too, anti-semitism received a strong impetus from the economic crisis of 1873 which caused the failure of leading banks, and great misery among the small people of the capital. It was easy to find a scapegoat in the Jews who were very prominent in Vienna's cultural and economic life. Schönerer started his political career as an admirer of Bismarck's Germany, and the 'Watch on the Rhine' was the favourite song of the Austrian student corporations among whom he found his most enthusiastic pupils. From German nationalism Schönerer soon moved to anti-Habsburg propaganda and anti-semitism. As a member of the Austrian parliament, the *Reichsrat*, he proposed in 1887 the adoption of a new law which was to prohibit the immigration of foreign Jews and was to be a preliminary to another law directed against Austrian Jews. As Schönerer put it : 'the customs and ways of life of these alien parasites are hostile to the Aryan descent of the German nation and to its Christian culture.'[25] On another occasion Schönerer exclaimed : 'I hold reconciliation with the Slavs to be a useless effort. . . . One hears of equality between Germans and Slavs. It is as if one compared a lion to a louse because both are animals.'[26]

Schönerer engaged in strident propaganda against the Catholic Church and urged his followers to leave the Church and to become Protestants. But he also tried to revive Germanic customs and festivals. Celebrations were organized to commemorate the battle of Noreia, where the Cimbri had defeated the Roman legions in the year 113 B.C., as well as the battle of the Teutoburg forest of the year 9, which Kleist had celebrated eighty years before. A new Germanic calendar was to start with the year of the battle of Noreia, the year 1888 becoming the year 2001, and Germanic names were to replace the Latin months of the Christian calendar. One of Schönerer's favourite slogans was :

> 'Without Juda, without Rome,
> We will build Germania's dome!'

We are told that this was the slogan which the young Hitler put framed over his bed.[27] But anti-Catholicism was not popular in Austria. In Vienna itself Schönerer's popularity was soon overshadowed by that of another anti-semitic politician, Dr. Karl Lueger, who at the end of the nineteenth century became Vienna's most popular mayor and the founder of the Christian Social Party. His anti-semitism was less violent than that of Schönerer whose followers sported a badge depicting a Jew hanging from the gallows.

Lueger was a non-racialist, and always remained a loyal Catholic and pro-Habsburg.

In the early twentieth century the main area of Schönerer's influence shifted from Vienna and Lower Austria to the German-speaking districts of northern Bohemia which were more indus-trialised. There the position and the standard of living of the German population were threatened by the influx of Czech workers who were seeking employment in the growing industries of the area and were willing to accept lower wages than the German workers. In opposition to the Czechs a *Deutsche Arbeiterpartei* was founded there in 1904 by German workers from Bohemia and Moravia and some Austrian towns : the party programme combined nationalist with radical social demands and was strongly opposed to Marxist 'international' Social Democracy. A few months before the collapse of the Habsburg Monarchy the party adopted the name of German National Socialist Workers' Party; it was comparatively strong in northern Bohemia, but much weaker elsewhere.[28] It was the first National Socialist party, but—needless to say—this fact was never acknowledged by Hitler. As early as December 1919 the 'National Socialists of Greater Germany' held their first common deliberations in Vienna which were attended by representatives of the National Socialist parties of Austria, Czechoslovakia and Germany, parallel with a party conference of the Austrian National Socialists. A representative from Bohemia, Hans Knirsch, spoke on 'the future of Germandom in the unredeemed lands'. Among the groups represented at the conference, those from Bohemia clearly were by far the strongest.[29] There the seed sown by Schönerer had germinated—but it also germinated in the mind of another Austrian, Adolf Hitler, who in *Mein Kampf* expressly acknowledged his debt to Schönerer and to Lueger. It was the fierce national struggle between Germans and Slavs in the Habsburg Monarchy which gave rise to National Socialism in its original form and very deeply influenced the young Hitler.

Anti-semitism acquired a new lease of life when, with the end of the world war and the creation of an independent Poland, many thousands of Jews migrated from Galicia and Posnania to Vienna and to Berlin. They feared the uncertainty and the strong anti-semitism of Poland and preferred, usually speaking German, to settle in German surroundings; yet after the lost war the conditions prevailing in Vienna and Berlin were extremely unsettled, and violence was never far from the surface. One year after the outbreak of the revolution the Viennese police noted in a comprehensive report that anti-semitism was becoming more and more marked :

'The exasperation with the eastern Jews who either engage in food-smuggling and overcharging or do nothing whatever grows daily; so does the hatred of the Jewish Communists. . . .'[30] In December 1918 a socialist newspaper reported that Jews and Christians who looked like Jews had been publicly assaulted in Berlin. A leaflet distributed in Berlin at that time claimed that the seat of the executive committee of the workers' and soldiers' councils was the synagogue in the house of deputies, and its private address was to be found in the Jewish quarter behind the Alexanderplatz, 'for short: in Jewish Switzerland'.[31] In February 1919 the leaders of the Pan-German League founded a new mass organisation, the *Deutschvölkischer Schutz und Trutzbund*, to take up the fight against the Jews on a larger scale, to eliminate their influence and thus to 'save' German culture. Within eighteen months this new League had almost 100,000 members and had attracted into its ranks many of the older *völkisch* organizations.[32]

With the collapse of the Hohenzollern and Habsburg monarchies Jews for the first time acquired ministerial office in Germany and Austria. The new government of People's Representatives in Berlin had two Jewish members, Haase and Landsberg; also Jewish were the prime minister of Prussia, Hirsch, and the prime minister of Bavaria, Eisner, as well as several prominent members of the new Austrian cabinet, for example Bauer and Deutsch. Jewish too were very prominent leaders of the nascent Communist parties, such as Rosa Luxemburg and Paul Levi. Perhaps even more striking to the public mind was the fact that, when Soviet Republics were proclaimed in Budapest and Munich in the spring of 1919, the leaders in both cases were almost exclusively Jewish. The slogan of the 'Jewish World Conspiracy', the slogan first coined by Lagarde, acquired a new and sinister meaning. The fear of Bolshevism became rampant among the middle and lower middle classes—until Hitler was able to ride to power in exploiting this fear. The fact that the new Communist parties of Germany and Austria were extremely weak and very easily defeated, that the Munich Soviet Republic only lasted for a few weeks, counted for little. These were conspiracies hatched by alien elements in which no good German could possibly participate—although in reality many good Germans, and even many good Bavarians, did participate in such ventures. The right-wing propagandists too made no difference between Communists and Social Democrats; to them they were all birds of a feather—although in reality Jewish Social Democrats, Landsberg in Germany and Bauer and Deutsch in Austria, took a very determined stand against Communist adventures and attempts at a *coup d'état*, which were very quickly suppressed. In the process many of the most prominent Jewish leaders of the extreme left were murdered, such as Luxemburg and Jogiches in Berlin and Landauer and Leviné in Munich. Murdered too was the Bavarian prime minister, Eisner, when on his way to the Diet to which he intended to submit his resignation.

Political violence indeed became rampant in central Europe. The world war had elevated violence to a patriotic duty : the killing of as many enemies as possible became the aim of every good soldier. After the end of the war the psychology of trench warfare could be transmitted to political life, and the 'internal enemy' became the object of similar violent action. There were many thousands of professional officers and NCO's who were unable to return to civilian life, and for whom there was no employment in the much reduced armies of the vanquished states. They were only too eager to continue the good fight, be that against the Communists at home, or against the Poles and Russians on the eastern frontiers. It was from these elements that the Free Corps were recruited; they committed political violence on a scale hitherto unknown, by no means only against Communists. Some of the most notorious Free Corps wore the swastika, the symbol of 'Aryan' Germanism, painted on their steel helmets and were openly anti-semitic. As early as March 1920 the Ehrhardt Brigade felt strong enough to resist a government order for its dissolution and to march into Berlin with the aim of deposing the government which had to escape to the south. Officers of the Ehrhardt Brigade in 1921 murdered a former minister, Erzberger, and in 1922 the Foreign Minister Rathenau, a Jew. Officers of the same brigade were used in the early 1920s to organise and to train Hitler's Storm Troopers in Munich. It was from the Free Corps and their successors that the National Socialist Party gained many of its earliest and most enthusiastic recruits. Among a random sample of men who joined the party between the years 1925 and 1927 as many as 20 per cent had been active in the Free Corps.[33] In Austria the same part was played by the *Heimwehren* which sprang up like mushrooms in the countryside in the years after 1918.

The fight of the Free Corps against the Poles in Upper Silesia and against the French in the Ruhr became a heroic legend, potent far beyond the circles of the extreme right. A Free Corps officer, Albert Leo Schlageter, who was shot by the French for sabotage, became a national martyr whose name was venerated by hundreds of thousands and exploited for purposes of early National Socialist propaganda. Hundreds of thousands hoped that the French occupation of the Ruhr would lead to another 'war of national liberation', like the war hailed by Arndt and Jahn one hundred and ten years before. When Hitler in November 1923 started his *Putsch* in Munich, not so much against the French as against the allegedly Marxist government in Berlin, it was a Bavarian Free Corps, *Oberland*, that marched together with his Storm Troopers and lost several of its members in the shooting at the Felderrnhalle. Although Hitler never acknowledged this, he and the rapid growth of his party owed a tremendous debt to the Free Corps, and equally to the earlier *völkisch* organisations.

In general the rise of the National Socialist Party was greatly facilitated by the strident and aggressive nationalism which permeated the Germany of the Weimar Republic. This affected all classes of the population, and even the Communist Party, which in 1930 published a programme 'for the national and social liberation of the German nation', in which national came first, and social only second.[34] This nationalism affected in particular the university students and secondary school teachers and their pupils, and the ex-servicemen of the world war, many thousands of whom joined the para-military associations, such as the *Stahlhelm* and the *Jungdeutscher Orden*. At many a Prussian secondary school even the one republican holiday, 'Constitution Day', was converted into an event to commemorate the great victories over the French, Rossbach and Sedan. Nationalism was particularly rampant in the German Nationalist People's Party, whose leaders so greatly aided Hitler's rise and combined with him in violent political campaigns, in particular against the acceptance of the Young Plan, against the Prussian government, and in the presidential election of 1932. And the German Nationalist Party was a party of the respectable middle class, of academics and industrialists: its support made Hitler acceptable. German nationalism was, of course, fanned by the terms of the Treaty of Versailles and by the virulent propaganda directed against it. But German nationalism had been extreme ever since the years of French domination under Napoleon. German unification under Bismarck had not abated it, but in the Second German Empire its voice became louder and shriller. In a country defeated and humiliated, plagued by one crisis after the other, it surpassed itself. That Stresemann successfully dismantled the terms of Versailles, that Germany again became a great power and a member of the League of Nations, made no impact on the masses. 'The Chains of Slavery' must be broken, and the very real achievements of the Republican governments counted for nothing.

The lost war and the revolution of November 1918 destroyed not only the old order, but at the same time the stability and security which it had guaranteed. This was a system in which everybody knew his place, in which the lower classes were firmly kept down, a hierarchical order, as it had existed for centuries. Indeed, the old ruling class, the nobility, kept its leading position at court, in the army and in the bureaucracy which occupied the commanding heights of society up to 1918. Members of the middle classes gradually penetrated into the leading groups, but did not dispute power with them and were rather assimilated and absorbed by them. There was a successful intermarriage between the owners of the broad acres and the industrial barons. Now this whole order seemed threatened by upstarts from the working class, such as Ebert who had been a mere saddler's apprentice. In the eyes of respectable bourgeois Germans Ebert cut a ridiculous figure, and it was a liberal middle-class illustrated paper which published on its front page a photograph of Ebert in bathing outfit to reinforce that impression. Although the Social Democrats, in both Germany and Austria, lost their position in the government as early as 1920, and re-entered it only for very short periods during the following years, there was 'red' Prussia where the SPD remained the leading party in the government until Papen's *coup d'état* of July 1932; and in Austria there remained 'red' Vienna whose surrender had to be forced by artillery fire two years later. As long as they existed 'red' Prussia and 'red' Vienna were equated with the dangers of Bolshevism by an assiduous propaganda. They personified to the middle classes a working-class victory achieved in November 1918, achieved as Hitler put it, by the 'November criminals'.

In general, of course, democracy was far from popular. The governments of the post-war period were extremely weak and ever-changing. There was no important statesman to give a lead, no leader to inspire any enthusiasm. The slow inflation of the mark destroyed whatever confidence in the government there might have been, and deprived the middle and the lower middle classes, the pensioners and all those who had something to lose, of the remnants of their security. These *déclassés* blamed the Republic for their loss of social status. It was a miracle that the Weimar Republic survived the crisis of 1923 when slow inflation became galloping inflation, when the printing machines could not keep up with the demand for more and more notes of ever greater denominations, when 'emergency money' had to be issued by countless local authorities, only to lose its value over night, when houses and whole streets could be bought for a few dollars. It is not surprising that eighteen months after the end of the inflation the Germans elected as their new president not a politician, but the old Field-Marshal von Hindenburg, who had liberated East Prussia from the Russians in 1914, a father figure, who might, after all, one day hand over the throne to a new Emperor. Not that monarchism was all that strong in the Germany of the 1920s : much more potent was the longing for a strong and paternal leader, who would lead the Germans back to the days of strength and glory, of order and stability, who would do away with the squabbling of the political parties. The French, in a very similar situation after their defeat of 1870, turned to the father figure of Marshal MacMahon and elected him as their president. That both marshals had been defeated, did not seem to affect the issue.

Hindenburg no doubt represented to most Germans the forces of the old Prussia. The 'day of Potsdam', when the new German parliament was ceremoniously opened by Hitler in the Garrison Church of Potsdam, where the Prussian kings lay buried, seemed to symbolise the union of the old Prussia with the new order of National Socialism. Hindenburg, in the resplendent uniform of an Imperial field-marshal, and many other former generals in dress uniform lent their image to the great occasion. Yet in reality National Socialism owed comparatively little to the old Prussia, and comparatively little to so-called Prussian militarism—except perhaps the love of so many Germans for military uniforms which affected even the political left. The leaders of the German army, the *Reichswehr*, certainly did not welcome the National Socialists with open arms, although some generals were much more sympathetic towards them than others. What might be said, however, is this. Centuries of absolute government—not only in Prussia, but in most German principalities—and the continuation of semi-absolute methods of government after 1871 had not permitted the slow growth of a genuine parliamentary tradition. There were many parliaments in Germany from the early nineteenth century onwards, but the governments were not responsible to parliament but only to the local prince. The leaders of the political parties did not learn how to wield political responsibility and did not share in political power. When power fell into their lap through the collapse of the old régime, not through their own efforts, they were totally unprepared for it and totally at a loss how to handle the reins of government. A glance at the protocols of the meetings of the government of People's Representatives of 1918–19 shows how pathetic the new 'rulers' were, how totally helpless, how dependent on the senior civil servants and the generals of the old régime. This in a way was the worst legacy which the old Prussia and the Empire left to the

Social Democrats and to the leaders of other political parties who soon joined them in a coalition government.

It is not surprising then that in these conditions democracy was unable to strike root in Germany, that the anti-democratic forces soon recovered from the shock, that the three democratic parties were never able to gain a majority in a general election after the year 1919. The first German republic suffered from fatal weaknesses, defects created at its birth, which permitted its enemies to destroy it.

Among these enemies were not only the National Socialists, but also the old conservatives and nationalists, Pan-Germans and Völkische, who all combined forces against the hated republic. Many of them were to realise later what régime they had helped to create, but by then it was too late. The roots of National Socialism reach far back into the nineteenth century, but not into the dim Germanic or medieval past. I have tried to show here that they are manifold, that there is no single cause to which this historical phenomenon can be attributed, and that has been the purpose of my paper.

NOTES

1. Karl Dietrich Bracher, *Die deutsche Diktatur*, Cologne-Berlin, 1969. English transl. London, 1971.
2. Sir Robert Vansittart, *Black Record: Germans Past and Present*, London, 1941, pp. 1–2.
3. Ibid., pp. 21–3.
4. Rohan D'O Butler, *The Roots of National Socialism, 1783–1933*, London, 1941, p. 283.
5. Ibid., p. 134.
6. A. J. P. Taylor, *The Course of German History*, London, 1945, pp. 213–14.
7. Wolfgang Foerster (ed.), *Ein General kämpft gegen den Krieg—Aus nachgelassenen Schriften des Generalstabchefs Ludwig Beck*, Munich, 1949, p. 12: letter of 28 November 1918.
8. *Heinrich von Kleist's gesammelte Schriften*, Berlin, 1891, ii, p. 613: 'Germania an ihre Kinder'.
9. Ernst Moritz Arndt,, *Volk und Staat*, Selected writings ed. by Paul Requadt, Stuttgart, s.a., pp. 81, 92: written in 1815–16.
10. The quotations according to Günther Scholz, 'Patriotische Klimmzüge auf der Hasenheide: Friedrich Ludwig Jahn', in Karl Schwedhelm (ed.), *Propheten des Nationalismus*, Munich, 1969, pp. 23, 31.
11. Bracher, op. cit., p. 26; for Arndt see: Gabriele Venzky, *Die Russisch-Deutsche Legion in den Jahren 1811–1815*, Wiesbaden, 1966, p. 69.
12. Paul de Lagarde, 'Über die gegenwärtigen Aufgaben der deutschen Politik' (1853), *Deutsche Schriften*, Göttingen, 1886, pp. 27, 31, 34.

13. 'Über die gegenwärtige Lage des deutschen Reichs' (1875), ibid., pp.111–12.

14. 'Die Finanzpolitik Deutschlands' (1881), ibid., p. 308.

15. 'Programm für die konservative Partei Preussens' (1884), ibid., p. 359.

16. 'Die nächsten Pflichten deutscher Politik', ibid., pp. 390-1.

17. 'Die Stellung der Religionsgesellschaften im Staate' (1881), ibid. pp. 255–6.

18. Richard Wagner, 'Was ist deutsch?' (1865), *Ausgewählte Schriften über Staat und Kunst und Religion (1864–1881)*, Leipzig, s.a., p. 206.

19. 'Erkenne dich selbst' (1881), ibid., p. 358.

20. Heinrich von Treitschke, 'Unsere Aussichten', *Preussische Jahrbücher*, November 1879, quoted by Gerd-Klaus Kaltenbrunner in Karl Schwedhelm (ed.), *Propheten des Nationalismus*, p. 50.

21. Peter Pulzer, *The Rise of Political Anti-Semitism in Germany and Austria*, New York and London, 1964, pp. 109, 112, 121, 190.

22. For details see Pulzer, op. cit., pp. 227–9, 305–6; George L. Mosse, *The Crisis of German Ideology*, New York, 1964, pp. 219–24; Alfred Kruck, *Der Alldeutsche Verband, 1890–1939*, Wiesbaden, 1954.

23. Houston Stewart Chamberlain, *Die Grundlagen des 19. Jahrhunderts*, 2nd ed., Munich, 1900, pp. 503, 520.

24. *Ibid.*, p. 324. An English translation, *The Foundations of the Nineteenth Century*, was published in 1911.

25. There is no good published work on Schönerer and the Austrian Pan-Germans. But there is a very interesting London Ph.D. thesis of June 1963 : J. C. P. Warren, The Political Career and Influence of Georg Ritter von Schönerer, from which the above quotation is taken.

26. Quoted by Arthur J. May, *The Hapsburg Monarchy 1867–1914*, Cambridge, Mass., 1960, p. 211.

27. Joseph Greiner, *Das Ende des Hitler-Mythos*, Zürich-Leipzig-Vienna, 1947, p. 81.

28. For all details see Andrew G. Whiteside, *Austrian National Socialism before 1918*, The Hague, 1962; and his 'Austria' in Hans Rogger and Eugen Weber (eds.), *The European Right—A Historical Profile*, Berkeley and Los Angeles, 1965, pp. 308 ff.

29. Details in *Deutsche Arbeiter-Presse—Nationalsozialistisches Wochenblatt*, Folge 49, Vienna, 6 December 1919. A copy in Landesregierungsarchiv Tirol, Innsbruck, Präsidialakten 1920, XII.77. The issue of 24 December 1919 contains the speeches of two other representatives from Czechoslovakia, Dr. Schilling and Rudolf Jung, as well as the speech of the Austrian 'leader', Dr. Walter Riehl, a Viennese lawyer. For Riehl see the unpublished Vienna Ph.D. thesis of Rudolf Brandstötter, Dr. Walter Riehl und die Geschichte des nationalsozialistischen Bewegung in Osterreich, Vienna, 1969.

30. Police report, 17 November 1919, signed Schober: Verwaltungsarchiv Vienna, Staatsamt des Innern, 22/gen., box 4860.

31. Hermann Müller, *Die November-Revolution*, Berlin, 1931, p. 109; Emil Eichhorn, *Über die Januar-Ereignisse—Meine Tätigkeit im Berliner Polizeipräsidium*, Berlin, 1919, p. 14.

32. For all details see Uwe Lohalm, *Völkischer Radikalismus—Die*

Geschichte des Deutschvölkischen Schutz—und Trutzbundes, Hamburg, 1970, pp. 15, 20–2, 81, 84, 89, 176–7.

33. Theodore Abel, *Why Hitler came into Power—An Answer based on the Original Life Stories of Six Hundred of his Followers,* New York, 1938, p. 81. A very large number of the top-ranking party and SA leaders had served in the Free Corps.

34. *Programmerklärung zur nationalen und sozialen Befreiung des deutschen Volkes,* issued by the Zentralkomitee der Kommunistischen Partei Deutschlands, 24 August 1930.

National Socialism, its Social Basis and Psychological Impact

by MARTIN BROSZAT

The rise of National Socialism between the two world wars has its causes on the one hand in general circumstances and developments of the period, the 'age of Fascism' as Ernst Nolte has called it; it was also due, on the other hand, to conditions specific to German history and society. The existence of non-German fascist movements in this period cannot and must not absolve us from the critical study of the peculiarly German preconditions of Nazism, particularly since none of the simultaneous non-German fascist movements or régimes in Europe developed anything like the totalitarian force, aggression and cohesion of Nazism. The transient importance acquired by fascist movements outside Germany, for instance by the Quisling party in Norway, the Mussert or Rexist movements in the Netherlands and Belgium after the German occupation, but also some of the potential which the Iron Guard in Rumania or the Hungarian Arrow Cross had already gained prior to the Second World War must be ascribed to direct or indirect German influence. Even some aspects of Mussolini's later domestic and foreign policy and especially its radicalisation was due to his dependence on Hitler.

Nevertheless fascist movements outside Germany had their native origins and were not only imported from Germany. The comparative analysis of European fascism between the wars may help us to comprehend their common elements during this period, and may enable us to isolate from their different national contents and aims the typical features of these movements as well as the typical social and psychological mechanisms behind their appeal.

Some of these common features are obvious: the para-military organisation, the exceptionally important rôle of charismatic leaders for the integration and mobilisation of the followers of fascism, the pseudo-religious, missionary type of propaganda and rhetoric, the high degree of activism exhibited by these movements and their functionaries, paralleled only by revolutionary communism, the strength of young people within fascist movements, and so on.

Fascist ideologies, notwithstanding their national orientation, also show striking similarity : the identical reversion to a past of national heroism and greatness, the striving for national purity and revitalisation, the proclamation of social renewal along the lines of more or less vague corporative ideas, the preaching of a new simplicity in cultural and social life, the fanatical condemnation of international Socialism and Marxism, deep disdain for political liberalism and democratic systems of government in the name of a new élite-cult and a strong authoritarian state, based on the principle of leadership and voluntary obedience.

All these elements in fascist ideologies illustrate that there is a common ground of motivation behind them. These ideologies, including Nazism, cannot therefore be adequately understood, if interpreted only in the framework of their respective national history of political ideas. And they cannot be adequately understood as primary forces shaping political attitudes by themselves, but have to be looked at in the context of social and psychological transformations and conflicts and the psychological requirements and depressions connected with them. To look at fascist ideologies from the viewpoint of their underlying social and psychological demands does not mean that the strength or predominance of special ideological patterns within the heritage of political thought in a particular nation is irrelevant. But the tracing back of ideologies into history needs to be supplemented by the explanation of social and psychological predispositions regulating the adoption and selection of ideas out of this heritage in a specific period.

Although the elements of fascist ideology, in Germany as in other countries, have their roots in nineteenth-century nationalism, genuine fascism arose only in the twentieth century, after the First World War and the Bolshevik revolution. These two overwhelming events put an end to nineteenth-century rationalism and liberalism and destroyed the optimistic bourgeois belief in security and continuous progess. They caused a revolution of consciousness especially among the middle classes of the nations which took part in the war, undermined social and economic stability and brought about a broad stream of new social unrest, out of deep frustrations, disappointments, fears and privations. Up to this time it was inconceivable that decent middle class people should take to the streets, enroll in uniformed squads of blackshirts or brownshirts, and follow the example of proletarian movements, should attack red-dominated districts or housing estates and organise illegal expeditions to terrorise Communists or Jews. It shows to what extent war and the real or imaginary danger of proletarian revolution had changed habits of mind and norms of social and political behaviour within the middle classes in Germany and other countries.

War and warfare, the mass killing on the battlefields all over central Europe, honoured as heroism and bravery and sanctioned by the Churches, had severely damaged the image of man, humanity and humane culture and had discredited the nineteenth-century values and endeavours of humanist education and civilisation. The greater or lesser historical strength of this educational tradition in the various countries was of course essential for the success or failure of its restoration after the war. The particular weakness of humanist morality in the tradition of German political and national thinking, compared with the Western democracies, now proved a decisive disadvantage. There were, however, also other factors responsible for the greater or lesser capacity for normalisation after the war. It made an important difference to be on the side of the victors or the losers of the war. During four years of war soldiers and civilians made a great investment of national devotion and idealism, of readiness to endure massive privations and severe sacrifices, and psychologically this investment demanded reward and recompense. Wherever this reward failed, grave disappointment and frustration arose. Disappointment turned into stubborn national defiance and into a feeling and suspicion of betrayal, when national humiliation and prolonged material suffering proved to be the result of the war. The more the initial expectations, passions and war aims differed from the real end of the war, the greater was the psychological disposition to ignore political reality and to take refuge in psychological evasions, leading to a defiant attitude of aggressive national resistance which bred new and illusory hopes. The German stab-in-the-back legend and its implications, as well as comparable attitudes in Hungary or Italy were typical examples of this psychology of national frustration.

The social renormalisation of soldiers in civilian life was greatly affected by the conditions under which the demobilisation of armies took place. National and economic conditions could be favourable for the return to civilian life or they could produce persistent social unrest among ex-soldiers, who might feel encouraged or obliged to seek opportunities for new warfare in volunteer corps like that of the German volunteer corps in the Baltic states or Upper Silesia, the Italian squads in Fiume under d'Annunzio, or Horthy's volunteer corps in Hungary. Ex-soldiers went on fighting at their own risk in national, territorial or counter-revolutionary actions and it was through these volunteer corps and private armies that the style and mode of open warfare was transferred to civilian politics. There developed the type of semi-illegal, paramilitary organisation, new social formations of fighting brotherhoods under charismatic leaders, which later on became the models for Mussolini's *fasci di combattimento* or Hitler's storm-troopers. The moral and psychological attitudes bred in them contempt for legal order and for the interests and values of liberal-bourgeois society, the stimulating experience of comradeship and conspiratorial solidarity while executing secret or even criminal actions in the name of great national goals, these laid the groundwork for those mental and moral perversions, which could then be magnified and systematised by fascist ideology, agitation and action.

Another consequence of the war which later favoured fascism was the socialisation of millions of soldiers from different classes, denominations and provinces within an army under the national flag. Their common national war effort, the requirements of the first total war with its mass-mobilisation for the front as well as at home for war production, fused the different groups of the nation into an emotional 'Volksgemeinschaft', seemed to suspend the sharp social dividing lines of peacetime and to produce a new national equality, a kind of national socialism. Even functionaries of socialist parties or trade unions were impressed by this phenomenon and mistook the war for a promoter of socialism. This was especially the case because in Germany and elsewhere the hitherto despised officials of the parties of socialist 'revolution' became partners of the military bureaucracy in the organisation of manpower and production, and they could regard some of the consequence of this partnership as a genuine social achievement. Moreover, the totalitarian mobilisation of manpower during the war, supported by the national passions of the people, showed the degree of efficiency an industrial bourgeois-society was able to attain, if organised and spiritually inspired in this way. It was from this experience that Mussolini and Hitler developed their concepts of national socialism, totalitarian organisation and ideological manipulation.

The general process of mobilisation and emotional nationalisation brought about by the First World War was of particular significance for those strata of the population which until then had either not at all or only rather marginally participated in the national life of their respective countries. It was true above all for millions of European peasants and agricultural labourers who before had lived

a stagnant social life in remote provinces. Military service in war
proved a decisive factor for their national integration and political
socialisation. For many of them the war, leading them into distant
regions or foreign countries and throwing them for four years into
a community with people from different social classes in their own
nation, was and remained the only extraordinary event in their
lives, the only opportunity to see the world and the only great
social mobilisation they experienced. They returned from the war
with a changed national and social consciousness, with a greater
awareness of their interests, they questioned their former social and
political quietism, and were more receptive towards social promises
and national propaganda. It was disastrous that much of the
agrarian population experienced their political and national
socialisation under the spell of war chauvinism.

Given the great success which fascism gained in the countryside
and especially with the most backward strata of the rural population in Germany, Italy, Hungary or Rumania, the importance
of this process can hardly be overestimated. In all these countries
fascist movements discovered and used the new national and
political potential of the small peasants or labourers who previously
had either not taken part in political elections or had mostly voted,
according to paternalist tradition, for the conservative platforms of
the socially and politically dominant élites of the landed aristocracy.

As has been shown in the work of Eugen Weber the Rumanian
fascist movement won many adherents in remote and backward
agrarian provinces of the country, which had been largely neglected
by all other national parties. Similar evidence can be drawn from
the success of the Italian fascists in the backward agricultural
regions of Southern Italy or of Nazism in East Prussia or Pomerania.
In many parts of these regions small peasants clearly started to
vote for the fascists mainly because they were the first national
party which came to their villages and identified themselves with
the peasant's interests and feelings. The sudden response of whole
peasant districts, with previously very low voting participation, to
the fascist appeal cannot be explained only by the deterioration of
the peasants' economic situation. It bears the typical signs of a
popular socio-psychological revivalist movement, comparable to the
appeal of the Russian Narodniki in the nineteenth century, within
a population which felt deeply neglected, whose former unreflecting
social passivity had been broken down by an awakening of national
and social consciousness, but which had not found any firm
orientation within the political system of its country. Their emergence did not, however, lead to genuine emancipation, but only to

the creation of a potential for the pseudo-emancipation of fascism. A comparable process of politicisation and nationalisation brought about by war and revolution and later benefiting the fascist appeal took place within the younger generation of the middle class. Young people of the age of sixteen to twenty-five are normally less interested in politics and less ready to engage actively in the tedious daily routine of party politics than people of the age of thirty or forty. Especially the German middle class youth movement before the First World War was entirely a-political or even anti-political. Their protest against the older generation and the bourgeois world had expressed itself in deliberate social and political escapism, in the form of a romantic cult of nature, personal friendship and search for individual originality and creativity. The First World War and its national passions changed this attitude completely. Many adherents of the former Wandervogel Youth Movement now became either revolutionary socialists or ardent nationalists. The political movements of the extremist left or right, emerging from the experience of war and revolution, with their strong appeal to revolutionary activism and rigorism, so befitting to the mentality of youth, became the main instruments for the political socialization of the young generation. The more than proportional presence of young people among the fascist or communist parties, compared with the liberal, conservative or social democratic parties, clearly confirms this. Especially fascism proved a highly successful medium for the politicisation of the younger age-groups which normally would not have been ready for political commitment. The structure of fascism displays many typical features of youth mentality.

The spirit of adventure and idealism, romanticism, spontaneity, group activities, rigorous disdain for the values of the older generation, for established society and morality, the quest for emotional rhetoric and demonstration—all these and other psychological dispositions encouraged by the Nazis and other fascist movements, attracted great parts of middle class youth. As early as 1929, at a time when the Hitler movement in Germany in Laender or municipal elections did not on the average gain more than between 5 and 8 per cent of the total vote, it managed to gain 20, 30, 40 or more per cent in the elections for student representation at the German universities.

In view of the fact that the extraordinary wave of irrational aggressiveness and ardent longing for leadership that favoured fascism in Germany in the 1930s was evident especially among the age group that had experienced the First World War as children, psychoanalysts have tried to find out which psychological deprivations had affected the early childhood of these young people in wartime and might help to explain their later fascist disposition. The prolonged absence of fathers, the overburdening of mothers who had to take over full responsibility for their families, corresponding neglect of education and family-life, frequent loneliness and premature self-reliance, early confrontation with national hatreds and wartime atrocities and above all the experience of hunger and material deprivation—according to such inquiries these are all likely to have affected the psychological state of these young men and women, especially in countries like Germany, where there was extreme malnutrition in the second half of the War. Recent psychohistorical research seems to indicate that severe deprivations in childhood induced infantile regression, particularly when fifteen or twelve years later the same people, now young adults, had to experience the new social and economic dislocations of the Great Depression. It was again in Germany that the most severe consequences resulted from the economic crisis, especially for the age group whose childhood had coincided with the war, and who, now aged fifteen to twenty-five, suffered most from unemployment and social despair.

Although the historian may doubt the weight of these arguments, they certainly deserve consideration and are confirmed by other evidence. One of the few documentary sources capable of quantitative analysis of psychological motivation towards Nazism is a collection of about six hundred autobiographies of individual Nazis which the American Sociologist Theodore Abel collected after 1933. The frequent mention of intense hunger and childhood privation is particularly striking in these adult memories of subsequent Nazi adherents. In any case there can be little doubt about the youthful character of the Nazi movement, 'a political youth rebellion of violent virulence which seems to have no equal prior to our own age'. It must be admitted that it is a weakness of this kind of historical research that it cannot rank in their due order of importance the various psychological and social factors creating a predisposition towards fascism.

These few, very fragmentary observations may be sufficient, however, to give some evidence of a general social and psychological pre-disposition towards fascism resulting from the upheavals of war and revolution, which left traces in nearly all European nations though more strongly in some than in others. Let us now change our perspective and consider more specifically the circumstances of Nazism in German society. In doing so we are deliberately neglecting the ideological antecedents of Nazism and concentrating on the psychological and social conditions which formed the basis for the creation of ideology and for political behaviour.

Compared with many small and middle-sized European countries, in which parliamentary democracy collapsed between the two wars and gave way to authoritarian or fascist régimes, as in the Baltic states, Poland, Rumania, Yugoslavia, Greece, Spain and Portugal, Germany seemed to have a reasonably sound socio-economic base for a stable democracy. In so far as the existence of a bourgeois-industrial society and broad well-educated middle class is the precondition for a democratic constitution, Germany had no need to fear comparison with England or France. There was a solid tradition of legality in the use of administrative power. The rule of law in public life had been established and improved in Prussia and other German states since the period of enlightened absolutism at the end of the eighteenth century. Constitutional restriction and control of monarchical government by an elected parliament, though late and hesitantly introduced and stubbornly resisted in Prussia by the monarchical and feudal powers until the second half of the nineteenth century, seemed no longer a major problem after the unification of the German Reich in 1871 and the introduction of the then relatively progressive universal equal and secret suffrage for elections to the Reichstag. But above all, Germany had, by the revolutionary speed of industrial development in the second half of the nineteenth century, become one of the most efficient industrial societies, with a broad middle class and with national codes of civil and penal law conceived in the spirit of liberalism. Freedom of the press, of association and assembly, and control of the executive by the judiciary were about as well guaranteed in Bismarck's Germany as in the Western democracies.

It is true that the political and constitutional structure of the Reich was becoming increasingly obsolete before 1914: the continued monarchical prerogatives in military and foreign policy, in the nomination of the cabinet and the recruitment of the military and civil service, the restrictions on the Reichstag in controlling the budget and domestic legislation, the stagnant class-franchise in several German states, especially in Prussia, which prolonged the social and political predominance of the feudal Prussian aristocracy, all this contrasted more and more sharply with the rapid emergence of an industrial society. The enlargement of parliamentary power seemed urgent long before 1914. The growing sense of the inadequacy of this semi-absolute monarchical system, a feeling that was frequently expressed in Germany before 1914, contributed greatly to the sudden break-down of the system at the end of the war and to the absence of any resistance.

The German Revolution of November 1918 and the new constitution of Weimar, so it seemed to their authors and so it was often expressed in the early months of 1919 by leading social democratic or liberal speakers in the Constituent National Assembly, had achieved no more than that reform of the political system which had been long overdue and had been prevented only by the stubborn resistance of the military monarchy and its conservative allies in the army, government and bureaucracy. The German middle class, so it appeared in January 1919 from the result of elections to the Constituent National Assembly, was going to adjust in its majority to the belated attempt to establish a liberal parliamentary democracy in Germany, which had failed in 1848. The *Deutsche Demokratische Partei*, newly founded under the impact of the Revolution, and dedicated to the unity of the former right-wing and left-wing liberals on a unanimous democratic platform, gained almost 20 per cent of the total vote. Forming together with the right-wing Social Democrats and the Catholic Centre of the Weimar Coalition, it seemed to create a solid foundation for a democratic, bourgeois republic. Even parts of the lower middle class voted in this election for the Social Democrats. This, too, seemed to indicate that the way was now open for an improvement of the political relations between industrial workers and the middle class, which had been so severely poisoned before 1914 under the pressure of the monarchical system. Now that the great majority of the German working class had proved their national loyalty, and the Socialdemocratic majority leaders in the revolutionary period had resolutely resisted the Spartacists and the Communists and their aim of Bolshevik revolution, it seemed no longer possible to ostracise the Social Democrats as unpatriotic. This used to be the habit under the monarchical system, in the days when the upper class alliance of feudal and industrial élites identified class interest with patriotism.

This time *seemed* to be over, but it seemed so only for a very short period. By 1920 the impact of the humiliating Treaty of Versailles, the recovery of counter-revolutionary forces of restoration and the demands of the democratic government for a common front against revolutionary Marxism on the left had produced a situation in which the German Democratic Party lost more than half their voters of 1919. The majority of the middle class voters left the liberal-democratic platform and turned to the right, partly to the *Deutsche Volkspartei* dominated by the representatives of commerce, industry and capital, partly to the conservative *Deutschnationale Volkspartei*, dominated by the big landed proprietors, by sections of heavy industry as well as by the traditional élites of the civil servants and protestant clergy. This was however only the first step in the political migration of the German Protestant middle class during the Weimar Republic. In 1924, after the experience of the inflation, the French occupation of the Ruhr and the leftist or rightist putsches in Saxony, Thuringia and Bavaria, there was a further move to the right. This benefited mainly the conservative *Deutschnationale*, but also those newly emerged groupings of extremists organised by Hitler or other nationalist fanatics. They offered release from social hardships and the restoration of national and political health through an aggressive counter-revolutionary campaign against socialism and democracy, whom they denounced as agents of an international Jewish conspiracy.

Another four years later, by 1928, after the consolidation of the currency, the revival of economic prosperity and the recovery or new establishment of powerful industrial combines, there had been a further upsurge of the forces of restoration within the political system, marked by the election of Hindenburg as president of the Reich in 1925 and by the formation of coalition governments purely of the right-centre and without social-democratic participation. A great section of the middle class vote, however, now left the right-wing parties; their domination by traditional values and élites had evidently proved insufficiently attractive to small farmers, to the lower strata of the civil service or to the masses of the old and new commercial and industrial urban middle class and white collar workers. But those who had left the parties of Hugenberg and Stresemann did not, in 1928, return to the Social Democrats or liberal Democrats but went to newly formed small peasant parties or special interest parties of the urban middle classes, which now gained 14 per cent of the total vote. This splintering of the bourgeois political centre, evident in these elections even before the Great Depression, was clearly due to the fact that numerous sections of the socially and culturally insecure middle class saw itself threatened simultaneously by socialism and capitalism. They were looking for the utopia of a third way, which was to bring back, by means of struggle and opposition, the good old days, and for this purpose the established liberal and conservative parties of the 'system' seemed useless. Hence this remarkable, impatient search of the middle class for constantly new parties offering apparently new recipes for success. From this it can be seen why the Nazis found it so easy, once the economic depression was under way, to become the collecting basin for the protestant middle class.

The subsequent course of development of the German party structure is well known : as a result of the world-wide economic crisis and the simultaneous erosion of the parliamentary system, which was now no longer able to integrate the diverging sectional interests and the pluralism of the political parties, the decline of the conservative and liberal parties accelerated and at the same time the Nazi party made continuous progress. In the Reichstag elections of September 1930 the German protestant middle class, about 45 per cent of all voters, was politically divided into three almost equally strong groups. Only one third of it still voted for the conservative or liberal parties (DDP, DVP, DNVP). The second third remained attached to the newly formed interest parties, and another third voted Nazi (more than 18 per cent of the total vote). The following two years were marked by a further deepening of the depression, by an enormous radicalisation of the political atmosphere and by unsuccessful attempts to fight the crisis by way of authoritarian cabinets based on the prerogatives of the Reichpresident, but lacking any political and social support among the masses. The Hitler movement now managed to outbid the temporary appeal of the small interest parties, which in 1932 decreased to 3 per cent of the total vote, while the right- and left-wing liberals were reduced to the derisory remnant of one per cent each. Only the reactionary Hugenberg Party kept its reduced following of 6 per cent after 1930. The entire remaining voting potential of the protestant German middle class, altogether 37 per cent, had gone over to Hitler.

This review of the changes in the German party structure during the Weimar period has been deliberately confined to the non-catholic and non-socialist parties. It was in this social sector that the decisive change in relation to Nazism took place before 1933. Neither the socialist left-wing parties nor the Catholic Centre party lost any considerable portion of their following until the end of 1932, but proved remarkably immune to Nazism. It may rightly be doubted how firm this immunity remained after 1933. In the Centre party, for example, resistance certainly did not amount to clear-cut opposition, but for great sections of it only to a temporary refuge behind social and political conservatism in traditionally strong Catholic regions. The party embraced many elements of a social and political ideology of restoration and of anti-liberal, anti-socialist and even anti-semitic doctrines, which after 1933 could be used as a bridge to Nazism and which helped to induce

German Catholic bishops to welcome Hitler and make their peace with him.

Nevertheless, from the perspective of Hitler's success within German political society before 1933, the attitude of the German Protestant middle class, the main bearer of German nationalism since the nineteenth century, was quantitatively the focal point for the breakthrough of Nazism. All sociological studies agree on this point : German Nazism was an 'extremism of the middle' (Lipset), it was based on the very social strata normally regarded as the natural social base of liberalism and democracy in industrial societies.

The social and psychological disintegration of the middle classes has been, as I tried to show, a general precondition of fascism. The penetrating force of the crisis of the middle class in Germany, however, demands further explanation. Let me try to explore, without pretending to be exhaustive, at least some important aspects.

The economic reasons for the severe psychological disturbance and panic of the German middle class in the Weimar period are closely connected with socio-cultural changes and reactions. A first severe blow to great sections of the German middle classes resulted from the material consequences of the war and the complete breakdown of the German currency in 1923. The planned economy during the war had already hit the independent commercial middle classes hard; in addition to the loss of their professional and material independence they were faced by the simultaneous rise in the status of the industrial workers. The workers had during the war and the revolution transformed the trade unions into successful champions of their interests, to whom neither the state nor the employers could now deny recognition as bargaining partners. Many documents from the activities of middle class economic interest groups after 1918 lead one to the conclusion that achievement of bargaining status by the unions in November 1918 and the agreements reached on that basis between unions and employers, often through official arbitration, caused far greater disturbance to the small independent trader than they did to heavy industry.

In hundreds of thousands of small workshops and enterprises management was still on a paternalist pattern. The rights conceded to the trade unions by the Weimar Republic were regarded by many small middle class businessmen as a flagrant interference in the sphere of personal property and control. The older commercial middle class had been threatened by industrial competition for decades; they made up for the reduction in their economic strength by developing a socially conservative middle class ideology. This ideology had received official sanction and favour from the 1880s onwards through the policy of state protection and had been used to broaden the social basis of the conservative and national-liberal parties. The change of system in November 1918, which made the social-democratic workers the social mass basis of the new state, was therefore felt very acutely. The furious reaction against socialism was not solely caused by economic factors, such as higher wage demands by employees or higher taxes for social welfare, it was also a protest against the raised social status of the workers. This threatened to undermine the class difference between petit bourgeois master craftsmen or small traders and the dependent proletariat, a difference which was in any case ideological rather than economic.

In addition there were the consequences of inflation which forced many members of the middle class to sell inherited capital or acquired house property to raise cash for consumption. Although the material and social results of the inflation of 1923 have so far not been fully investigated, it is safe to assume that the property position of many middle class families was hit hard. War and inflation destroyed much of the property on which they had relied for their security before 1914, and reduced the living standards of many of the well-to-do to a petit-bourgeois or even proletarian level. A strong feeling of loss and cultural pessimism was produced among this class as well as a deep longing for restoration, an atmosphere evoked in much contemporary literature about the decay of middle class culture and values, for example in Thomas Mann's novel *Unordnung und frühes Leid*, published in 1925. A great tide of social envy and hate arose, directed against those who had made large profits from the inflation as they had previously done from the war. Here was a further motivation for the irrational search for conspirators and alleged 'Jewish usury' that had already been invoked by the Fatherland-party at the end of the war and was taken over into the 25-point programme of the early Nazi party.

The German middle class underwent further structural change through the numerical growth of white collar workers. This was the result of rapid progress in the formation of large scale industrial and commercial enterprises, banking and insurance companies and the growth of the public service in the 1920s. The emerging broad strata of white collar workers, the 'neue Mittelstand der Angestellten' as they were called in contemporary analysis, did not differ very much in material standards from industrial blue collar workers both in their dependence on employment and in the level of their wages. Nevertheless they clung jealously to what distinguished them socially from the workers, their non-manual work, demanding special abilities and training, their educational background and their cultural and social aspirations. They ardently wanted to belong to the middle class, from which they either came by family tradition or to which they eagerly aspired to climb from their former proletarian background. The socio-psychological fear of proletarianisation among this group of German white collar workers, who were severely hit by unemployment, wage cuts and social insecurity as a result of the Great Depression after 1929, was particularly strong. And they obviously contributed a great many adherents to the Nazi movement.

In this case specifically German socio-cultural attitudes, values and aspirations, more than economic and material hardships, motivated the flight to the radical right and this explains why most of the depressed members of this group, in spite of their economic degradation, did not go to left wing revolutionary parties. Recent comparative sociological studies have shown how differently German and American white collar workers reacted politically to the depression. In the United States, with its high degree of social mobility and lack of rigid class structures and distinctive cultural class norms, white collar workers tended under the impact of the depression to vote more or less unanimously for the democratic left, while in Germany the reaction was quite the opposite.

Another important group among the German urban middle classes, representing about 15 per cent of the total population at the beginning of the 1930's, consisted of artisans and small traders. This group experienced a slump even before the Great Depression : growing competition from the bigger industrial and trading concerns led to a reduction in the number of small firms and traders even in the relatively normal years between 1924 and 1929. The rapid advance of capitalist concentration during the middle years of the Weimar period, on the one hand, and the taxation, tariff and wage policies of the democratic welfare-state as well as the strengthened position of the trade unions, on the other hand, were regarded as the two great threats to this old urban middle class. Theodor Geiger wrote in 1932 of this 'double threat' to the old middle class in his book, *The Social Stratification of the German People*. It is remarkable, however, that this old middle class, contrary to the requirements of its 'objective' economic plight, which should have made it into an ally of the proletariat, reacted so much more sharply and emotionally against the supposed threat of 'socialism' than it did to the capitalist threat.

In this stratum, as well as among millions of small farmers, the superior competition from the great capitalist and industrial combines increasingly led to the demand for state interference against the whole democratic political system. The strong emotional rejection of public social welfare policies, simplistically identified with socialism, raised a growing irrational protest especially against the influence of the Social Democrats and trade-unions, which had improved the social security, the rights and incomes of the workers. Paternalistic social attitudes and values deeply ingrained in the mentality of artisans and farmers, and nourished by the conservative monarchical system before 1914, were fundamentally affronted by the mass-democracy of Weimar and this resulted in the irrational desire for the restoration of a sound national morality and strong public authority. Just because these depressed strata of the old non-industrial middle class could not compete against industrial efficiency they compensated for their loss of significance by ideological evasions, stressing the value of farmers and artisans and their work for the moral and social health of the nation. National Socialism skilfully took up this theme and cured the depression of these groups by loud propaganda, promising the revaluation of creative German work and the restoration of its historical image by a new *ständische Gesellschaft*.

A deep economic slump like the Great Depression usually leads to political radicalisation. But the degree and the direction of radicalisation cannot be deduced from economic factors alone. It is deeply rooted in the socio-psychological structure of a given group. The particularly violent economic and social changes, which the German middle classes had to undergo in the Weimar period, may explain their striking lack of stable political orientation as expressed in their continuous pilgrimage from one party to another. But it cannot in itself explain the whole extent of panic reaction to economic depression and the reason why the German Protestant middle classes so speedily disengaged from the liberal-democratic platform and turned to the right, and why their political radicalisation ended almost entirely in fascism, not in revolutionary socialism.

The extraordinarily sensitive political reaction to the fluctuations of economic life, which it seems to me is even now still a remarkable indication of a particular kind of nervousness in German middle class society, is certainly related to the traditional lack of genuine political self-confidence among this middle class; it is also connected with the fact that the German middle class had failed to develop a political consciousness commensurate with the awareness of its economic role and interests.

Once German political liberalism had suffered its historic failure in 1848 and had further compromised with Bismarck after 1866, the political order of the national state was no longer the primary concern of the rapidly growing middle classes and of their main political vehicle, the *Nationalliberale Partei*. The monarchical national state, in which this newly established German middle class grew up, was seen by it mainly as a protector and promoter of economic development and a guarantor of the security and legality required for economic prosperity. The middle classes voted for the liberal parties as long as they helped to secure these aims. For as long as the translation of liberal ideas into legislation continued to be urgently necessary for economic progress, the liberal parties in fact promoted progress in this field against the forces of conservatism. But when unrestricted freedom of economic life became troublesome for sections of farmers, who wanted protective tariffs, or sections of artisans and traders, who wanted restriction of economic competition, and when the growing strength of the working class movement led to a demand for greater participation in industrial income and political influence, at that point compromise and arrangement between liberals and conservatives began to dominate the scene in Germany politically and socially. The German middle class, which in the nineteenth century had never gained political power and political self-determination and in the Bismarckian monarchical system had been excluded from real political responsibility, compensated for the lack of political self-determination by economic efficiency. In return for the benefits of economic progress, which they owed to the protection of the state, the middle classes largely adapted themselves to the semifeudal, military and bureaucratic political élites and their values which were dominant in this state. Their common interest in defending themselves against the apparently revolutionary aims of the proletarian movement formed the most real aspect of this alliance. The pursuit of one-sided economic and non-political cultural activities and interests by the German middle class of that time was one of the main reasons for the deep and persistent divisions between the upper and the middle classes on the one hand and the proletarian working class on the other. This division deeply poisoned the German political and social atmosphere before 1914 and prevented the common political interests and ideals of liberalism and socialism from being fused into more than very occasional common action.

We would be underestimating the significance of the historical ties which bound the German middle class to the traditional conservative ruling class and to conservative values and attitudes if we did not also take into account the spiritual, ideological and cultural elements by which they were supported and justified. Professor

Carsten in his article has given ample evidence of the predominance
of conservative and anti-democratic traits in the tradition of
German political and national thinking from the beginning of the
nineteenth century. Later on, when mass-education organised by
conservative school authorities and permeated with authoritarian
educational practices had taken over, these traits deeply influenced
the value systems of the well-educated German middle classes. I
will not go back over the whole complex of this ideological and
educational background, but because of the obvious responsibility
which the German Protestant tradition bore for the failure of
liberal democracy, I will mention only one more point : the role of
Lutheran Protestantism which was so dominant in German tradition
and culture. Through the historical alliance between throne and
altar Lutheranism had long bred a subservient loyalty to monarchical authority. It had moreover produced a special kind of individual
piety and devoutness—which in contrast to Calvinism or Puritanism
—did not strengthen the communal religious spirit nor the resistance
of religious communities to the demands of the state. It promoted a
deepening of private spiritual devotion and submission, in cultural
as well as social matters, a private attitude of service sanctioned by
religion. Lutheranism taught that there was spiritual benefit in the
pursuit of knowledge, scholarship and philosophy, but it neglected
social and political actions which were considered inferior to the
intellectual and cultural achievements of the Germans. This deeply
rooted religious tradition, handed on by thousands of Lutheran
clergymen as the most influential element in the cultural and spiritual life of the nineteenth century, was one of the great arsenals
from which the spiritual content of German national culture and
virtue and the dedication to the pursuit of national aims in the
German middle class could be nourished and justified; but it also
provided justification for their cultural and moral contempt for the
proletarian way of life and subculture.

In the social psychology of the Protestant German middle class
of the Weimar Republic these cultural motivations served to under-
pin a rigid inherited class structure. The middle class was depressed,
but it was just because of this material decline that they aggressively
defended their social standards based on educational and cultural
values and fanatically opposed socialism associated with the image
of a proletarian subculture.

The syndromes of cultural despair and fear of social degradation,
prevalent among the German middle class in this period, coincides
and overlaps to a large extent with the stereotypes of National
Socialist ideology and propaganda. The general prospectus pre-

sented by Nazism, however vague its terms, was a mixed promise of renewal and restoration. Romantic memories of the past were transposed into the affirmations of a young popular movement claiming to be the wave of the future. Regression to the norms and values of a pre-industrial society and an élitist aristocracy was reinterpreted as the new social ideal of a disciplined modern *Volksgemeinschaft*. Inherited subordination to traditional authority, after war and revolution no longer satisfying to the middle class longing for more social and political participation, was transformed into the ideal of voluntary obedience to a plebiscitarian leader.

The charismatic leader, representative of the same depressed middle class and a living expression and confirmation of their feeling, enabled the old monarchical loyalties to be renewed in a concept of leadership closer to the masses and seen as the incarnation of the true will of the people. Democratic participation was thus replaced by plebiscitarian assent. For the old, but by now weakened deference to the political and social upper classes, there was substituted the appeal to the new racist notion of a *Herrenrasse*, accessible to all sections of the population regardless of their economic and social status.

National Socialism, the most extreme form of fascism, arose in an age of violent intellectual and social transformation and in a nation whose broad middle class was, owing to its political and socio-cultural traditions, badly adjusted to the needs and values of democracy in an industrial society. The rise of Nazism cannot be ascribed mainly to the ingenious will of a satanic demagogue, but was largely caused by a broad complex of social and psychological disintegration in the German middle class.

To explore these processes is not to deny that the decision of single individuals and individual responsibilties had no part in this development. Hitlerism was not an inevitable outcome, but the decisions of individual men can change things only within the narrow parameters set by super-individual historical and social factors. There is much good evidence that the factors which favoured Nazism in Germany have changed since 1945. The critical historical reassessment of German history and tradition since the end of the war has become a means of cultural and political reorientation and may itself be a tribute to this change.

Germany's Strategic Position in the European Power Balance

by THEO SOMMER

I

In the world of the 1970s Germany is a geographical term rather than the description of a politico-military entity. After a brief interlude of unified statehood, forged by Bismarck in the heat of the Franco-German War of 1870–71 and buried, seventy-five years later, by Hitler in the holocaust of the Second World War, the Germans have once again reverted to the habit of division against themselves, of internecine strife and quarrel, a habit that had marked the first thousand years of their history. The pattern is simplified now, for instead of a multitude of German states there are only two contenders, the Federal Republic of Germany and the German Democratic Republic. At the same time, the pattern is more complicated, for the line of national partition coincides with that great international divide which is both the main result and the chief remnant of the Cold War.

As a consequence of territorial division, ideological confrontation, and the revolution of arms technology, the German role in European power politics has undergone a drastic change. Germany is no longer a cockpit of specific conflict, causing unrest either by tempting the twelve neighbouring countries with its weakness or over-powering them with its strength. The present German Question, however unresolved, is no longer going to cause a war; the harsh logic of the nuclear age has put paid to any idea of armed revision. Finding a solution to the problem, or bringing about a tolerable non-solution must be left to the tides of history rather than to the arbitrament of the sword. About this there is no quarrel in either Germany. It is a fact that the two successor states to the old *Reich* have been so thoroughly integrated in the opposing power blocs that neither could start or conduct a war on its own. Both of them are part of larger battle orders. If they were to get involved in an armed conflict the cause and scope of that conflict would certainly be general and global, not parochial and limited.

There is a corollary to this. Just as the two German states can no longer make war at their own discretion and risk, so they are no longer capable of independently ensuring peace. They have to rely for their security on the protection afforded them by their respective alliances. For this reason alone, ideological considerations apart, neither is tempted by the notion of one neutral Germany or two neutral Germanies. Neutralisation would put them beyond the effective balance of power between NATO and the Warsaw Pact, and it would threaten the new identity they have acquired in the past quarter of a century. This risk they are not going to run. The gains of interdependence within their different spheres are patent under any conceivable circumstances, the profits of independence doubtful at best. The need for self-preservation is clearly felt more strongly in both Germanies than the impulse towards unification. To the extent that self-assertion is their aim, it is, for all practical purposes, self-assertion within the larger groupings they have joined since the Second World War, not self-assertion in terms of a reunited Germany.

It would be tempting to pursue the analogy between West and East Germany and to investigate whether the two German states share the same apprehensions, preoccupations and basic tenets *vis-à-vis* their respective allies. I shall withstand the temptation to speculate on this. Any analogy is defective in the first place, because it compares the perception of the ruling élites in Bonn and East Berlin, that is two kinds of *raison d'état*. The heart may have its own reasons, and in the East most certainly has, for there is still no congruence between the aspirations of the people and the ambitions of their rulers. Whatever mirror-image symmetry might exist with regard to strategic thinking and fundamental military attitudes is warped by this basic asymmetry. Furthermore, we have no way of proving the assumption of even apparent symmetry; we know far too little about the thought processes of the East German leadership. Therefore, I shall limit my discussion strictly to the topic of the Federal Republic.

II

The main feature of West Germany's defence policy is the fact that it is not a national defence policy viable on its own, but strictly a national contribution to a wider, international security effort. As the White Paper on Defence of 1970 put it: 'An effective policy of maintaining and organizing peace presupposes the inclusion of the Federal Republic of Germany in the global balance of power; it precludes any course leading into isolation.' Willy Brandt made the same point in slightly different phraseology when he told Parliament on 28 October 1969 : 'For our security we need friends and allies.'

This has indeed been the basic political tenet of Bonn's defence policy ever since the early fifties when, at the climax of the Cold War, both Chancellor Adenauer and the Western allies concluded that some kind of West German rearmament was inevitable. In a memorandum submitted to Adenauer on 14 August 1950, General Hans Speidel addressed himself to the question : 'What to do if the Russians came?' After a professional analysis of the military situation, Speidel arrived at the 'basic political insight' that West Germany would never be able to maintain its security all by itself. For this reason he proposed that the European nations co-ordinate their defence systems. This was tantamount to the renunciation of any purely national security effort.

Indeed, from the very beginning there was never the slightest doubt in Bonn that any Federal Army would have to find its place within a larger grouping. At first, Adenauer's advisers hoped this grouping could be provided by an integrated Western Europe. The 'Himmerod Memorandum', drawn up in October 1950, summed up a discussion about the 'creation of a German contingent in the framework of a supranational force for the defense of Western Europe'. This was a force obviously very similar to the one envisaged in the Pleven-Plan, which was published shortly afterwards—a force integrated at division, battalion or even company level.

It is a matter of historical record that in the end both Pleven's proposal and the concrete plans which it inspired for a European Defence Community foundered in the French National Assembly. But it is also a matter of record that in Bonn the craving for a wider framework never slackened. When French nationalism killed European supranationalism in the military field, the West Germans resisted any temptation of going national themselves. Rather they pressed for the establishment of some different international context. In the end, NATO and the Western European Union took the place of the abortive E.D.C. as the receptacle of the new German army that was founded in 1955.

The point is that the Bundeswehr was created not as an independent national force within an oldfashioned coalition of states. To this very day it is an alliance force—incapable, on its own, of holding the front, let alone of independently conducting war for any meaningful length of time. It does not even have a body that might properly be called a national General Staff. Its military philosophy, its doctrine, its operational plans are all alliance issue; so is its logistical base. The Bonin Plan for a conventional border defence system and the Heye Proposal for coastal defence were both rejected during the fifties precisely for the reason that they would have jeopardised the vital and indispensable backdrop of integrated alliance support.

Integration is not only a word; it is an absolute necessity. In isolation from their NATO allies, the Federal Armed Forces would not be able to accomplish their mission.

This is self-evident with regard to nuclear deterrence. Even if there were not plenty of weighty political arguments militating against the establishment of a national nuclear force, an autonomous West German nuclear deterrent just would not make strategic sense in view of the country's geography and demography, quite apart from the financial limitations. It would be beyond the political, economic and military capacity of any single European country to provide a full panoply of deterrence. I, for one, harbour grave doubts whether even by pooling Western Europe's nuclear resources a deterrent of sufficient credibility could be created to make reliance on the American arsenal superfluous.

The same goes for defence proper. More than half of the Federal Republic's land border with the Warsaw Pact—1,346 kilometres of frontage *vis-à-vis* the GDR, 356 kilometres *vis-à-vis* Czechoslovakia —is manned by allied forces. NATO's emergency defence plans provide for a sort of layer-cake : In multiple tiers, troops from Denmark, the Netherlands, Great Britain, Canada, Belgium, the United States and, perhaps, France, would fight side by side with Bundeswehr units. Even now, there are nearly as many allied soldiers stationed in the Federal Republic as there are Bundeswehr soldiers. Not only for deterrence but also for territorial defence West Germany depends heavily on its allies. In the last analysis, the Bundeswehr is primarily the entrance ticket to common deterrence, joint crisis management, and collective defence. It is hard to see how this situation could fundamentally change. It is, it seems to me, and will remain a fact of life.

III

If it is the political purpose of NATO's Armed Forces to prevent an outsider from imposing his will on any member of the alliance, it is their military mission, as the Ministerial Guidance of 1967 phrases it, to guarantee security through credible deterrence or else, in the event of aggression, to preserve and restore the integrity of the territory by appropriate means.

This Guidance does not, of course, provide precise answers to such crucial defence questions as : Where? When? How? By what means? Any expert knows that not even the military documents drafted on the basis of the political guidelines are completely un-equivocal. It is relatively easy to agree on strategic principles like proportionality of means, adequacy of forces or limitation of ob-jectives; it is much more difficult to agree on the modalities of their implementation. There is always room for interpretation, and it is here that specific national interests can be brought to bear.

Before investigating what the specific interests of the Federal Republic are, it might be useful to cast a glance at the situation from which they arise.

A hundred years ago, Germany was the centre of Europe, living in perpetual fear of encirclement; Bismarck used to lie awake at night haunted by his *cauchemar des coalitions*. Nowadays, Germany is divided, and its free part leads a precarious existence at the outer edge of the Western world. If the former position in the centre of things seemed risky, the new location on the borderline between two antagonistic systems is certainly no less fraught with danger. No other country in Western Europe is more vulnerable than the Federal Republic, for the simple reason that it can neither trade space for time nor use weapons of mass destruction on its territory without destroying its own national substance.

It is against the foil of these grim facts that the four specific interests have to be seen which, according to the White Paper on Defence of 1970, the Federal Republic upholds within the Atlantic Alliance.

First, there is the overriding interest in what has since come to be called Forward Defence. The territory of the Federal Republic is a narrow strip of land. The maximum distance between the eastern and western borders is 480 kilometres, the minimum distance 225 kilometres—just a few minutes' flying time as modern fighter aircraft go. Seventeen million people out of 60 million live within 100 kilometres west of the border, 42 million within 200 kilometres. Of these, 5.5 million work in industry—a figure that equals roughly 70 per cent of all industrial manpower. For this reason, the freedom of manoeuvre for the West's armed forces is greatly restricted. There is simply not enough room for defence in depth.

No defence doctrine can hold the slightest attraction for the West Germans if it does not give them a reasonable assurance that their country will be defended as close to the eastern border as possible.

The prospect of being liberated after the terror of occupation is unlikely to engender any allegiance to NATO. While conceding territory in order to gain time may be sound policy in the unpopulated areas of Northern Norway or Eastern Turkey, a strategy based on the same premise in Central Europe could only cause the Germans to turn their backs on the alliance. When NATO was founded in 1949, the first line of defence ran along the Pyrenees. It was then progressively pushed forward to the Rhine; by 1958 to the Weser, Fulda and Leck Rivers and finally, in the autumn of 1963, as close to the Iron Curtain as militarily feasible (30 to 60 kilometres). This, in the eyes of the West Germans, marks the main achievement NATO has to its credit. Going back on the principle of Forward Defence could only incline them towards defeatism.

The second specific German interest refers to nuclear weapons. They are today an indispensable means of deterrence—not only on the strategic plane but on the tactical level as well. Several thousand of these weapons are today stored on West German soil. (The Bundeswehr is equipped with delivery means, the nuclear warheads are kept in American custody.) Any opulent use of nuclear weapons, however, would clearly threaten the physical survival of the country, causing irreparable damage to the people which they are intended to defend.

After many years of hesitation, the Federal Government has now taken the unequivocal stand that because of their escalatory and devastating effect, nuclear weapons must not be used except as a last resort, and even then only with great constraint and on a very selective basis. This is in line with the new NATO doctrine adopted in December 1969. Any other doctrine would tend to produce a state of mind in which the fear of aggression might be subordinated to the fear of nuclear war. I for one, am unable to imagine that any continental European could bring himself to bow to the concept of a 'theatre nuclear war' limited to Europe which has been bandied about in the Pentagon for the past four years. It would be just as unacceptable to them as a return to the old Massive Retaliation Doctrine would be to the Americans—and, incidentally, equally incredible in the eyes of the Russians.

The third specific West German interest has to do with the requirement for a multi-national presence on the territory of the Federal Republic. It is based on the principle that any aggressor in Central Europe must, from the very outset, expect to engage the forces of as many allies as possible. A multi-national presence in forward positions, in normal times and especially after mobilisation, is the manifest expression of NATO's indivisibility.

Obviously, if the strength of the various national contingents fell below a certain minimum level, the present set-up, according to which each of eight nations covers part of the border frontage, would have to be overhauled. This goes in particular for the Americans. Were they to withdraw as much as, say, half of their garrison from Germany, a drastic redesigning of today's layer-cake type of defence structure would become inevitable. The remaining U.S. forces might then have to be concentrated in the rear as a central reserve for counterattack. It is hard to say how the gaps along the Iron Curtain could be filled—perhaps by German militia forces or, hopefully, by defence contingents from a European Army which has yet to emerge. There is no denying the fact, however, that any general re-deployment of troops would pose grievous problems if it were implemented according to the principle 'The Germans to the front, the others to the rear'. The net result of any such upheaval could only be a definite security deficit. The certainty that an aggressor will be actively engaged by a number of allies right on the border rather than by only one is a crucial part of the Western deterrence posture.

There is a fourth, and final, specifically West German interest. We believe in integration. Integration means three concrete things : an integrated command structure with multi-national headquarters even in peacetime; joint operational exercises; joint operational command in war. These are the factors which distinguish NATO from all previous alliances in history. They enable the allies to harmonise their military resources, to co-ordinate their employment in an emergency, and to react in the nick of time to any crisis or aggression. Again, this is an absolutely indispensable feature of both deterrence and defence if deterrence should fail.

Personally, I cannot help feeling that whatever loosening of NATO's integration structure we might live to see would have to be compensated for by a greater degree of integration within the West European framework. This presupposes, of course, a French willingness to accept the principle of integration in the context of building Europe rather than rejecting it as an instrument of American paramountcy.

These, then, are the four points in which the Federal Republic takes a particular interest. For the rest, our problems are common to all allies.

IV

La Germania farà da se, Germany will go it alone—this nineteenth-century slogan is today only a very far and faint reminiscence. The Federal Republic will not go it alone. It is finally one of the crowd—and that is a historical novelty of the greatest import.

There are doubts about this in some quarters, especially in view of the Ostpolitik pursued in recent years by the government of Chancellor Brandt and Foreign Minister Scheel. But it would be quite wrong to consider Ostpolitik an alternative to Westpolitik. It is not an alternative but a supplement. In fact, Ostpolitik would be doomed to failure if Westpolitik did not provide a firm and durable basis.

The rationale of Brandt's eastern policy is easy enough to understand. At its root lies the recognition that security through deterrence is one essential element of stability, but that security through lessening tension is a supplementary one, no less essential. For many years, West Germany pursued vis-à-vis the East a basically revisionist course. However justified its revisionist claims may have been, it created specific points of German-Eastern friction in addition to the general conflict between East and West. As the nuclear stalemate hardened into nuclear parity, it became quite obvious that the Western Allies of the Federal Republic were not going to back up Bonn's claims for territorial change. The goal of reunification, originally endorsed by the allies in the treaties of 1954/55, became more and more of an embarrassment. It was allowed to remain on the prayer books, but at the same time it was dropped from the agenda of practical politics. Brandt drew the consequences from this state of affairs : He dismantled the specific quarrels the Federal Republic has with Communist Eastern Europe. The remaining degree of tension is identical with that reigning between East and West in general—no more, no less.

East and West have established, for all practical purposes, a military equilibrium; both recognise the futility and the riskiness of attempts to change it. They must now try to create a political equilibrium, desist from pressing their maximum demands and accept restrictions on the nature of political settlements. In practice this means : putting up with the status quo while trying to improve it; not necessarily ratifying the present situation but at any rate pacifying it; trading formalisation for normalisation.

This has been the rationale of Western detente policies since the days of John F. Kennedy ('Peace Strategy'), Charles de Gaulle ('détente, entente, co-operation') and Lyndon B. Johnson ('bridge-building'). The same considerations motivate Chancellor Brandt in his Ostpolitik. Since the partition of Germany and Europe cannot be overcome, at least we must try to overcome the separation of the peoples; since borders cannot be shifted about any longer, we must aim at making them more permeable; since a European peace settlement cannot be forced, we must bend all our efforts to render its absence more tolerable and less poisoning. Realities are accepted as they have developed since the end of the war.

In practice this amounts to a recognition by Bonn of all present frontiers, especially Poland's Western frontier and the border between the two Germanies. It is also tantamount to factual recognition of the East German state. If a modus vivendi can be worked out between Bonn and East Berlin, the Federal Republic, while not itself according the GDR recognition as a totally foreign state, would seek closer contacts with East Germany and would no longer object to the German Communists establishing relations with third countries or joining international organisations. The degree of recognition granted by Bonn to East Germany will depend on the degree of amelioration permitted by East Berlin in the every-day relations between the two states.

Can a programme of improvement along such lines be implemented between East and West? The signing of the Soviet-German Treaties and the conclusion of the Warsaw Treaty first justified some cautious hopes. The Quadripartite Agreement on Berlin, the supplementary inter-German agreement, and the recent negotiations between Bonn and East Berlin on a step-by-step normalisation have further brightened the horizon. For the first time since the mid-fifties, something may budge. This something will definitely not include frontiers, systems, allegiances. Rather it will be composed of what one might call 'tangible imponderables' : attitudes, judgements, opinions, myths, mystifications. New avenues of access may open, channels of communication broaden, areas of contact widen. A process might be started, a dialogue unfolded, machinery set up —all of which would not undo the division of Europe but could help to soften the dividing line. A propitious climate could thus be created for a positive evolution towards compromise and conciliation.

Of course, the road ahead is not easy. There will be difficulties within the Western alliance, for the game we are now playing on several boards simultaneously is likely to be complicated and may be resented by administrations which are already plagued by bureaucratic overload. Similarly, we have to expect difficulties in the East. The Czech crisis of 1968 underlined the paranoid touchiness of the Kremlin leaders. Whenever detente becomes serious, they tend to view it as the 'export of counterrevolution'. The problem is to assure them that counterrevolution is not what the West is aiming at, while at the same time refraining from putting the stamp of approval on their heavy-handed hegemony over Eastern Europe. To this end, Soviet security interests in the area must be recognised. The same goes for the stake Moscow has in the political and economic order of the region that forms its *glacis*. Yet this cannot and should not preclude the evolution of the Communist system towards less autocratic, more 'liberal' versions. Reducing Soviet concerns without foreclosing such evolutionary options will be a difficult enterprise. It takes two to tango. But the West has no other choice than trying to institutionalise, over time, a common economic, political and military framework within which change could be encouraged without raising suspicions that would put paid to the entire détente process. It is first and foremost in this perspective that the project for a Conference on Security and Co-operation in Europe ought to be seen.

v

The point bears reiteration that Ostpolitik is no solitary West German venture. It is in line with the predominant trend of our epoch : the endeavour to break the sterile pattern of confrontation while at the same time reinsuring against the failure of that enterprise. Thus it is not aimed at dismantling the security structure erected since 1949 but rather at cashing in on it. The balance on which our survival rests is not to be destroyed; all that is intended is to establish it at a lower level of risk and expenditure.

It is here that the Conference on Security and Co-operation comes in. Signals have been exchanged for some time now, but I frankly doubt whether enough common ground has been found already to warrant the calling of a conference that would assemble thirty-odd European countries including the Vatican State and San Marino, plus the Soviet Union, the United States and Canada, for fruitful negotiations about the future organisation of military security on the European continent.

This, after all, is what a European Conference would have to be about in order to be at all meaningful. Just a big propaganda jamboree would serve little purpose. No Conference that limited its agenda to vague political or economic questions without getting down to the hard facts of the military situation would be worth the effort.

On the one hand, both sides admit meanwhile that the threat— actual or perceived—of an armed aggression is now rather hypothetical. We have plenty of official testimonies for this in the West; and the Russians admitted it in so many words when they signed the

Moscow Treaty with West Germany. On the other hand, both sides feel that only the present balance of forces, as guaranteed by NATO and the Warsaw Pact, offers security against a possible renewal of the threat. In the eyes of the West, this balance provides the guarantee that peaceful coexistence is not just the synonym for a Communist take-over by stealth; in the eyes of the East, it makes sure that détente is not simply roll-back in disguise.

Thus both East and West regard the Alliance system as the best insurance against expansionist intent or temptation on the part of the opposite camp. Both, however, consider it basically only a second-best solution. The Soviets have long clamoured for the dissolution of the two military pacts and the creation of a new system of collective security. In the West, President Johnson said as far back as 1967: 'In Western Europe we shall maintain in NATO integrated common defense. But we also look forward to the time when greater security can be achieved through measures of arms control and disarmament and through other forms of practical agreement.'

The difficulty lies, as usual, in getting from here to there. If the creation of a new security system serves only the purpose of toppling the present balance, then we are not going to have such a system. But if both sides are prepared to accept the present balance and build any new structures on its foundation, then there is hope for a gradual, pragmatic rapprochement between the two Pacts, for an infusion of détente elements also in the military relations between East and West, and for the growth of mutual confidence. It is only on the basis of such confidence that a new system over-arching and eventually replacing the old can be built. At best, then, it would come at the end of a very long process. Such a process presupposes the readiness of both sides to find security through compromise rather than confrontation, to mitigate antagonisms instead of exploiting them; and to settle for the political and territorial realities no matter how imperfect or unsatisfactory they may appear to either side.

Such readiness can meanwhile be counted on everywhere in the West. The Soviets may still have their reservations in this regard. Their traditional attitude has normally prompted them to seek security through confrontation; thus the main thrust of Moscow's European policy has long aimed at expelling the Americans from the continent and isolating the Federal Republic. Only recently have there been signs that the Kremlin leaders may have decided to try a different approach, accepting the American presence in Europe and working *with* Bonn rather than *against* it in pacifying the status quo. These signs are encouraging, but it is too early to tell whether they really spell a major break with past habits.

The main test of Russian sincerity will be provided by their attitude to the problem of Mutual and Balanced Force Reductions. In this issue the West must take an active interest for the very compelling reason that Mutual Force Reductions are the only alternative to Unilateral Reductions—and such unilateral reductions will be inevitable in many countries, not only in the United States. MBFR might well be the European way of reducing the levels of uncertainty, cost and potential violence, a corollary to SALT, as it were. The present balance of forces would be lowered, not changed; America would not be pushed out of Europe but could retain a foothold; and in the process an insurance against miscarriage would still be maintained.

There are problems, to be true. One is the locus of MBFR negotiations. Where should reciprocal troop withdrawals be talked about, and by whom? Personally, I think a Security Council Conference would be as good a place as any (in fact, if there were no MBFR discussions at such a conference, the security issue would not figure on the agenda at all, which would turn the gathering into a rather inane and vain affair). Of course, it is quite unthinkable that San Marino, Malta and the lot could fruitfully address themselves to a topic of such import. A subcommittee would have to be created to deal with the matter at the conference and afterwards. Conceivably, this would be a permanent commission, made up of representatives of at least those NATO and Warsaw Pact nations who either station troops abroad or host them, perhaps complemented by one or two European neutrals whose territory, knowhow or all-round acceptability might be useful for verification purposes. It would be the task of this commission to work out various security arrangements including reciprocal troop withdrawals, to submit them to further full-dress Conferences for ratification, and to monitor the arrangements agreed upon.

Another problem is posed by the negotiating stance the West ought to take. NATO has been working on models ever since the Reykjavik meeting in 1968. A number of models have been completed, some symmetrical, some asymmetrical. I could never help feeling that all of these models were rather naive—either inconsequential and negotiable or, more often than not, so favourable to the West that their negotiability dropped to zero. To my mind, the percentage approach used by the model-builders was perhaps illustrative but held no diplomatic promise; so I have long argued that rather than entering into negotiations with a cut-and-dried offer one should evolve certain firm criteria and then engage the other side in an exercise of mutual mind-probing and mutual education much in the same way that Americans and Soviets probed and educated each other at the SALT table. In the end, the percentage approach will most certainly be superseded by mixed packages containing comparable but not necessarily equal or identical pieces of equipment and numbers of men or units. Whatever military measures may be agreed upon would, however, have to be flanked by a number of confidence-building, political measures : improved communications; limits on freedom of movement or deployment of troops; observation of agreed rules of behaviour.

The question is whether the Soviets are at all seriously interested in a Security Conference which would be more than a propaganda exercise—one, in other words, that would include MBFR on its agenda, or provide for MBFR negotiations in some in some different but related arena. At least we ought to find out whether they may not now have motives of their own to favour balanced force reductions. Three such motives suggest themselves : ever more pressing Asian preoccupations; growing internal demands on their resources; and the conclusion from the Czechoslovak operation in the summer of 1968 that presence on the ground is not, perhaps, absolutely necessary for controlling and policing an area—potential presence, quickly mobilised in times of crisis, is just as effective. It does not take twenty-two Soviet divisions to keep the GDR in line; and the troops withdrawn from East Germany might usefully be transferred elsewhere. In my view, at any rate, there are enough genuine motives that might favourably incline the Kremlin leaders towards an MBFR scheme to justify an honest Western effort.

Let me conclude by leaving the dreary military detail and return once more to the point I made at the outset. The Federal Republic is closely tied up with the West today. It has no military interest outside the Atlantic Alliance; what specific interest it has, it realises within the framework of NATO. Likewise its political interests coincide with that of the larger Western groupings that were constructed from the ruins of the last world war : the North Atlantic Pact and, even more notably, the European Community. Anyone who assumes West Germany could simply drop out of these groupings again and retire into isolationist neutrality has not understood the most important lessons of the past two decades : that there is no future in separatism and that it is already far too late to tear up the tightly woven fabric of the West's economic, social and military integration of which the Federal Republic is an integral part. From here on, there can be no distinct West German policy except within the Western Community. If that community crumbled, or if for some odd reason it decided to reject the West Germans, things might be different, of course. But this is as unlikely a contingency as that of a West German Chancellor taking 60 million West Germans out of an association which provides them shelter, affluence and the only chance of softening the European dividing line to the point where it becomes tolerable though unchangeable.

Experts and Critical Intellectuals in East Germany

by PETER C. LUDZ

Preliminary Remarks

It is only since the early sixties, or more precisely after the VIth SED Congress, that experts and critical intellectuals in the GDR have developed their present characteristics with regard to their social role, their societal function and their conflicting relationships among each other. There were, of course, experts as well as artists and intellectuals before the erection of the Berlin Wall in 1961, the VIth Party Congress and the introduction of the 'new economic system' in 1963; but both groups lived under completely different conditions. The minorities in both groups actively committed to the SED régime had little contact with each other. The same can be said of the majorities of SED opponents within both groups. Moreover, the intelligentsia was not integrated into the earlier GDR social and political system. In the forties and fifties, representatives of the intelligentsia were, of course, among those courted by the SED and given privileges, at that time probably more so than today. Before 13 August 1961, however, flight to the West was a more attractive alternative than acceptance of the privileges offered to those who believed themselves to be indispensable or to those others who still hoped to be able to build the socialism of their vision in the GDR.

While experts, e.g. technocrats and managers in the factories or the state and party administration, were more or less isolated from their colleagues and from the intellectuals, for instance those in cultural life, mutual contact among the latter group seemed to have been quite frequent, especially in the cities of East Berlin, Leipzig, and Dresden. According to Gerhard Zwerenz, for example, a writer who is living in the FRG now, professors and students from some university institutes, most of them working in the disciplines of philosophy and Romance and Slavonic language and literature, were meeting regularly with other intellectuals who shared their beliefs and were working for the media or the publishing houses.

In those days, Wolfgang Harich was one of the leading intellectuals.[1] There was a specific and commonly shared mentality among these intellectuals evidenced by a growing criticism of the system, by attempts at a counter concept, and—most of all—by literary documents expressing disappointment, disillusion and lost hopes. In other words, there existed a certain solidarity among those who later were sent to prison for longer or shorter periods. The SED stigmatised them as 'party-hostile revisionists'.

These intellectuals of the fifties differ considerably in their attitudes from their present counterparts. In that earlier period the intellectuals did not yet feel uncertain about their right to legitimate criticism. With the Second World War only ten years behind, they were able to rely upon the international community of fighters against fascism, i.e. of those who in the name of humanity and civilisation adhered to values which only in western industrial societies have developed into commonly agreed standards of social behaviour. Also, many of the early intellectuals felt their critique to be legitimate because they could put their trust in the values of socialism which—at least until the XXth Congress of the CPSU (1956)—had remained intact.

It should be realised that today even such loosely connected groups of critical intellectuals can hardly be found in the GDR. Instead there now are many individuals who know of each other and agree on certain central issues. They can make their unity of view known, however, only indirectly, for instance through the dedication of literary works to each other, or by quoting a friend's name in a poem, or in occasional interviews which, if at all, are mostly published in the West. Nevertheless, these intellectuals have a certain consciousness of continuity which, for example, is demonstrated by a shared allegiance to Bert Brecht, whom many refer to as their mentor.

In contrast to these intellectuals, the new generation of scientists and technocrats is much more integrated into GDR society. Among them reflective individuals who express themselves critically, such as Uwe-Jens Heuer, are an exception.

Definitions

Marxist terminology in the GDR does not provide clear definitions of how to distinguish between scientific-technological experts or 'scientifically and technically trained personnel', cultural functionaries and critical, i.e. literary, artistic or philosophical-sociological, intellectuals. On the contrary : The members of these three groups, although representative of completely different social functions, are flatly subsumed under the category 'intelligentsia'. Already in Lenin's work the intelligentsia was defined as a 'social stratum' (or sometimes an 'intermediate stratum') existing alongside the two 'main classes', i.e. the workers and peasants. Thus part of the class structure, the intelligentsia—so it is frequently argued by contemporary East European ideologues—is supposed to provide society with the intellectual, not the political premises for its development, and it is assigned the task of guiding and developing social relations as well as directing work in some social organisations.[2]

Further distinctive elements of the intelligentsia, as defined by the official dogma of Marxism-Leninism, include the following assumptions : The intelligentsia is not a uniform social stratum; rather, its members stem from various social groups. Therefore among the members of the intelligentsia one cannot find either a common class consciousness or shared feelings of solidarity. On the other hand, the intelligentsia is said to practise intellectual work that requires 'high qualifications' and is exercised within, but more frequently outside the productive sectors of the economy. The SED officially propagates that the intelligentsia is today an integral part of socialist society. This includes the notion that the intelligentsia is entitled to a share in 'people's property' and—like all other parts of the work force—to participation in the planning of state, economy, and society.

The intelligentsia does not, however, as Kurt Lungwitz, for instance, emphasised years ago,[3] play an independent role in production; it is not a representative of a specific mode of property relations and thus lacks the capacity required to change a social system. Consequently, it is argued that the intelligentsia does not play the leading part in social development; this part is reserved for the 'main classes', i.e. the workers and peasants. Thus, direct exercise of political power by the intelligentsia is clearly rejected. Nevertheless, the intelligentsia is growing in social importance since its members are supposed to provide the ideological, scientific, technological and organisational know-how for socialist societies committed to the principle of economic growth. This ambivalence towards the intellectuals in the GDR may be compared to the 'ambivalence and structurelessness' assigned to intellectuals as a social stratum in Western industrial societies by the West German sociologist M. Rainer Lepsius.[4]

The assignment of comprehensive tasks to the intelligentsia in the GDR points to the fact that in socialist industrial societies the 'tertiary sector' is growing by leaps and bounds, too. As in Western industrial societies, the intelligentsia in socialist systems is more and more functioning as a 'service class'. This 'service class', which should be distinguished from both the workers and the employees, was first described by the Austrian Marxist Karl Renner. Following him, Ralf Dahrendorf has created the term *Dienstklassengesellschaft* (service class society).[5] His proposition that the intelligentsia conceived as one service class among others may bridge the gap between the rulers and the ruled, is difficult to verify with regard to GDR society. For verification we would need an exact description of the societal functions of scientific-technical intellectuals on the one hand, bureaucrats of the state and party apparatus and qualified party functionaries on the other. Furthermore, detailed information would be required about possibilities and observable manifestations of social change in large-scale organisations in general and the bureaucracies of the East German party and the state in particular. Also, the specific influence of the service class on social change would have to be investigated.

All these attempts to define the term 'intelligentsia' were pursued in the spirit of Lenin. This doctrinal compliance results in a number of serious shortcomings. Firstly, official Marxism-Leninism is not in a position to grasp either the various ideological and dogmatic or the actual sociological problems which GDR society has been confronted with for years. On the other hand, official Marxist-Leninist dogma is characterised by its strong demand for a definition of the socio-economic 'nature' of the intelligentsia. Such a definition is needed in order to check up continuously on the 'historic mission' and the functions of the working class in a changing industrial society; for the new socialist intelligentsia is believed to be representative of the permanent process of progressive occupational evolution which the working class is undergoing. Secondly, the proclaimed unity of the 'socialist' and the 'scientific-technological' revolution cannot be described if sociological work on attitudes, behaviour and functions both of the various groups of intellectuals and of the working class is missing. Moreover, who is to be included in the stratum or intermediarie stratum of the intelligentsia? Do all managers, all qualified personnel in the state apparatus, the mass organisations as well as journalists, artists—and do activists and innovators belong to the intelligentsia? Are all graduates from the universities and (technical) colleges included; are those who enrolled with trade or technical schools members of the intelligentsia too? Sometimes, the argument runs as follows: The intelligentsia is composed of all graduates from universities, colleges, and trade or technical schools.[6] If this is so, where should the functionaries of the SED be listed? And a final problem : Is there a definition of the intelligentsia that permits a line to be drawn from older and formerly 'bourgeois' intellectuals to the younger ones grown up and educated in the GDR?[7]

The primary purpose of all efforts to identify those belong to the intelligentsia as separate from others who may be part of the working class has been to demonstrate that a new intelligentsia submissive to the authority of the working class has evolved. In accordance with this general intention, the following were numbered among the core groups of the new intelligentsia in the GDR : activists and innovators, graduates from the so-called workers' and peasants' faculties at the universities, and the cadres educated at schools and colleges run by the SED. In addition to these groups, however, others have been identified as members of the new intelligentsia, especially since the introduction of the 'new economic system' in 1963. In the fifties, the intelligentsia was usually seen as being composed of 'artists', 'scientists', 'technicians', 'pedagogues', etc. and thus defined by its constituent occupational parts. But in the course of the ambitious measures of decentralisation in the GDR economy which were started in 1963, the intelligentsia was defined in a much more adequate way, by considering occupational functions as well as positions. In addition, a tendency has developed to distinguish between two groups of the intelligentsia : the scientific-technical intellectuals on the one hand and the cultural intellectuals, i.e. the professional expositors of the Marxist-Leninist ideology, of agitation and propaganda, of the 'socialist culture', on the other hand—with the critical intellectuals as part of the latter-named group.

While the representatives of the scientific-technical intelligentsia are mostly still listed by professions, although a more specified code is used, the definitions of those who represent the Marxist-Leninist ideology concentrate on functional criteria. Or more specifically, the scientific-technical intelligentsia is subdivided into doctors, scientists, mathematicians, statisticians, technicians, etc., while the cultural intelligentsia is supposed to be composed of individuals performing different functions, mainly the functions of guidance, mobilisation, justification, and critique. In recent times, the term 'socialist intellectuals' has been created for both groups. Professor Max Burghardt, in a speech delivered at the 8th National Congress of the Cultural Association (*Kulturbund*) in October 1972, describes the 'socialist intellectual' as follows: 'A young socialist intellectual distinguishes himself by his high cultural standards, his wide knowledge, and his loyalty to the international socialist movement.' Burghardt adds further items to this characteristic: 'To be a member of the intelligentsia involves a special commitment; it implies the individual's adoption of specific and commonly shared standards and qualities. It further includes the command of the theory of Marxism-Leninism in order to convincingly defend and—together with other parts of the work force —to materialise the political goals of the workers and peasants in power. Also, a member of the intelligentsia should be a master in his field and make use of collective experiences; he must acquire the faculties of both a researcher and an experienced organiser.'[8]

This programmatically extensive description of the socialist intellectual is highly revealing from a political as well as a sociological aspect. From the political point of view, the discussion of a 'socialist intelligentsia' is interesting because this terminology reflects the attempts by the party to win over for cultural-political work that social group which by tradition rejects the bureaucratic apparatus. From the perspective of sociology, the discussion turns on the competence and legitimacy of the critique by intellectuals. The intellectuals can be regarded as 'competent' because the existence of an occupational stratum or profession, not only the cultural-political intelligentsia but the socialist intelligentsia as a whole, is now recognised. Thus, critique by intellectuals can be based on norms which are valid as professional norms. An attempt has also been made to create a basis of legitimacy for the critique of the intellectuals. Because they are now nominated the 'socialist' intelligentsia, they can to that extent appeal to values which for at least *one* sub-system of the GDR, namely the SED, can lay claim to a general consensus as guidelines for social behaviour.

While new and important distinctions with regard to the intelligentsia are being brought forward in the GDR, a number of links and connections between the various social groups can also be observed. Indeed, East German sociologists have been devoting increasing attention to such phenomena. For example, they put much emphasis on the tendency of members of the scientific-technological intelligentsia to adopt working class behaviour and, consequently, to integrate into the social order of the GDR. Thus the behaviour, the attitudes and needs of the workers serve as standards for social integration. The constant 'upward' evolution of the working class, mentioned earlier, has, of course, in this connection to be taken into consideration.

Some Aspects of the Intelligentsia's Integration into Society

The ideological demands for the intellectuals to integrate into GDR society comply with certain realities of the East German scene. In principle, the intellectuals—whatever individual group may be taken as an example—are more fully integrated than parts of the Western intelligentsia by tradition or the 'intelligentsia' in Russia or Poland before World War I. The marginal intelligentsia of the past and the present is characterised as a type by its total lack of direct responsibility for the solution of concrete tasks. Herein lies one of the most significant differences between Western societies, e.g. the FRG, and socialist systems such as the GDR : all social strata and groups have reached a degree of societal integration that is much higher than in Western societies and makes the GDR a much more homogeneous system. This is not to overlook the existing and developing tendencies towards hierarchism in the GDR; but for the matter under discussion such tendencies are not relevant.[9]

It is necessary, however, to emphasise that social integration in the GDR is achieved by the direction and control through the SED of all processes by which individuals or groups become assimilated to various organisational systems, such as to the party itself, but also to the numerous mass organisations the following of which were designed especially for the intelligentsia : The Cultural Association (*Kulturbund*), the Chamber of Technology (*Kammer der Technik*), the *Urania*, the GDR German Writers' Union (*Deutscher Schriftstellerverband/DDR*) et al. Furthermore, societal integration of the intelligentsia is also achieved by the coincidence of positions and functions in individuals : those intellectuals who hold positions in the cultural-political sector simultaneously exercise a number of concrete—mostly ideological-political—leadership functions. Such functions include : activation and direction, interpretation (of one's own system as well as the outside world) and information, anticipation and justification, further—although within a close framework set up by the party—the functions of critique and utopia. These functions may provide their holders with a high degree of societal integration.[10]

The Experts: Competence and Social Functions

In the following pages the discussion will concentrate on the scientific-technical and economic experts within and outside the SED apparatus. The essential fact is the GDR's general tendency to develop towards an expertocratic career-orientated society :

those who have obtained certain qualifications are given the chance of further training and—with the assistance of 'science', seen as 'productive force'—reach the visionary state of the *Gesamtarbeiter* (comprehensively trained worker). In this connection several aspects are worthy of note : firstly, qualification is a value in itself : it is potential performance, as it were. Moreover, the tendency towards an expertocratic career-orientated society has been foreshadowed by Lenin's vision of the 'worker engineer' and the notion that human activity in the production process should attain to scientific standards. This tendency was further reinforced by the official philosophy of man which equates man's gradual acquisition of scientific knowledge with his development towards an ideal, harmonious personality. Finally, the lack of qualified scientific and technical personnel has been decisive in this development in the GDR.

These factors, namely the concrete socio-political pressures, the political and social effects of the officially proclaimed image of man, and the lack of qualified personnel, carry some social implications. In the first place we should mention the system of rewards with its multifarious ranks of status and prestige. As far as this system is concerned, the concept of a 'socialist performance-orientated society' is realised most significantly in the experts' role. In the GDR the performance principle receives a specific interpretation in the following maxim (which was incorporated into the 1968 GDR Constitution) : 'From each individual according to his abilities, to each individual according to his performance.' This interpretation stresses the notion of equivalence inherent in the performance principle.

The role of the experts is, however, as ill-defined as the performance principle. Under the rule of the 'new economic system' and the 'economic system of socialism' (1963–70), performance was based on measurable (occupational) achievements much more clearly than in subsequent years when the principle became diluted. Since 1970 performance has been linked more with political implications. This can be demonstrated from the wages and incomes policies. It can also be found in discussions on the responsibilities of directing personnel. Indeed, these discussions reveal a considerable extension in meaning of the performance concept which has gradually been losing its definite character. Thus today specialists find themselves confronted with a pattern of role expectations which may in part react negatively upon their professional efficiency. Not only is it difficult to combine the roles of expert and member of the party or mass organisation, particularly in the upper middle ranks of leadership; the expert role may also shelter the individual from too much control by the party apparatus. Furthermore, the expert role offers a strong possibility of inertia, which is due to the experts' high-ranking position in the SED status hierarchy. This high prestige is guaranteed to the experts by their occupational competence. In the GDR, very much as in every industrial performance-oriented society, a variety of professions enforcing professional norms have established themselves. They have created continuously expanding opportunities of competent critique. Such critique is not only 'socially defined' but also accepted politically.[11] The acknowledged and approved expert in East Germany does not, naturally, occupy the highest rank in the prestige and income hierarchy, in contrast to the officially proclaimed ideal type of the *Gesamtarbeiter* who is conceived as the personified synthesis of white-collar and blue-collar work, of *partiinost* and professional qualification. But the experts rank sufficiently high to enable them to refrain from stepping out of their expert role.

With these remarks we reach one of the limitations inherent in the 'professionalisation' so typical of life in East Germany today : in nearly all its sectors the socio-economic system lacks policy-oriented expert leaders capable of taking risks. Thus again and again the leading SED functionaries point out that experts should learn how to 'lead', that they should refrain from too narrow an interpretation of their expert role. In other words, they are supposed to meet additionally the challenges and risks of planning and critique that is beyond their professional norms : the qualified technical-scientific personnel must take over leadership roles. In the GDR, much more than in Western industrial societies, these leadership roles are characterised by unspecified norms and, in addition, by role expectations that are totally different from those of the expert role. The norms for leadership roles are unspecified for two inter-connected reasons : they consist of empty formulae, i.e. formulae which can assume whatever meaning is desired, and, as a consequence, are highly susceptible to incalculable sanctions by the SED.

Since experts lack a uniform and pragmatic political orientation, they hold on to their politically and socially well-defined professional competence. Thus the occupational transfer from administrative expert positions to political leadership positions involves considerable complications; there is less interchangeability from the top echelons in the bureaucracy to the real political élite in the GDR than in any Western industrial society. This, of course, is not only due to the fact that top political positions, i.e. those within the SED Politbureau, the SED-Central Committee, and the GDR Council of Ministers are spread thinly. It is caused rather by the wide field of unspecialised social norms and thus by patterns of politically and socially unprotected behaviour. The leap to the top is successfully achieved only by a small minority. One of them was Dr. Günter Mittag, who in 1967 became a member of the political élite proper. When entering the SED Politbureau as a full member, he had, however, to abandon his expert role which he had been able to keep as long as he had been merely a candidate member of the Politbureau.

This 'bar' blocking top experts from rising to genuine political positions represents an objective feature of the SED ruling system : the party has to secure room for itself in order to retain its command over all sectors of the social system. On the other hand, this implies that leadership positions as such are mistrusted by the expert intelligentsia. We know from a variety of discussions that, for example, in East German scientific organisations, the leaders of 'interdisciplinary research collectives' do not meet (and often do not want to meet) the roles expected from them. For their job specialised professional skills are less important than organising abilities such as developing research objectives and planning research programmes in accordance with the resources at their disposal.[12] Their hesitation to take over and properly fulfil such organising tasks results, as previously mentioned, from the general principles of SED politics as well as from the fact that they are, if at all, ill-trained for leadership work. The very conditions and actual demands of the performance-oriented career society have shaped training programmes which, apart from political indoctrination, give priority to professional specialisation rather than to managerial expertise. Training programmes adopted by the party academies and institutes constitute no exception to this rule. Even now, when the teaching of management classes is increasing, the content of courses tends to remain tied to doctrinal axioms.

The Critical Intellectuals: Critique and Legitimacy

First it should be noted that a critical intelligentsia does exist in the GDR, now as much as before. But more than at an earlier period its contemporary representatives have to be singled out of the officially proclaimed 'socialist' intelligentsia; they should be distinguished from the experts within and outside the SED as well as from the official and officious parts of the cultural intelligentsia. The latter-named group is assigned mainly the task of 'satisfying the cultural needs in a socialist way'. In addition they are ordered to direct 'the class competition' in the cultural sphere.[13]

Compared with these parts of the cultural intelligentsia and with the experts, but even with the intelligentsia as a whole, the critical intelligentsia is a less coherent social group. It is composed of individual philosophers, sociologists, political economists as well as writers, poets, and dramatists. Indeed, different authors—such as the philosopher and scientist Robert Havemann, the writers Christa Wolf, Werner Bräuning, Manfred Bieler (who emigrated to the West), Hermann Kant, the poets Wolf Biermann, Günter Kunert, Peter Huchel (who is also living in the West now), Reiner Kunze and Volker Braun—cannot be regarded as members of an organised group; but their work reveals some group feeling, or some—although latent—solidarity. Most of the individuals named here include a political dimension in their work. Biermann calls himself a 'political song-writer'; others, like Kunze, resort to parables. All of them have a feeling of freedom and justice; but they cannot agree among themselves on a general definition of freedom, justice and truth. In order to achieve such an understanding, constant discussions would be needed among those who tend to unite in political opinion. Such contacts, however, can hardly be made, for political reasons. But there are additional reasons why these intellectuals and artists cannot agree on a common programme. Given the collective experiences of Stalinism and the necessity of surviving as an individual in that era, each of them has developed a basic political outlook which has become a component part of his personality. For example, according to Leszek Kolakowski, in each case when people believe they are standing up for 'justice', the term expresses a different meaning so that it is hard to arrive at a common concept.[14]

The adjective 'critical', as it is used here to identify a group of intellectuals, covers a great variety of attitudes and activities characteristic of this opposition: deviant opinions on general political and/or cultural-political issues; a general loyalty towards the régime; attempts to re-interpret parts of the ideological dogma and to proclaim counter-utopias. This broad range of attitudes and activities indicates that this 'critique' is not grounded in professional competence. Thus, it is often rejected as 'incompetent' by the SED. But is this 'critique' illegitimate too?

The critique ranges from a criticism of the system based on immanent principles to a criticism that openly rejects and fights some component features of the existing system. Immanent criticism, for instance, is defined in a sentence that the poet Volker

Braun (born in 1939) wrote : 'We do not write against society but for it, for its change by inherent qualities.' Others, e.g. Havemann and Biermann, stand up for democratic socialism, for the freedom of speech and writing and especially of critique. Their position is thus at the extreme end of immanent criticism. They demand independent thinking and the possibility for artists and philosophers to express themselves in a personal, subjective manner. Christa Wolf, who at the time was a candidate member of the SED Central Committee, put these wishes into words when she stated at the 11th plenary session of the SED Central Committee in December 1965 : 'Now as much as before, the arts cannot give up (their claim) ... to be subjective, i.e. to reflect the artist's style, his language and intellectual world.'[15]

Havemann, Biermann and Christa Wolf, all three are committed to socialism and loyal to the GDR—even though their loyalty can hardly be 'proved'. There is, however, at least one strong proof of their faithful allegiance : although they probably had the opportunity, they did not emigrate from the GDR. In the cases of Havemann and Biermann, many a top SED functionary would presumably have breathed more freely if they had left. For it is Havemann's and Biermann's idea that the 'socialist revolution' in the GDR be completed.[16] They struggle against the cult of personality, the party bureaucracies and a dogmatised ideology; they want especially to break the SED's monopoly in ideological matters. The code word for all these hostile targets is 'Stalinism'. In addition, Biermann and Havemann fight what they call *stalinistischer Gulaschkommunismus* (Stalinist stew communism), or the socialist consumer society. They strive for total nationalisation of the consumption sector; they make absence of desire the guiding principle of their philosophy of man. These aims are combined with their longing for general freedom and equality, which includes the call that in the GDR social classes and strata be abolished.

It is an open secret that in the wake of the XXth Congress of the CPSU (1956), the meaning of Stalinism and the nature of their personal involvement became clear, at least to the political brains of the critical intelligentsia, such as Havemann and Biermann. Therefore, they frankly welcomed the events of the Prague Spring as bringing new hope for the implementation of democratic socialism. Moreover, apart from all the criticism which they level at the Federal Republic, they are much more open to 'socialdemocratic reformism' than the SED leaders.

Under these circumstances, it is hardly surprising that Biermann and Havemann were isolated from their fellow intellectuals by the

SED and have been placed under constant surveillance. Their demands and confessions involve the negation of some aspects of political rule in the GDR. Such negation is intolerable to the SED because it is not only based on a utopian vision but also an actual criticism of the GDR and on sympathy expressed for the SED's arch enemies : the Dubcek Régime and the Social Democratic Party in the Federal Republic.

Leaving aside Havemann and Biermann, the question has to be posed what are the political, social and ideological functions of contemporary critical intellectuals in the GDR? What is their self-understanding? How can they secure a legitimate basis for their critique? Certainly, in the GDR satements by the critical intelligentsia do not directly merge in the process of the formation of public opinion. Their critique of the system, including their visions of a socialist democracy, undoubtedly remains outside the narrow framework of party-licensed opinions. Nevertheless, in its questioning of the SED's claim of legitimacy, the critique gains an additional dimension. The critical intelligentsia moreover fights the purism of those who officially and officiously represent ideological criticism —thus attacking the party's autocracy from another end.

Because it is not absorbed into public opinion on the one hand and because it is comprehensive on the other, the intellectuals' critique is very effective indeed. It makes the ideological strategists create mechanisms of defence and justification and forces them at times to accept the visionary democratic socialism, however disguised. Owing to such pressures by the critical intelligentsia, the top functionaries in the ideological and cultural-political sectors attempt to modernise both the dogma and the operative ideologies and to adjust them constantly to new situations. Hence it appears that the real relationship between the maintenance of political power and the preservation of a pure dogma does not only call for open rejection of all new ideological interpretation, but also for a continuous transformation of critical or rather 'revisionist' thinking into the official party language; it demands a semantic purge, so to speak. This purge should not, however, be understood as implying purification from all substantial elements. Thus the exertion of pressure to provoke the party into reacting may be regarded as the societal function of the critical intelligentsia in the GDR and, likewise, as a proof of its legitimacy.

In the long run, the strategic leading clique of the SED cannot develop the GDR into a convincing alternative to the FRG unless it adopts—at least in part—some advanced ideas of the critical intelligentsia and unless it gradually and without using coercive measures de-activates some criticism raised against its methods of rule. In general, this reception by those in power of alien ideas should be seen as a long and continuous process the individual aspects and stages of which may not always be observable at once.

Again, the critical intellectuals are effective, although not in the straight sense of the word. Their political-ideological influence is a hidden phenomenon and can be ascertained only indirectly, i.e., by analysis of the defence strategies of the official and officious ideologues.

The social functions of the critical intelligentsia are determined by these general conditions. Individual members of the intelligentsia, although kept separate from each other and from a wider public, live at liberty. In contrast to their personal and political friends in the fifties, they are not jailed. And they have a great public. This holds for Biermann, who is now forbidden to appear on stage and to publish his work in the GDR, as well as others, who may get their works published, but in small editions only. In the case of Biermann, we may speak of some kind of influence on partial publics or group publics. His songs are being sung, his records played, and his poems read. This is, of course, not the picture of a real ideological and, even less, of a political underground. On the whole, it rather shows a dimension of everyday life independent of the actual political and social controls of the SED, a social setting in which opinions, hopes and illusions are blossoming. And the critical intellectuals are well aware of the responses they get from the people, especially the young, and of being regarded as trustworthy. This, in turn, produces additional momentum and strengthens their will to survival.

The self-perception of the critical intelligentsia is substantially marked by this will to survive and to accept the self-imposed responsibility to speak out openly on problematical issues. The word "open" stands for critical-utopian—probably the most important dimension of the intellectuals' mode of expression in the West; but in the GDR it includes especially the additional meanings of : sceptical, melancholic, resigned, pessimistic, sad, serenely detached. Thus fundamental moods of human nature which lie deeper than the level of political programmes and social behaviour are being handed down, preserved and hence kept alive. Biermann is completely conscious of this dimension of his work, when he says : 'In order to live here, we need a complete arsenal of socialist ideas, hopes, illusions and passions. I notice of at least some of my songs and poems that they belong to this arsenal; they help to bring about a situation that permits us to live our unpartitioned lives in this half of a country, and not just to struggle for our survival.'[17] The recourse to the moods and forms of behaviour which so far have not been absorbed by the norms of either the party or the experts may provide Biermann with additional legitimacy. For now as before he is giving expression in his songs to values which in the GDR may be representative of commonly accepted guide-lines for social behaviour.

Some Common Characteristics

In the GDR the expert role and the role of the critical intelligentsia are closer together than in Western societies. Although in social reality and in the SED's self-perception the East German technical-scientific intelligentsia is separate from the critical intelligentsia, both groups have some common characteristics and these are not merely peripheral: firstly, there is a similar basic feeling of loyalty towards both the idea of socialism and the social reality of the GDR in general. Further common characteristics include negative criticism as well as appreciation of the West—hence an attitude of distance and ambivalence towards Western systems. Thirdly, there is a proximity through daily experience. Day by day, both groups probably experience the bureaucratic inefficiency and slowness of political rule in the GDR. Fourthly, the experts and the critical intellectuals can be characterised by a basic attitude which highly values the willingness to learn, the readiness to take risks and the faculty to perceive and integrate new perspectives. They both are compelled constantly to re-orientate themselves. Thus they resemble each other in their propensity towards a, perhaps somewhat forced, optimism. Finally, both groups of intellectuals are convinced that such values as personal responsibility, self-reliance, self-determination and responsible co-operation should be given wider scope in the society of the GDR.

Two, although a little remote, examples shall serve as illustrations of these propositions: the interpretation of cybernetics which Uwe-Jens Heuer, a professor of public and economic law, published between 1965 and 1967; and the statement Christa Wolf made at the 11th plenary session of the SED Central Committee in 1965.[18] Both authors expressed their loyalty to the GDR and, at least in my estimation, did so not for the purpose of paying lip service. Heuer wishes to strengthen socialism in the GDR by new combinations of co-operation and conflict. Christa Wolf, when talking about her meetings with other writers from foreign countries, speaks of 'our country here,' 'our feelings for this country'. Both want to pave the way for the 'development of the socialist personality' : Heuer by trying to encourage new forms of co-determination in firms and other organisations; Christa Wolf, in referring to discussions about her book *Der geteilte Himmel* (1963), by encouraging her listeners to develop feelings of appreciation and responsibility for the GDR and to commit themselves. Heuer and Wolf criticise the bureaucrats, especially those in the party apparatus. They courageously break through the barriers of written and unwritten laws on 'criticism and self-criticism', while advocating their views in public.

These examples may illustrate that, however different in function, role and self-perception, the experts and the critical intellectuals have certain characteristics in common. Their proximity is a matter of similar views and attitudes; of adherence to a specific combination of pragmatic critique and reality-bound vision; of common possibilities to combine competent with legitimate critique; and last but not least it is a matter of personal courage which each individual must have when exposing himself. Thus, behind the official ideological patterns, the mechanisms of anticipation and justification in the SED's programme, and apart from the actual policies in science and culture, some contours of potential modernisation have shown up in our picture of the GDR. This potential should be taken even more seriously, since, in their personal and professional lives, the representatives of modernisation stand firmly on the ground of their society. By their mental attitudes and belief systems these groups of the 'service class' display themselves not as members of a 'class without consciousness'; they rather make clear that, while remaining in the system's framework, they want to present proposals for alternative developments to the party leadership. Given further rapid socio-economic change in the GDR, some of the devices of contemporary critical intellectuals may not be as unrealistic in the future as they appear at present.

NOTES

1. Gerhard Zwerenz in his contribution to *Das Ende einer Utopie: Hingabe und Selbstbefreiung früherer Kommunisten—Eine Dokumentation im zweigeteilten Deutschland*, ed. Horst Krüger (Olten, Freiburg: Walter-Verlag, 1963), esp. p. 184.

2. Cf. Kristo Dimitroff, 'Die soziale Struktur der Gesellschaft und die Struktur der Intelligenz', *Soziologie im Sozialismus: Die marxistisch-leninistische Soziologie im entwickelten gesellschaftlichen System des Sozialismus*, ed. Wissenschaftlicher Rat für Soziologische Forschung in der DDR (Berlin: Dietz Verlag, 1970), pp. 415–17.

3. Kurt Lungwitz, *Über die Klassenstruktur in der Deutschen Demokratischen Republik: Eine sozialökonomisch-statistische Untersuchung* (Berlin: Verlag Die Wirtschaft, 1962), p. 112.

4. M. Rainer Lepsius, 'Kritik als Beruf: Zur Soziologie der Intellektuellen', *Kölner Zeitschrift für Soziologie und Sozialpsychologie*, XVI (1964), pp. 75 ff., esp. p. 77.

5. Ralf Dahrendorf, *Konflikt und Freiheit. Auf dem Weg zur Dienstklassengesellschaft* (München: R. Piper & Co., 1972), esp. pp. 136 ff.

6. Cf. Siegfried Grundmann, 'Arbeiterklasse und Intelligenz: Aktuelle Probleme ihres sozialökonomischen Wesens', *Soziologie im Sozialismus* (op. cit., n. 2), pp. 417–19.

7. Cf. Hans Reinhold, 'Über die führende Rolle der Arbeiterklasse auf geistigem Gebiet', *Sozialismus und Intelligenz: Erfahrungen aus der Zusammenarbeit zwischen Arbeitern und Angehörigen der Intelligenz*, ed. Institut für Gesellschaftswissenschaften beim ZK der SED. Lehrstuhl für Philosophie (Berlin: Dietz Verlag, 1960), esp. pp. 107 f.

8. *Neues Deutschland*, 27 October 1972, p. 4.

9. Cf. Karl Müller, 'Die Integration der jungen naturwissenschaftlichtechnischen Intelligenz in die Arbeiterklasse', *Soziologie im Sozialismus* (op. cit., n. 2), pp. 342 f.

10. In other publications, in order to identify such integration, I have used the term 'identification' and described the 'institutionalized intelligentsia' in detail. Cf. my *The Changing Party Elite in East Germany* (Cambridge, Mass.: The MIT Press, 1972), pp. 43 ff.

11. For the sociological significance of competent critique cf. Lepsius (op. cit., n. 4), p. 83.

12. Cf., for instance, the report on the scientific conference on 'Kollektiv und Persönlichkeit in sozialistischen Forschungseinrichtungen', held on 14/15 October 1971, at the Technische Hochschule für Chemie 'Carl Schorlemmer' in Leuna-Merseburg), published in *Deutsche Zeitschrift für Philosophie*, XX (1972), p. 343.

13. Cf., for instance, Hans Koch, 'Die Kultur in der entwickelten sozialistischen Gesellschaft', *Weimarer Beiträge*, XVIII (1972), pp. 33 ff.

14. Leszek Kolakowski, *Der revolutionäre Geist* (Stuttgart etc.: Verlag W. Kohlhammer, 1972), p. 33.

15. *Neues Deutschland*, 19 December 1965, p. 12.

16. Thus Havemann writes: 'We are committed to the completion of the socialist revolution.' Cf. Robert Havemann, *Fragen und Antworten: Aus der Biographie eines deutschen Marxisten* (München: R. Piper & Co., 1970), p. 155.

17. Wolf Biermann in an interview, published in *Frankfurter Rundschau*, 30 December 1972, feuilleton section, p. viii.

18. Cf. Heuer's book *Demokratie und Recht im neuen ökonomischen System der Planung und Leitung der Volkswirtschaft* (Berlin: Staatsverlag der DDR, 1963) and my evaluation of his position in my *The Changing Party Elite* ... (*op cit.*, n. 10), pp. 400 ff.—For Christa Wolf cf. note 15 above.

Epilogue: Germany in our Time

by ALFRED GROSSER

It is naturally tempting to take the beginning and end of a period of a hundred years as the limits of a historical epoch; particularly when this beginning and end happen to coincide precisely with significant breaks in the continuous flow of history.

16 April 1871 : 'We, William, by the grace of God, German Emperor, King of Prussia, etc, hereby ordain in the name of the German Empire, and with the consent of the Federal Council and the Reichstag, as follows :

§1 In place of the constitution agreed between the North German Confederation and the Grand Duchies of Baden and Hesse, and in place of the treaties concluded on 23 and 25 November 1870 with the Kingdoms of Bavaria and Württemberg concerning their adhesion to this Constitution, the attached constitutional instrument is promulgated.'

21 December 1972 : 'The High Contracting Parties ... conscious that the inviolability of borders and respect for the territorial integrity and sovereignty of all the states of Europe is a basic condition for peace ... have agreed as follows :

Article 1 : The Federal Republic of Germany and the German Democratic Republic will develop normal good-neighbourly relations with each other on a basis of equality.'

In the first place, however, such breaks are only milestones in a continuous evolution, and secondly, the selection of some landmarks over others gives special importance to a specific aspect of the total socio-political reality. From the point of view of the German workers the foundation of the SPD or the Socialist law of 1878, in point of time on the far and the near side of the *Reichsgründung*, was perhaps more important than that event itself. And has anything changed fundamentally for the inhabitants of either Germany as a result of the treaties of 1970–72?

A radical break is rare and indeed almost inconceivable; even the most total political revolution embraces a society and an economic system which do not disappear in its wake, it affects human beings, whose ideas and convictions are not being completely transformed. Today, forty years after Hitler's appointment as Chancellor, historians are still at loggerheads on the extent and nature of the changes wrought by the Nazi seizure of power and its consequences on Germany and the Germans. The Judges of the Federal Constitutional Court have in their basic judgement of 17 December 1953 dealt in detail with the problem of continuity and discontinuity in the public service.

There are, however, moments when discontinuity prevails to a degree that makes it advisable to be very cautious in adopting an interpretation based on the assumption of continuous evolution. These are the moments when changes in the organisation of society, in the distribution of power and in the dominant ideas take place on a very broad front. In Russia the year 1917 was such a moment. In Germany 1945 did constitute a genuine break.

This is, however, not to be taken for granted. It is not difficult to show that the break of 1945 means more in German than in English or even French history. But to what extent was there genuine continuity in the social order, in the value systems of the three western zones of occupation? In the fifties there was much talk of restoration. It was not so much a matter of the return of past authorities and structures, as of the discovery that the collapse of 1945 had not produced a total change. Organised groups, such as the Churches or the Social Democratic Party, have a continuous existence across breaks and personal changes which makes it impossible to regard 1945 as an absolute zeropoint.

And yet it is natural today to compare the German past with 1945, rather than with 1871, 1919 or 1933. For the impression is justified that the end of the Second World War marks not only the beginning of an entirely new development, but that no comparable discontinuity has occurred since. This does not mean this development is easy to describe or to assess. It is, indeed, possible to point to two completely differing results.

1945 : a Germany in ruins, annihilated, hated, dominated by the victors. 1973 : two powerful German states, prosperous, respected, whose economic and political power counts for much in international affairs. What a transformation!

1945 : the unity of the victors is only an illusion; the Soviet Union takes possession of its part of Germany, the other three take over their part. 1973 : the integration of the two parts into their respective hostile blocs is completed and accepted. It is possible to speak of a transformation, when after a quarter of a century the same situation has become stabilised and recognised?

The contrast can be taken further. The Germans are today the only nation in the world who live under two totally different international systems—the system of East/West conflict which arose in 1947 and the four power system of 1945, created only for and in Germany and which continues only there.

The German Democratic Republic did its utmost for many years to reject and get rid of the system of 1944–5. Between 1950 and 1964 it seemed to have strong support for this policy from Moscow. But then it had to put its signature to the Berlin Agreement of 3 September 1971, to which the victor powers gave their blessing. They were 'acting on the basis of their rights and responsibilities as the four Occupying Powers and in accordance with relevant agreements and decisions of the Four Powers arrived at during and after the war, which remain in force'. Accompanying the basic treaty there was a note from the GDR to the Soviet Union :

> The German Democratic Republic and the Federal Republic of Germany affirm with reference to article 9 of the Treaty ... that the rights and responsibilities of the Four Occupying Powers and the relevant four power agreements, decisions and practices remain intact.

The Federal Republic had already in the Paris treaty of 23 October 1954, by which the three Western powers had given the state created in 1949 internal and external sovereignty, approved of article two, which gave the three powers sole responsibility in the great national problems of reunification and Berlin. The will to full sovereignty was for many years counterbalanced by the fear that the abolition of the system of 1944–5 would make the German division irrevocable and would undermine the defence of Berlin—Berlin, which it was desired to see recognised as an integral part of the Federal Republic but which was at the same time still protected by the Four Power Agreement of 1944–5. Finally there was point five of the joint resolution of 17 May 1972 of the parties in the Federal Parliament :

> The rights and responsibilities of the Four Powers with regard to Germany as a whole and to Berlin are not affected by the treaties. The German Federal Parliament considers it essential, in view of the absence of a settlement of the German question as a whole, that these rights and responsibilities should continue.

In the meantime it was the system of 1947 which first called the Federal Republic as well as the GDR into existence and then gave them power and influence : the East/West conflict transformed the defeated into respected Partners. It was not until the sixties that the Federal Republic felt so secure in their partnership, that it believed it could afford to prosecute a policy of detente without running the danger of again becoming a passive object of four-power politics. And it had to take the risk of such a policy if it wanted to prevent the split in the German nation caused by the Cold War from becoming ever deeper.

The question where the discontinuities occurred in the foreign policies of the Federal Republic is not easily answered. Was 1954–5 a turning point with the Paris treaties, the accession to NATO and Adenauer's journey to Moscow? Or was it 1969 with the arrival of Brandt's Government and Ostpolitik? Or was it not rather the 13th of August 1961? The Wall destroyed many illusions and it is quite possible to establish a continuity from Gerhard Schröder's Ostpolitik under Adenauer and Erhard, through Kiesinger's declaration of Government policy and his letter to Willi Stoph, to the three treaties of Moscow, Warsaw and Berlin.

It is possible to feel the continuity of events so strongly that turning points become non-existent. Was not the surrender of the territories east of the Oder-Neisse line implicit in the decision of the first federal Government to absorb the expellees economically and socially? Certainly Willy Brandt abolished the Ministry for Expellees in 1969, which was not in line with the weekly speeches of Theodor Oberländer and Hans-Christoph Seebohm through many years. But Brandt only put the finishing touches to a continuous development which could only have been different if Adenauer had behaved like the rulers of the Arab states towards the Palestinian refugees : to frustrate any kind of absorption deliberately, in order to prepare for return and vengeance by force of arms as a desired possibility.

The gesture of the Federal Chancellor Brandt in kneeling in front of the Ghetto Memorial in Warsaw has rightly been admired as a sign of human and statesmanlike stature. What he expressed in a particularly touching way was, however, based on the same principle as the Treaty with Israel of 1952 : in contrast to the GDR the Federal Republic has from the beginning accepted the collective responsibility (not to be confused with the rightly rejected idea of collective guilt) for the crimes committed in the name of Germany.

The SPD accepted after 1955 the French and European policies of Adenauer, because it recognised at last that it was pointless to oppose a popular Chancellor in the very policies that made him most popular. In the same way the CDU has been undergoing a transformation since 1971 in order to escape from a domestic and international position of weakness which is very comparable with that of the SPD in the early fifties—so that a possible future replacement of the SPD by the CDU would not bring about changes in Ostpolitik any greater than the transition from Schröder to Brandt; the difference between Brentano and Schröder was if anything greater.

The domestic affairs of the Federal Republic developed similarly, even if not in a very straight curve. 1949 marked the end of a first phase which led from the Left to the Right centre, from the Ahlen Programme to Ludwig Erhard. The Catholic Convention of Bochum and the Co-determination Law were left-overs of the new spirit which was largely extinguished by the fog of the Cold War, until in the course of the sixties a new phase began. Was it new? The victorious SPD of 1973 appeals not to the slogans of the Jusos, but to the Godesberg Programme of 1959 composed under the shadow of Erhard. Were the fundamental freedoms so much in danger in the period of remilitarisation, when there was a Defence Commissioner and guarantees for conscientious objectors? And today, is there, in spite of left-wing extremism among the young, any real attack on the infra-structure of social inequality and economic power—even in respect of the land laws and the educational system?

The election results of 19 November 1972 put the SPD in the lead and this was undoubtedly a turning point. But the trend which has progressively concentrated the vote in the three liberal-democratic constitutional parties has remained and the on-going sociological changes, for example the diminution of Church influence among women, have not produced any different results than in 1960, but have merely reinforced them. These sociological changes, to what extent can they be regarded as elements in a society specifically German? Is not society in the Federal Republic today more comparable to the French and that of the GDR to the Polish, than either of them to each other? To what extent are the factors most relevant to change of a transnational nature? It is not only the delimitation of a timespan and the search for turning points in the past that is difficult. The spatial determination of the object under investigation can by no means be taken for granted, particularly in the case of the open societies of today.

Perhaps Germany no longer exists, because there are two German states. If Germany is to be not merely an abstract concept, but is to have cultural, economic and societal content, then there can be no two 'Germanies' : both of them are already in many of their contents closely integrated with the relevant elements in other countries. From Bismarck to Brandt : it is a change transcending the political-constitutional sphere.

Suggestions for Further Reading

(Only titles available in English appear in this list;
place of publication is London, unless otherwise stated)

Imperial Germany
Golo Mann, *The History of Germany since 1789*, 1968
A. J. P. Taylor, *The Course of German History*, 1945
E. J. Feuchtwanger, *Prussia: Myth and Reality. The Role of Prussia in German History*, 1970
A. J. P. Taylor, *Bismarck*, 1955
Werner Richter, *Bismarck*, 1964
Ludwig Dehio, *Germany and World Politics in the Twentieth Century*, 1959
Hans Kohn, *The Mind of Germany: the Education of a Nation*, 1961
G. L. Mosse, *The Crisis of Germany Ideology*, 1966
Fritz Stern, *The Politics of Cultural Despair*, U. of California P., 1961
J. A. Nichols, *Germany after Bismarck. The Caprivi Era, 1890–94*, Cambridge, Mass., 1958
J. C. G. Röhl, *Germany without Bismarck. The Crisis of Government in the Second Reich, 1890–1900*, 1967
Michael Balfour, *The Kaiser and his times*, 1964
G. A. Craig, *The Politics of the Prussian Army, 1640–1945*, Oxford, 1955
Martin Kitchen, *The German Officer Corps, 1890–1914*, Oxford, 1968
Fritz Fischer, *Germany's aims in the First World War*, 1960
J. W. Wheeler-Bennett, *Hindenburg, the Wooden Titan*, 1936

Social Democracy
Evelyn Anderson, *Hammer or Anvil. The Story of the German Working-Class Movement*, 1945
Helga Grebing, *History of the German Labour Movement*, 1970
Carl E. Schorske, *German Social Democracy, 1905–17. The Development of the Great Schism*, Harvard U.P., 1955

Douglas A. Chalmers, *The Social-Democratic Party of Germany. From Working-Class Movement to Modern Political Party*, Yale U.P., 1964
Peter Gay, *The Dilemma of Democratic Socialism. Eduard Bernstein's Challenge to Marx*, New York, 1952
J. Joll, *The Second International 1889–1915*, 1955
F. L. Carsten, *Revolution in Central Europe*, 1972
A. J. Ryder, *The German Revolution of 1918. A study of German socialism in war and revolt*, Cambridge, 1967

The Weimar Republic
E. Eyck, *A History of the Weimar Republic*, 2 vols., Oxford, 1962–4
Arthur Rosenberg, *A History of the German Republic*, 1936
A. J. Nicholls, *Weimar and the rise of Hitler*, 1968
A. J. Nicholls and Erich Matthias (ed), *German democracy and the triumph of Hitler: essays in recent German history*, 1971
R. N. Hunt, *German Social Democracy, 1918–1933*, Yale U.P. 1964
T. Eschenburg and others, *The Road to Dictatorship. Germany 1918–1933*, 1964
F. L. Carsten, *Reichswehr and Politics, 1918–33*, Oxford, 1966
F. L. Carsten, *The Rise of Fascism*, 1967
K. v. Klemperer, *Germany's New Conservatism*, Princeton U.P., 1968
Istvan Deak, *Weimar's Left-Wing Intellectuals. A Political History of the Weltbühne and its Circle*, U. of California P., 1968

Nazism and the Third Reich
K. D. Bracher, *The German Dictatorship*, 1971
Alan Bullock, *Hitler: A Study in Tyranny*, 1952
Helmut Heiber, *Adolf Hitler, A Short Biography*, 1961
H. Mau and H. Krausnick, *German History, 1933–45*, 1962
W. L. Shirer, *The Rise and Fall of the Third Reich*, 1960
R. Butler, *The Roots of National Socialism*, 1941
J. L. Fest, *The Face of the Third Reich*, 1970
F. Meinecke, *The German Catastrophe*, 1950
H. Rauschning, *Germany's Revolution of Destruction*, 1939
Peter Pulzer, *The Rise of Political Anti-Semitism in Germany and Austria*, 1964
Franz Neumann, *Behemoth, The Structure and Practice of National Socialism*, 1945
A. Speer, *Inside the Third Reich*, 1970

David Schönbaum, *Hitler's Social Revolution. Class and Status in Nazi Germany*, 1966

Christopher Sykes, *Troubled Loyalty*, 1968

Hans Rothfels, *The German Opposition to Hitler*, 1961

Eberhard Zeller, *The Flame of Freedom: The German Struggle against Hitler*, 1967

Post-War Germany

Alfred Grosser, *Germany in our Time*, 1971

Karl Jaspers, *The Question of German Guilt*, New York, 1947

Ralf Dahrendorf, *Society and Democracy in Germany*, 1967

Terence Prittie, *Adenauer*, 1972

Uwe Kitzinger, *German Electoral Politics. A Study of the 1957 Campaign*, Oxford, 1960

David Childs, *From Schumacher to Brandt. The Story of German Socialism, 1945–65*, 1966

Willy Brandt, *In Exile. Essays, Reflections and Letters, 1933–1947*, 1972

Joachim Braun, *Gustav Heinemann: The Committed President*, 1972

Karl Kaiser, *German Foreign Policy in Transition*, Oxford, 1968

Wolfram F. Hanrieder, *West German Foreign Policy*, Stanford U.P., 1967

Helmut Schmidt, *The Balance of Power*, 1971

Philip Windsor, *Germany and the management of detente*, 1971

David Childs, *East Germany*, 1969

Hans Axel Holm, *The Other Germans*, 1971

David Shears, *The Ugly Frontier*, 1970

R. B. Tilford and R. J. Preece, *Federal Germany—Political and Social Order*, 1969

Michael Freund, *From Cold War to Ostpolitik—Germany and the new Europe*, 1972

Hanns Werner Schwarze, *The GDR Today, Life in the "other" Germany*, 1973

Contributors

Professor Wolfgang Abendroth   *Marburg University*

Professor Martin Broszat   *Institut für Zeitgeschichte, Munich*

Professor F. L. Carsten   *University of London*

Dr. E. J. Feuchtwanger   *University of Southampton*

Professor Alfred Grosser   *Institut des Études Politiques, Paris*

Professor R. Hinton Thomas   *University of Warwick*

Professor Walter Jens   *Tübingen University*

Professor Peter C. Ludz   *Bielefeld University*

Professor Golo Mann   *Zürich-Kilchberg*

Dr. Theo Sommer   *Deputy Editor 'Die Zeit', Hamburg*

Professor Kurt Sontheimer   *Munich University*